CATHOLICS
AND POLITICS

Religion and Politics Series

JOHN C. GREEN, TED G. JELEN, AND MARK J. ROZELL, *series editors*

Bonds of Affection: Civic Charity and the Making of America—Winthrop, Jefferson, and Lincoln, MATTHEW S. HOLLAND

The Catholic Church and the Nation-State: Comparative Perspectives,
PAUL CHRISTOPHER MANUEL, LAWRENCE C. REARDON, AND CLYDE WILCOX, EDITORS

Catholics and Politics: The Dynamic Tension between Faith and Power,
KRISTIN E. HEYER, MARK J. ROZELL, AND MICHAEL A. GENOVESE, EDITORS

The Christian Right in American Politics: Marching to the Millennium,
JOHN C. GREEN, MARK J. ROZELL, AND CLYDE WILCOX, EDITORS

Faith, Hope, and Jobs: Welfare-to-Work in Los Angeles,
STEPHEN V. MONSMA AND J. CHRISTOPHER SOPER

From Pews to Polling Places: Faith and Politics in the American Religious Mosaic,
J. MATTHEW WILSON, EDITOR

Of Little Faith: The Politics of George W. Bush's Faith-Based Initiatives,
AMY E. BLACK, DOUGLAS L. KOOPMAN, AND DAVID K. RYDEN

The Origins of Christian Anti-Internationalism: Conservative Evangelicals and the League of Nations, MARKKU RUOTSILA

Politics in the Parish: The Political Influence of Catholic Priests, GREGORY ALLEN SMITH

Reaping the Whirlwind: Liberal Democracy and the Religious Axis, JOHN R. POTTENGER

School Board Battles: The Christian Right in Local Politics, MELISSA M. DECKMAN

Uncompromising Positions: God, Sex, and the U.S. House of Representatives,
ELIZABETH ANNE OLDMIXON

The Values Campaign? The Christian Right and the 2004 Elections,
JOHN C. GREEN, MARK J. ROZELL, AND CLYDE WILCOX, EDITORS

CATHOLICS AND POLITICS
The Dynamic Tension between Faith and Power

Kristin E. Heyer
Mark J. Rozell
Michael A. Genovese

EDITORS

GEORGETOWN UNIVERSITY PRESS
Washington, D.C.

Georgetown University Press, Washington, D.C. www.press.georgetown.edu

Library of Congress Cataloging-in-Publication Data

Catholics and politics : the dynamic tension between faith and power / Kristin E. Heyer, Mark J. Rozell, Michael A. Genovese, editors.
    p. cm. — (Religion and politics series)
  Includes bibliographical references and index.
  ISBN-13: 978-1-58901-216-5 (hardcover : alk. paper)
  ISBN-13: 978-1-58901-215-8 (pbk. : alk. paper)
  1. Catholic Church—United States—Political activity. 2. Christianity and politics—United States. I. Heyer, Kristin E., 1974– II. Rozell, Mark J. III. Genovese, Michael A.
  BX1407.P63C37 2008
  261.7088'28273—dc22   2008003050

∞ This book is printed on acid-free paper meeting the requirements of the American National Standard for Permanence in Paper for Printed Library Materials.

15 14 13 12 11 10 09 08   9 8 7 6 5 4 3 2

First printing

Printed in the United States of America

CONTENTS

ILLUSTRATIONS

Tables

INTRODUCTION

Kristin E. Heyer and Mark J. Rozell

*I*N EARLY 2003 under the leadership of then-prefect Joseph Cardinal Ratzinger (now Pope Benedict XVI), the Congregation for the Doctrine of the Faith (CDF) issued a "Doctrinal Note on Some Questions Regarding the Participation of Catholics in Political Life." The note asserts, "The Christian faith is an integral unity, and thus it is incoherent to isolate some particular element to the detriment of the whole of Catholic doctrine. A political commitment to a single isolated aspect of the Church's social doctrine does not exhaust one's responsibility toward the common good."[1] As the chapters in this volume indicate, the CDF's call to moral coherence in Catholic politics, reflecting the integral unity of the faith and the issues upon which it touches, both shapes and tests Catholic political engagement in domestic and global contexts. In practice, given the complexities of political realities and the human nature of such institutions as church and government alike, we encounter a more fractured reality than the pure unity depicted in doctrine, disclosing fallible departures from a commitment to Catholic universalism and the transcendent nature of its values.

As social scientists and theologians alike have repeatedly noted, Catholic political identity and engagement defy straightforward categorization.[2] This book takes up the political and theological significance of this "integral unity," the universal scope of Catholic concern that can make for strange political bedfellows, confound predictable voting patterns, and leave the Church poised to critique narrowly partisan agendas across the spectrum. This comprehensive, Catholic scope can be politically beneficial as well as divisive, depending on the context and one's perspective. This volume integrates social scientific, historical, and moral accounts of persistent tensions between Catholicism and politics over the past generation, in the context of the Vatican as well as that of the United States. Its accounts of the implications of Catholic universalism for voting patterns, international policymaking, and partisan alliances together reveal complex intersections of Catholicism and politics.

In the post–Vatican II era, public engagement of questions of Catholic identity, orthodoxy, and hierarchy of values indicates that Catholicism constitutes an evolving political force on the international scene. The ways in which Catholic organizations and members intersect with political life are shaped significantly by the fact that theirs is a global institution with a tightly organized hierarchy and clearly defined official Church teachings. Catholic political engagement benefits from institutional strength and the Catholic tradition's rich history of intellectually and socially engaging polit- ical issues.[3] That said, there persists a significant degree of political and even moral pluralism amid believers, particularly in the U.S. context. Furthermore, the Catholic Church has a long and controversial history of political activity in the world. Some perceive that today the Church has lost some of its direction by involving itself so deeply in matters of state and politics, whereas others see such activity as a natural extension of the effort to propagate Catholic teachings.

Given the North American political landscape, this comprehensive scope does not provide Catholics with a comfortable home in either major political party. Many have noted that Catholic politics generally tend to defy strictly partisan boundaries, frequently serving as a bridge between liberal Protestant and Evangelical approaches to social issues, due in part to their positions on welfare and immigration, on the one hand, and abortion and sexual morality on the other. Mary E. Bendyna, RSM, refers to one result of this phenomenon as the "Goldilocks effect" in which Catholic posi- tions serve to moderate political discourse and constrain extremism; her studies with Mark M. Gray in chapter 5 bear out these tendencies during recent years in Catholic political attitudes. The volume's social scientific analyses of political alliances (chap- ter 2) and of Catholic voting (chapter 6), along with its historical narratives of Catholics and U.S. politics (in chapters 9 and 10) that trace relationships to the White House and Supreme Court, bear out patterns of Catholic "political homelessness."

As Margaret Ross Sammon points out in chapter 1, on the politics of the U.S. bishops, Joseph Cardinal Bernardin—the Catholic architect of the influential seam- less garment approach to a consistent life ethic—emphasized the ecclesiological and moral significance of preserving this comprehensive agenda as against a more reduc- tionistic approach. Bernardin noted, "Morally, a single-issue strategy forfeits many of the resources of the moral teaching of the Church. To highlight one question as the primary and exclusive objective in the policy process is to leave too many issues un- attended and risks distortion of the single issue itself."[4] For his view, while there are limits to both competency and energy that point to the wisdom of defining dis- tinct functions, the Church "must be credible across a wide range of issues; the very scope of our moral vision requires a commitment to a multiplicity of questions."[5] Gregory A. Smith's research (see chapter 3) demonstrates that Catholic parishioners are exposed to a variety of moral and social issues messages from the pulpit, depend- ing on where they happen to attend services.[6]

Yet as Sammon's chapter emphasizes, the recent history of Catholic politics in the U.S. context is marked by disproportionate attention to and distinct modes of anti- abortion rights advocacy. This development in part has led to what Streb and Frederick trace as a shift in alignment of the Catholic vote from Democratic to Republican leanings, the emergence of Catholic and Evangelical fledgling alliances (see chapter 2), and some authors' caveats regarding the single-issue litmus tests characterizing several highly publicized bishops' statements during the 2004 presidential campaign and in other election cycles as well (see especially chapter 1).

Hence, patterns of Catholic political engagement in recent decades have threatened to upset the delicate balance of "politically homeless" engagement. Reports in the Catholic press on the U.S. bishops' semiannual meetings in recent years suggest polarizing divisions between the "social justice" and the "pro-life" sides of the Church in their elections and deliberations. A tendency toward narrowly selective "cafeteria Catholicism" can be found on both the Left and Right, with leaders and laity alike becoming vulnerable to single- or narrow-issue politics and the distortion that ensues. The results of Gray and Bendyna's surveys in chapter 5 offer ample evidence of widespread selective adherence to Church teachings, at least in part linked to partisan divides in U.S. politics.

American Catholics' prioritization of any one issue can blind them to the cause of others and the inherent interrelatedness of "life" and "justice" issues: those who work with the poor may remain silent or even favor legalized abortion due to their "progressive" alliances on poverty issues; those who prioritize anti-abortion work may ignore socioeconomic factors that contribute to unwanted pregnancies or may support the use of force when a "pro-life" administration goes to war.[7]

For example, the director of the U.S. Conference of Catholic Bishops' Office of Social Development and World Peace, John Carr, has argued that "Catholic progressives should be measured by how we stand up for human life, how consistently, how courageously, how persistently. And Catholic conservatives should be measured by how often, how consistently, how persistently, how courageously we stand up for human dignity. The consistent life ethic doesn't give anyone a free pass. It challenges all of us."[8] As maintained in chapter 4, on the ethics of Catholic political engagement, single-issue agendas of any stripe can blind Catholics to the fact that Catholic social doctrine is rooted in the dual reality of human life. As Bernardin's consistent ethic emphasizes, humans are both sacred *and* social, so Catholics are called both to protect human life and foster its development at every stage *and* to ensure social institutions foster such development. As noted in chapter 4, despite the difficulties in practice, "Catholic political practices must embrace this comprehensive scope," due to the breadth and depth of the Catholic moral tradition and the ecclesiological significance of a multi-issue approach.

As several of the chapters indicate, however, it is not simply conventional partisan configurations that confound the Catholic range of issues or consistent ethic of life, but also the cultural ethos and operative philosophical framework that challenges Catholic politics in the U.S. context, in particular. In his discussion of U.S.–Vatican relations in chapter 11, Paul Christopher Manuel identifies "clashing ideologies" that impact the relationship between Catholicism and "American-style capitalism," such as a deeply engrained economic liberalism fundamentally at odds with Catholic commitments to human dignity and an option for the poor and vulnerable. Chapter 4 also emphasizes how the communitarian personalism that shapes Catholic political engagement necessarily encounters a difficult reception in a democracy based on individual liberty, for while "the Catholic vision shares certain commitments of a democracy like the United States, it radically challenges a culture that prioritizes economic efficiency over solidarity with the weak and marginalized, or narrow national interest over global concern."

For example, the Catholic commitment to peace and the hierarchy's critique of most U.S.-led uses of military force in recent decades emerge throughout the volume as a point of contention in the midst of other areas of collaborative accommodation throughout administrations. Whereas some hail international peace as one of the Church's best contributions, Thomas J. Carty's historical narrative of White House outreach to Catholics, for example, in chapter 10, addresses clashes during the Cold War as well as fighting wars in Vietnam, Panama, the Persian Gulf, Afghanistan, and contemporary Iraq in ways that highlight this influential stream of "clashing ideologies."

Such dissonant philosophical currents may also help explain why American Catholics are more susceptible to influence by partisan loyalties than religious values. Streb and Frederick's chapter, for example, traces the loss of a discernibly distinctive Catholic vote. As previous scholars have pointed out, Catholics were once a reliable part of the old New Deal coalition that anchored the Democratic Party for years. Some leading authors maintain that the Catholics who came to the United States found jobs in the inner cities, joined labor unions, and were a part of the American immigrant underclass attracted to the Democratic Party primarily due to economic issues. But over time, as the children and grandchildren of these immigrants became better educated, many joined higher professions, moved to the suburbs, and warmed up to the Republican Party.[9] Thus, although much has been made of the impact on Catholic voters of the Democratic Party's identification with abortion rights beginning in the 1960s and 1970s, recent scholarship demonstrates that religious values have not been the main factor in driving many Catholics to the GOP. This finding is compatible with the research on Latino Catholics by Adrian Pantoja, Matthew Barreto, and Richard Anderson (see chapter 7). Latinos may have socially conservative beliefs compatible with the Republican Party, but they still vote heavily Democratic. The authors demonstrate that nonreligious factors continue to drive the political behavior of Latinos in the United States.

Gray and Bendyna's chapter 5 also confirms that ideology drives voting behavior more decisively than do religious values. Several other chapters shed light on patterns of cooptation of Catholicism for political ends, whether in the form of politicians' opportunistic symbolic gestures or ecclesial leaders' selective framing and shaming regarding properly "Catholic issues." The dominant model of a "public church" that navigates between cooptation by and utter conflict with wider society is exemplified in the U.S. bishops' characterization of appropriate Catholic political engagement as remaining "engaged but not used." In their recent "Forming Consciences for Faithful Citizenship" document issued in late 2007, the bishops explicitly warn that Catholics must not let dialogue with political leaders and candidates devolve into mere "photo-ops," but rather should work for policies that reflect Catholic values.[10] Catholic religiopolitical engagement walks this fine line with some human failures and prophetic successes in American and global contexts alike.

Contextualizing the navigation of these tensions throughout the chapters in their historical sweep of post–Vatican II U.S. Catholicism, the volume's authors narrate American Catholics' passage "from ghetto to mainstream," employing historical, social scientific, and normative perspectives. Some would hail this account as a triumphant victory of immigrant outsiders over Protestant suspicions and various barriers; others would argue that such assimilation simply represents an inevitable stage in any immigrant wave's progression. Still others, however, have raised concerns that this transition signals a decline in coherent identity, risking un-Christian accommodation.

Those who critique the aforementioned dominating model of a public church from a radicalist perspective, for example, charge that once U.S. Catholicism moved into the mainstream, it succumbed more readily to temptations to subordinate the Church's ethic to the state's agenda. Such critics perceive the ghetto-to-mainstream "arrival" of American Catholicism as signaling failure rather than success, because Christian distinctiveness and purity become compromised and Catholicism's proper ends become subordinated to worldly political ends.[11]

The chapters herein depict this ambivalent character of Catholics' mainstream "arrival" over the past forty years, analyzing both the new opportunities for influence and the risks of cooptation that have accompanied such shifts. Hence, for example, Streb and Frederick suggest that the shifts in the Catholic vote in this country indicate that perhaps Catholics have become like most Americans, for whom partisanship plays a greater role in shaping political behavior than group affiliation. Gray and Bendyna's confirmation that the link between party identification and ideology has strengthened over past generations may similarly point to the American indoctrination of Catholics.

While the analyses presented by Gray and Bendyna on the one hand and Streb and Frederick on the other depart somewhat in their overall alignment of Catholic voters and party preferences (with the former assessing the majority Catholic population as aligned with the Democratic Party platform and the latter emphasizing the population's Republican shift), they both conduct studies which show that partisanship and ideology influence U.S. Catholics' political decisions more than the Church's positions do. Specific findings herein seem to bear this out; for instance, Gray and Bendyna's studies reveal that abortion and the death penalty do not align as well as other issues. (The percentage of Catholics who state opposition to both abortion and the death penalty remains small). As they show, "If one factors in those who oppose each and who support social justice and welfare issues consistent with Church teachings, the number of Catholics in agreement with Church teachings and statements on these issues diminishes even further." This misalignment indicates not only a challenge to the Catholic Church's consistent ethic of life but also the priority of ideology or partisan affiliation to a comprehensive (if politically inconvenient) Catholic ethic.

The "mainstream" risk of religion becoming coopted for political ends is reflected not only at the level of Catholic voters in terms of the role of partisan ideology and cafeteria Catholicism of various stripes, but also on an institutional level in the Church's function as a mere interest group or in its manipulation by and susceptibility to symbolic overtures. Sammon frames much of the political activity of the U.S. bishops in chapter 1 in terms of protecting their own interests with respect to abortion, and others differentiate the Church's strategic advancement of aid to parochial schools from broader, value-based advocacy, for example.

Carty's discussion of different administrations' outreach to Catholics (in chapter 10) showcases different politicians' appeals to Catholic figures and images to distinct effects, noting carefully orchestrated Notre Dame appearances, the "soft power" of president-pope exchanges, and the opportunistic employment of the presidential "bully pulpit." The relationship of symbolism to substance reflects long-standing tensions between partisanship and principles inherent in the machinations of politics, yet the landscape of recent U.S. Catholic history augurs some significant changes in the terrain. Perry's analysis of Catholics on the U.S. Supreme Court in chapter 9, tracing the recent move from a "Catholic seat" to a "Catholic court," for example, signals a broader shift on the Court from electoral considerations (via symbolism) to ideological ones (in terms of the priority of establishing a conservative majority). This trend in considerations for nominating new members of the "priestly tribe" arguably mirrors a shift from religious considerations to ideological ones, risking accommodation.

The ethical analysis in chapter 4 evokes the eschatological tensions facing Christians, such that Catholics' status "in the world but not of it" should leave them uncomfortable within neat partisan confines as major political parties are currently construed in the United States, much less with symbolic overtures manipulated for narrow ends or politicians' (long-standing or upstart) pandering to values voters. Thus, "the great importance of the church witnessing to transcendent values and remaining independent demands its nonpartisanship in intent *as well as in effect.*" Hence there remain tensions between the Church operating as an institutional or moral actor, along with the ongoing temptations of cooptation.

As chapter 2 indicates, conservative, Protestant-led political organizations in the social movement known as the Christian Right have looked to so-called faithful Catholics as logical targets of political recruitment. Yet despite the shared values of these groups on some issues, such as abortion and federal aid for religious schools, even politically conservative Catholics have been hesitant about political recruitment by religious-based interest groups, and they maintain a somewhat distinctive identity within the Christian Right. Politically conservative Catholics who oppose abortion rights may vote for Republican candidates backed by the Christian Coalition or Focus on the Family, but they are not eager to join these organizations.

At a perhaps more basic level, these tensions highlight the complex interplay between sacred and secular matters, the mix of human and divinely inspired elements that comprise Catholic institutions and engagement. In chapter 12, on the organization of the Vatican throughout history, Thomas J. Reese, SJ, outlines concrete proposals for borrowing models from secular political practices as, he argues, the curia has done throughout its history. His insights reveal the limits of an all-too-human institution that could benefit from further incorporation of other secular practices such as the separation of powers. Given the inescapably human dimension of religion and politics and its ambivalent character, becoming informed about the complex realities regarding how Catholic values are actually perceived and shaped, as the social scientific chapters herein analyze, and how the landscape in the United States and worldwide has shifted for Catholics, as the more historical chapters show, is invaluable for any lasting analysis of the present and future state of Catholic politics.

This ambivalence also indicates that prudential discernment of particular secular contexts is a crucial aspect of any Catholic political engagement.[12] For any assessment taken to its extreme—total cultural corruption leading to unrelieved countercultural identity or understanding any secular ideology as merely one path among other equally valid paths—is problematic.[13] Catholic ethicist David Hollenbach, SJ, illustrates the ambivalence of context well. Citing the Barmen Declaration and *Dignitatis humanae* as examples of situations calling for distinct Christian responses, he notes that "an assessment of just what the larger culture is up to is essential to authentic Christian identity. There is no a priori way to determine whether resistance or learning is called for."[14] In theological terms, he frames this task of discernment as understanding "*when* the affirmation that 'Jesus is Lord' should lead to countercultural resistance and *when* 'God is creator of heaven and earth' should lead to cooperation with non-Christians in pursuit of a universalist agenda." He continues, "Theologically, [both statements are] true. Both are scriptural; both were employed in the formation of Christian identity during the Apostolic age that is still normative. . . . It is not possible on theological grounds to grant absolute primacy to one or the other of these two stances on the relation of Christian identity to its intellectual, social and political environment."[15] In addition to Reese's navigation of what secular political practices are worthy of adoption by the Vatican, chapter 4's analysis outlines what prudential discernment amid human constraints demands of Catholic politicians, in particular.

This volume's juxtaposition of more normative articulations of the integral unity of Catholicism and its political implications with social scientific and historical accounts of Catholic politics prompts questions for ongoing interdisciplinary research and reflection: Should all Catholic justices (and voters) properly constitute a swing vote? How should growing Catholic-Evangelical alliances (or Catholic-Republican tendencies) be assessed morally and politically? Were formerly Democratic Catholic tendencies simply self-interested politics of a different stripe even if more than Catholic socioeconomic status factors have contributed to partisan shifts? More broadly, does the shift from ghetto to mainstream signify arrival or failure? What gets sacrificed? What will be the role ideology plays relative to religion in the future? What does the changing role of religion in electoral politics mean for Catholics, shifting as they have from John F. Kennedy's insistence in Houston that his Catholicism would not interfere with his ability to lead Americans, to pressure on John Kerry and other Catholic politicians to prove their voting records are sufficiently Catholic? What tactics should Catholicism use to evince reverence for life across the spectrum amid new threats? Does the Catholic political diversity exhibited in these pages and in elected officials' postures across the spectrum threaten coherence of identity, imply a lack of orthodoxy, or appropriately reflect different applications of constant values in complex and evolving circumstances?

No one volume can definitely answer these questions. The essays that follow, however, offer a useful addition to academic understanding of key issues surrounding the dynamic tension between religion and politics in the Catholic community.

NOTES

1. Congregation for the Doctrine of the Faith, "Doctrinal Note on Some Questions Regarding the Participation of Catholics in Political Life," dated November 24, 2002 and released January 16, 2003, available in *Origins* 32, no. 30 (January 30, 2003): 537–43 at para. no. 21.

2. See, for example, William D'Antonio, James D. Davidson, Dean R. Hoge, and Katherine Meyer, *American Catholics: Gender, Generation, and Commitment* (Lanham, MD: Altamira Press, 2001); John J. DiIulio, "The American Catholic Voter," Program for Research on Religion and Urban Civil Society, University of Pennsylvania, 2006, available from http://www.prrucs.org/pdfs/PRRUCS_AmerCath.pdf; William Prendergast, *The Catholic Voter in American Politics* (Washington, DC: Georgetown University Press, 1999).

3. Kristin E. Heyer, *Prophetic and Public: The Social Witness of U.S. Catholicism* (Washington, DC: Georgetown University Press, 2006), xvii.

4. J. Bryan Hehir, "The Consistent Ethic: Public Policy Implications," in *Consistent Ethic of Life,* ed. Thomas G. Fuechtmann (Kansas City, MO: Sheed & Ward, 1988), 233.

5. Joseph Cardinal Bernardin, "A Consistent Ethic of Life: Continuing the Dialogue," in Fuechtmann, ed, *Consistent Ethic of Life,* 15.

6. See also Gregory Smith, "The Influence of Priests on the Political Attitudes of Roman Catholics," *Journal for the Scientific Study of Religion* 44, no. 3 (September 2005): 291–306. Also available from http://mutex.gmu.edu:2167/toc/jssr/44/3.

7. Heyer, *Prophetic and Public,* 197.

8. John Carr, "The Church in the Modern World: Learning Lessons, Making a Difference and Keeping Hope" (plenary address, Annual Catholic Social Ministry Gathering, February 21, 2005), available at http://usccb.org/sdwp/carrspeech.htm.

9. See Prendergast, *The Catholic Voter,* especially on this point.

10. U.S. Conference of Catholic Bishops, *Forming Consciences for Faithful Citizenship: A Call to Political Responsibility from the Catholic Bishops of the United States* (Washington, DC: USCCB, 2007). Also available at http://www.usccb.org/faithfulcitizenship/FCStatement.pdf (accessed November 30, 2007).

11. See Michael Baxter, "Writing History in a World without Ends: An Evangelical Catholic Critique of United States Catholic History," *Pro Ecclesia* 5 (Fall 1996): 465. For a fuller discussion of these trends, see Heyer, *Prophetic and Public,* esp. chapter 3.

12. See also Heyer, "Bridging the Divide in Contemporary U.S. Catholic Social Ethics," *Theological Studies* 66 (June 2005): 401–40.

13. David Hollenbach, "Response to Robert Gascoigne's 'Christian Identity and the Communication of Ethics'" (address, Catholic Theological Society of America Convention, San Jose, CA, June 9, 2000).

14. He does, however, insist that this excludes the possibility of viewing the Church as a self-contained narrative community, for it would bypass this necessary effort to discern and distinguish "cultural wheat from cultural chaff." Yet he admits that uncritical appeals to natural law, the universal human community, and reason are unacceptable as well. Hollenbach perceives this task as constitutive of life between the times. See Hollenbach, "Response to Robert Gascoigne."

15. Ibid.

PART I
Catholic Leaders in U.S. Politics

1

THE POLITICS OF THE U.S. CATHOLIC BISHOPS

The Centrality of Abortion

Margaret Ross Sammon

T HE POLITICAL ACTIVITY of the American Catholic bishops has been guided by the words of John Carroll, the first bishop of the United States, who asked that Catholic priests avoid political involvement unless the interests of the Church were in danger. Leaders of the Church adhered to this request, but when the U.S. Supreme Court legalized abortion in 1973, the bishops reacted with an unprecedented political response. Believing that abortion was a grave threat to the Catholic Church, the bishops devoted an extensive amount of time, money, and energy in an attempt to overturn legalized abortion. While abortion is not the only concern of the bishops, it has generated perhaps the most strategic and well-planned political involvement of the hierarchy. The fight against abortion clearly illustrates the hierarchy's ability to organize, raise money, lobby members of Congress, and address individual Catholics at the parish level. Activities surrounding abortion exemplify the skillful political maneuvers of the hierarchy.

POLITICAL INVOLVEMENT BEFORE THE 1960s

All previous threats to the Church had been dealt with on a local level and by individual bishops, but that type of problem solving was no longer feasible for the hierarchy. With the Supreme Court's decision, the abortion debate shifted to the national level and became particularly important in presidential elections. The bishops were drawn into those elections and eventually aligned themselves with the Republican Party. They have been very successful in ensuring that many Republican candidates are pro-life and have remained politically active to ensure that the best interests of the Catholic Church are served. Although participating politically in such a national manner was out of character for the bishops, protecting the Church was not. The bishops had always adhered to the belief that political participation was permitted so long as the Church was in danger. The American bishops did not choose to make abortion a national issue; that decision was out of their hands. What they did choose was to protect the Church from what they perceived as a grave threat.

As leaders of an immigrant church in the early twentieth century, the American Catholic bishops mainly provided education, spiritual guidance, and protection from anti-Catholic hostility. Before the 1960s, American Catholics were regarded as suspicious foreigners by Protestants. Protestants feared the growth of the Catholic Church in America, as they believed that its leaders would disregard the separation of church and state. Knowing that American Catholics faced hostility, the American bishops generally refrained from political involvement unless the interests of the Church were in danger. John Carroll asked that the Catholic bishops avoid partisan political struggles of the day, but he was "willing to enter the political arena to defend Catholic interests when he felt they were under attack."[1]

The relative inactivity of the American bishops lay in a stark contrast to their European counterparts, who benefited from blurred lines of separation of church and state. During the 1950s and 1960s, three major changes within the Roman Catholic Church and in the United States allowed the American bishops to expand their political involvement. First, the social and economic status of American Catholics increased. A 1957 Census Bureau survey found that the median income of Catholic families was 10 percent higher than the income of white Protestant families.[2] Second, John F. Kennedy's election signified mainstream acceptance of Catholics. Third, American Catholics no longer needed the bishops' protection from suspicion and discrimination.[3] The structural and doctrinal changes made during the Second Vatican Council (1962–65) moderated the Vatican's hard-line stance on church–state relations; altered its teaching on matters of religious liberty under the influence of American Catholic theologian John Courtney Murray, SJ; strengthened the importance of episcopal conferences; and urged a heightened concern for social issues.[4] All of these changes allowed the American bishops to focus on other areas of concern among American Catholics. Despite advocating other issues, the bishops' primary concern continued to be defending the interests of the Church. Protecting the interests of the Church initially drew the bishops into political involvement. Despite changes in their agenda, it is likely they will remain involved in the political process so long as the interests of the Church remain subject to secular politics.

A NEW ACTIVISM

A key impetus for the American hierarchy's new political activism was *Gaudium et spes* (1965). The encyclical was based on the social teachings developed by Popes Leo XIII,

Pius XI, and John XXIII. *Gaudium et spes* was written in broad terms, but it called on the Church to be a progressive force for social change instead of a reactionary partner with the state. The Vatican wanted the Church to look for changes that the government needed to make instead of reacting to problems after they had occurred.[5] During the 1960s American bishops, through the National Conference of Catholic Bishops (NCCB) and the United States Catholic Conference (USCC), paid increasing attention to civil rights, war, peace in the Middle East, Vietnam, and the plight of farm workers.[6] The NCCB and the USSC were organized in 1966. The NCCB was created to deal with canonical issues and the USCC to deal with public policy. In 2001 the NCCB and the USCC were combined to form the United States Conference of Catholic Bishops (USCCB). The USCCB does all of the work that was done by the NCCB and the USCC. In this chapter, the conference will be referred to as the NCCB/USCC or "the conference" until 2001, when the two were joined.[7] The NCCB/USCC released numerous pastoral statements on these issues, but soon the Church's attention turned toward the perceived moral decline of Americans. The bishops' social concerns increasingly concentrated on American Catholics' permissive view of birth control and abortion.[8]

The new prosperity of American Catholics was both a blessing and a curse for the American bishops. They had successfully aided a generation of Catholics to become accepted into American society; however, once Catholics were no longer isolated from the rest of the country, they were increasingly exposed to the secular aspects of American culture. American Catholics as a whole were not outraged by the expanding acceptance of birth control, nor did they share in the hierarchy's position that abortion was a grave sin. Believing that the Catholic Church was in danger, the bishops became publicly vocal about the evils of abortion, and they directed their message to all Americans, not just Catholics. Their public statements on abortion were a departure from the bishops' usual mode of operation. In the past, the American bishops had reacted on the local level and on an individual basis. Consensus was not required, and each bishop responded to problems according to his own judgment. When episcopal conferences were strengthened after Vatican II, the NCCB/USSC began forming a united front when addressing important issues. The initial response of the hierarchy was to release a pastoral message that detailed its position on a specific issue.[9]

The first statement issued by the NCCB/USCC regarding contraception was Human Life in Our Day, which was released on November 15, 1968. The conference defended Humanae vitae, an encyclical released on July 25, 1968, by Pope Paul VI condemning contraceptive methods. The encyclical stated that it was not a negative proclamation but a "defense of life and love" that challenged the sentiment of the times.[10] Human Life in Our Day was a stepping-stone allowing the bishops to expand their pro-life dogma to include abortion. The tone of the statements released by the bishops (Statement on Abortion [1969], Declaration on Abortion [1970], and Population and the American Future: A Response [1972]) became increasingly aggressive. As more states legalized abortion during the early 1970s, the bishops became more vocal in their opposition.[11] In Declaration on Abortion the American bishops stated, "The function of law is to support and protect the rights of every person. The unborn child's civil rights have consistently been recognized by American law. Proposed liber-alization of the present abortion laws ignores the most basic of these rights, the right to life itself."[12] The bishops instructed both Catholics and non-Catholics that the evil of abortion is not merely a sin but a part of a larger social concern. They believed that society often lacks compassion for expectant mothers, which may cause some women to seek an abortion. It was their belief that government and voluntary agencies should broaden counseling and care of expectant mothers in order to prevent them from re-sorting to abortion.[13] It was the belief of the bishops that abortions would be unnec-essary if women with unwanted and unplanned pregnancies knew other options were available to them.

THE IMPACT OF *ROE V. WADE*

The concern of the bishops turned to outrage in 1973, when the majority opinion in *Roe v. Wade* announced that the Supreme Court had found a constitutional right to abortion. The bishops responded by blasting the opinion as bad law and bad logic. Cardinal John Krol, then the NCCB/USCC president, called the decision "an un-speakable tragedy for this nation."[14] The NCCB/USCC formed an ad hoc committee on pro-life activities, which recommended that the bishops explore every legal pos-sibility to challenge *Roe*'s holding. The Committee concluded that the best way to over-turn the decision would be the passage of a constitutional amendment prohibiting abortion. They made it known that passage of this amendment would be the highest priority of the NCCB/USCC. To this end, the bishops took two steps. First, they es-tablished the National Committee for a Human Life Amendment (NCHLA), a lob-bying group separate from the Church's official bureaucracy. Despite the formal sep-aration from the hierarchy, it was funded exclusively by the bishops and never severed its ties from the Church. Second, the NCCB/USCC would send several bishops to tes-tify before the Senate subcommittee on constitutional amendments. In the two years following *Roe,* the bishops devoted all of their energy to the passage of a constitutional amendment banning abortion.[15]

Advocacy of Civil Disobedience

Roe produced an unprecedented reaction from the American bishops. For the first time in U.S. history, the bishops advocated civil disobedience. In a statement of the Com-mittee for Pro-Life Affairs of the National Conference, the bishops disregarded the legitimacy of the ruling: "Although as a result of the Court decision abortion may be legally permissible, it is still morally wrong and no Court opinion can change the law of God prohibiting the taking of innocent human life. Therefore, as religious leaders, we cannot accept the Court's judgment and we urge people not to follow its reason-ing or conclusions."[16] The Committee recommended that (1) all legal possibilities to overturn the decision be explored, (2) all state legislatures restrict the practice as much as they can, (3) the Catholic Church pledge support for a program presenting the case for the sanctity of the child's life from conception to birth, and (4) Catholic hospitals and health facilities not find the judgment of the Court compatible with their faith and morals. The Committee called the decision "bad morality, bad medicine and bad public policy" and urged that the Court's decision be opposed and rejected.[17]

In February 1973 the Administrative Committee of the National Conference of Catholic Bishops released a pastoral message in which it directly invoked the logic of Pope John XXIII's *Pacem in terris:* "Every man has the right to life, to bodily integrity, and to the means which are necessary and suitable for the proper development of life."[18] Using *Pacem in terris* as its rationale, the Administrative Committee of the NCCB refuted the legality of the Supreme Court's decision. It believed that the Court held the right to privacy, which was granted in *Griswold v. Connecticut* (1965), as more important than the right to life and defined an unborn child as not a person under the Fourteenth Amendment. The bishops stated, "If any government does not acknowledge the rights of man or violates them . . . its orders completely lack juridical force."[19] The pastoral message also expressed the bishops' belief that *Roe* was entirely contrary to the fundamental principles of morality. They believed that no one, "no court, no legislative body, no leader of government can legitimately assign less value to some human life."[20] They further stated that when a conflict arises between divine law and human law, Catholics are required to follow God's law; this, in turn, legitimized their call to disobey the Court's decision. The pastoral message of the Administrative Committee came to the same conclusions as the Pro-Life Committee: that abortion was immoral and that doctors, nurses, or hospital workers were not required to obey civil laws allowing abortion. The two committees also declared that every effort must be made to overturn the decision and urged unified and persistent efforts, beginning in churches, schools, homes, and the civic community, to "instill reverence for life at all stages."[21]

Participation in National Politics

The nationwide implications of *Roe* forced the American bishops to participate in national politics on an unprecedented scale. This was possible partly because Americans no longer feared the political involvement of the bishops. Despite the fact that American Catholics had become economically and socially prosperous, the bishops felt that their morals had declined, as had those of the American public in general. Taking their cue from the Vatican II document *Gaudium et spes,* they addressed what they felt was damaging the Catholic Church: the permissive view of birth control and especially abortion "as a matter of right" to all pregnant women. The bishops cited passages from the document during a March 7, 1974 hearing before the Senate Judiciary Subcommittee on Constitutional Amendments. In their testimony the bishops quoted a passage that they felt adequately expressed their feelings toward the protection of all human life: "Although as a result of the Court decision abortion may be legally permissible, it is still morally wrong and no Court opinion can change the law of God prohibiting the taking of innocent human life."[22]

As they did in previous statements regarding abortion, the bishops' testimony before the Senate subcommittee invoked principles of American law. Their testimony stated that according to the Founding Fathers, all law is based upon divine law and that in order for society to be just, civil law must not conflict with divine law. The best way to rid the country of this conflict would be the passage of a constitutional amendment to reflect a commitment to human rights. The bishops admitted that the passage of a constitutional amendment was only the first step in eradicating the need for abortions. Citing the fact that it has taken a century for the promises of the Thirteenth and Fourteenth Amendments "to begin to bear fruit in our present society," they acknowledged that it would be a long road to end abortion. The constitutional amendment would provide support and assistance to pregnant women and their unborn children. The support would include nutritional, prenatal, childbirth, and postnatal care plus nutritional and pediatric care for the child throughout its first year of life. In addition, subsequent legislation pursuant to the amendment would provide counseling services, adoption facilities, and financial assistance.[23]

The American Catholic hierarchy soon realized that in order to reverse the Supreme Court's decision, it would need to rely on more than pastoral statements, congressional testimony, and the founding of pro-life organizations. The bishops understood that it would require political action that was focused and coordinated.

In November 1975 the NCCB/USCC released the *Pastoral Plan for Pro-Life Activities*. The *Pastoral Plan* offered a strategic plan for defending human life.[24] According to the bishops, it was issued because in the preceding decade, respect for human life had been declining in society. The decline in respect for human life resulted in laws and judicial decisions that denied basic human rights. The Supreme Court's decision in 1973 to legalize abortion was the direct result of the loss of respect for human life.[25] The bishops believed that focusing on the sanctity of life in all its forms was the best method of protecting all persons: "In focusing attention on the sanctity of human life, therefore, we hope to generate a greater respect for the life of each person in our society. We are confident that greater respect for human life will result from continuing the public discussion of abortion and from efforts to shape our laws so as to protect the life of all persons, including the unborn."[26]

The bishops' fight against abortion has been emblematic of their approach toward secular political involvement. They chose abortion not only because of its moral implications but also because it epitomized all Catholic concerns. For the bishops, not focusing on abortion would mean ignoring the underlying cause of all other issues. The *Pastoral Plan* explicitly stated, "Indeed, the denial of the God-given right to life is one aspect of a larger problem. But it is unlikely that efforts to protect other rights will be ultimately successful if life itself is continually diminished in value."[27] The *Pastoral Plan* summoned all the resources of the Church to pursue the fight against abortion in four areas: public information and education; pastoral care; public policy; and prayer and worship. The bishops further divided the efforts among the national, regional, state, diocesan, and parish levels.[28]

With this new aggressive political plan, some of the bishops feared that the anti-Catholic hostility of the past would resurface, and others worried that the Church might lose its tax-exempt status. The hierarchy particularly feared that the creation of pro-life lobby groups in every congressional district would lead people to believe that the groups were puppets of the NCCB/USCC. To alleviate this perception, the final version of the *Pastoral Plan* defined a congressional pro-life group as "an agency of citizens operated, controlled, and financed by these same citizens" and that "it is not an agency of the Church, nor is it operated, controlled or financed by the Church."[29] However, many noted that the detailed list of objectives and guidelines effectively eliminated independence from the Church. In addition, some bishops worried that the Church was focusing too much on one issue. These concerns did not prevent the *Pastoral Plan* from being adopted. It was approved for publication in November 1975 and was updated and approved again in 1985 and 2001. The *Pastoral Plan* was considered to be "emblematic of the hierarchy's approach to political activism in the modern era."[30] The bishops, through the NCCB, presented their moral judgment on a public policy issue and devised a strategy to turn their judgment into legislative action.[31]

The American bishops hoped to recreate the role they had played on the local level in the early twentieth century. Yet now, the bishops' political efforts were not limited to Catholics. Their fight against abortion encompassed a broad grassroots movement and a growing social movement that was precipitated by a volatile political system. The collapse of the New Deal coalition, which was caused by the desertion of Catholics and white southerners from the Democratic Party, opened the door for new political coalitions.[32] A 1972 Gallup poll showed that 52 percent of Catholics voted for Richard Nixon, as compared to the 33 percent he received in 1968.[33] The American bishops benefited from these changes, and politicians began to take the implications—and opportunities—seriously.

The politicians appreciated the special position of the bishops. The American bishops were the leaders of the largest single religious denomination in the United States, which comprised one-fourth of the national electorate. Additionally, Catholics had become one of the largest swing voter groups in the United States. While politicians understood that the bishops did not control Catholics, they were also aware that the bishops held great influence over their flock. As Robert Beckel, Walter Mondale's 1984 campaign manager, noted, "If you are a bishop, you've got a lot of people, you've got money, places to meet, you've got a lot of things that any good politician would like to have at his disposal."[34] Politicians also appreciated the fact that the American bishops could devote substantial money, resources, and time to the issue of their choice. Additionally, the bishops' view on abortion allowed them to exert influence on Americans besides Catholics. Politicians and candidates acknowledged the influence of the bishops by seeking out and publicizing areas of agreement with them. Consequently, the bishops were drawn more actively into electoral politics.[35]

Before 1973 abortion was not a particularly prominent issue in national politics. It was not an issue in the 1968 presidential election, and although President Nixon had publicly opposed abortion and had reversed a federal regulation that expanded the availability of abortions in military hospitals, he preferred to leave the battle over the issue to the state legislatures. Nixon's opponent in 1972, George McGovern, refused to make abortion an issue and instead chose to focus on Vietnam, the economy, busing, and crime. He did, however, state that he felt abortion was a private matter and should be left to the state governments.[36] It was only when *Roe* was decided in 1973 that abortion politics became a major campaign issue for all presidential candidates.

THE 1976 ELECTION   The 1976 presidential election was the first post-*Roe* presidential contest, and the bishops asked abortion opponents for "well-planned and coordinated political action."[37] The president of the NCCB/USCC, Archbishop Joseph Bernardin, praised the support of prominent Republicans for a constitutional amendment prohibiting abortion, and he condemned Democrats for opposing it. Because Richard Nixon had won a majority of the Catholic vote in 1972, both Jimmy Carter and President Gerald Ford understood the importance of the bishops' role in the 1976 presidential election and actively sought their approval.

Carter tried desperately to show his alignment with the bishops' position on abortion. He attempted to distance himself from a Democratic platform that opposed an anti-abortion constitutional amendment. Carter tried, in effect, to have it both ways, saying he was morally opposed to abortion but that he also did not agree with proposals for a constitutional amendment to prohibit the procedure. The bishops, of course, did not accept this distinction. He also sought a face-to-face meeting with the Executive Committee of the bishops' conference. Carter tried to create an "intimate personal relationship" with the bishops in order to win over Catholic voters; however, he only succeeded in raising the bishops' political profile and drawing them further into the political debate. Carter's failures allowed President Ford to emphasize the differences between Carter and the bishops. Ford also attempted to show his own concern for Catholic issues. Additionally, he used Carter's unsuccessful attempts to show solidarity with pro-life leaders to announce publicly his support for a proposed anti-abortion plank in the Republican platform.[38] Ford invited the NCCB/USCC's Executive Committee to the White House so he could contrast his agreement with the bishops' position on abortion to Carter's public opposition to an anti-abortion constitutional amendment. The political involvement of the American bishops in the 1976 election showed how the bishops were able to capitalize on the collapse of old coalitions and the creation of new ones.[39]

THE 1980 AND 1984 ELECTIONS   During the 1980 presidential campaign, Ronald Reagan aggressively championed the pro-life cause and endorsed a constitutional amendment prohibiting abortion. Reagan promised to appoint federal judges who opposed abortion and vowed to prohibit the use of federal funds for abortions except when necessary to save the life of the woman. Reagan's election in 1980 heightened the importance of the abortion debate.[40]

By 1984 the Republican Party had fully aligned itself with pro-life supporters and with traditional religious values. Reagan's attempt to reemphasize his identification with the religious base gave the 1984 campaign a deeply religious tone.[41] The question became "not whether religion and Christian morality should influence public policy, but rather where that influence should begin and end."[42] The majority party candidates had different responses to that question. Reagan believed that morality was best expressed through emphasizing the issues of abortion and school prayer, whereas Mondale believed morality was best displayed through eliminating poverty and nuclear arms.[43] The American bishops had to decide the extent of Catholic morality's relationship with the American political agenda.[44]

The hierarchy was split over how to deal with the issue of morality in public policy. Cardinal Joseph Bernardin was concerned about the single-issue platform of the bishops. He stated that the hierarchy "would be severely pressured by those who wanted to push a particular issue with little or no regard for the rest of the bishops' positions."[45] To counteract this possibility, he articulated a "consistent ethic of life." Bernardin first addressed this issue during a lecture at Fordham University in 1983. The lecture elicited numerous questions about the consistent ethic of life theory; therefore, Bernardin explained the idea further during the 1984 Wade Lecture at Saint Louis University in March 1984. A consistent ethic of life was needed because of the dimensions of the threats to life posed by nuclear weapons and to examine the value of the moral vision of Catholics. Bernardin's theory of consistent ethic of life did not mean that all Catholics must advocate on behalf of the same issue, but rather that when an individual and a group pursue one issue, that issue should be advanced in a manner that promotes a "systemic vision of life." It also meant that groups pursuing different life issues should not be insensitive or opposed to the positions of those who advocate other moral issues.[46]

The consistent ethic of life contained four dimensions. The first was the need to identify a single principle with diverse applications. For example, the prohibition against direct attacks on innocent life is central to the Catholic moral vision and is related to a range of specific moral issues. A consistent ethic of life "encourages the specific concerns of each constituency, but also calls them to see the interrelatedness of their efforts."[47] The second level stressed the distinction among cases rather than their similarities. Different moral principles apply to diverse cases because "not all moral principles have relevance across the whole range of life issues."[48] The third level involved relating a commitment to principles to the public witness of life. While no institution can do everything, "the Church, however, must be credible across a wide range of issues, the very scope of our moral vision requires a commitment to a multiplicity of questions. In this way the teaching of the Church will sustain a variety of individual commitments."[49] The fourth level was the relationship between moral principles and concrete political choices. The moral questions of abortion, the arms race, and human rights are public moral issues that are not decided in the Church but in the political process. The consistent ethic of life would present a coherent linkage among a diverse set of issues. Bernardin intended this level to test party platforms, public policies, and political candidates.[50]

While the consistent ethic of life was accepted by a majority of the conference, several prominent bishops did not adhere to its underlying theory. They did not share Bernardin's concern that the Catholic Church would be solely associated with the abortion issue and instead embraced the ideas set forth in the *Pastoral Plan*. Some were concerned that it would be counterproductive to equate the potential threats of human life from nuclear war with the actual destruction of millions of human fetuses every year.[51] Archbishop Bernard Law of Boston called nuclear war "a future possibility" and called abortion the "critical issue" of the 1984 campaign. Archbishop John O'Connor of New York publicly stated "if the unborn in a mother's womb is unsafe it becomes ludicrous for the bishops to address the threat of nuclear war."[52] He also asked how a Catholic in good conscience could vote for a candidate who supported legalized abortion. This debate led to a larger issue beyond the 1984 presidential election.

The bishops did not disagree on the importance of abortion; rather, they disagreed on what place it would have within their public policy agenda. Some also feared how the hierarchy's politics would intersect with the platforms of national political candidates. The problem was that the Church disagreed with both parties on certain issues. However, there was a benefit to the bishops' political agenda, which "cut across partisan lines of a campaign in which the scope of religion's role in American public life had become a major national issue."[53] Bishops such as Law and O'Connor refused to include other social issues within their agendas. Their very public opposition to abortion only magnified its importance and provided a guide for Catholic voters. By publicly asserting the great importance of the abortion issue and proclaiming it the most important issue of the presidential campaign, the bishops tacitly supported one candidate over another. Ronald Reagan was fiercely pro-life and Walter Mondale was not. O'Connor stated at a right-to-life rally, "I didn't tell you to vote for Reagan did I?" He made this statement after a taped message of support from President Reagan had been played at the rally.[54] Despite the disagreement between members of the hierarchy about the place of abortion in their political agenda, Law's and O'Connor's public statements that abortion was the most important issue facing the nation made it a central issue during the 1984 campaign.

O'Connor repeatedly chastised Catholic politicians who supported abortion. He accused 1984 Democratic vice-presidential nominee, Geraldine Ferraro, of misrepresenting the Church's teaching: "Geraldine Ferraro has said some things relevant to Catholic teaching which are not true. . . . The only thing I know about her is that she has given the world to understand that Catholic teaching is divided on the subject of abortion. . . . As an officially approved teacher of the Catholic Church, all I can judge is that what has been said [by Ferraro] about Catholic teaching is wrong. It's wrong."[55] The criticism of Ferraro's statement was based on a letter she had signed two years previously from Catholics for a Free Choice. The group invited members of Congress to attend a briefing on the special problems facing Catholic politicians. The purpose of the meeting was to show that "the Catholic position on abortion is not monolithic and that there can be a range of personal and political responses to it."[56] O'Connor and Ferraro exchanged remarks for several days. Ferraro finally conceded that "the Catholic Church's position on abortion is monolithic." However, she stated, "But I do believe that there are a lot of Catholics who do not share the view of the Catholic Church."[57] Ferraro was subsequently criticized because the speech was given in Scranton, Pennsylvania, where O'Connor had previously served as bishop. His successor, James Timlin, rejected her views as absurd and not rational.[58] The back-and-forth exchanges showed that a large number of bishops rejected the consistent ethic of life theory and would make abortion the major issue in every election. Timothy Byrnes has asserted that the individual actions of the bishops regarding Bernardin's consistent ethic of life prevented "pro-choice Catholics from taking solace from their agreement with the bishops on issues other than abortion."[59]

As the NCCB/USCC had stated in the *Pastoral Plan,* failing to prevent abortion was far graver than failing to stop nuclear threats, poverty, or capital punishment. If the bishops could not protect life in its most innocent form, what hope would they have in advocating protection from other forms of harm? For the bishops, the most basic human right was "the very right to life." As Pope John Paul II stated: "In focusing attention on the sanctity of human life, therefore, we hope to generate a greater respect for the life of each person in our society. We are confident that greater respect for human life will result from continuing the public discussion of abortion and from efforts to shape our laws so as to protect the life of all persons, including the unborn."[60] The bishops sought to protect life at its most vulnerable stage and devoted an increasing amount of time, money, and effort to overturn *Roe*.

THE 1996, 2000, AND 2004 ELECTIONS   The 1984 presidential election was the pinnacle of the abortion debate, but the issue was never absent from subsequent presidential elections. In 1996 Cardinals Bernard Law of Boston and James Hickey of Washington urged Catholics not to vote for Bill Clinton after the president vetoed legislation banning partial-birth abortions. Cardinal Hickey asked "not only Catholics but all Americans to remember the veto on Election Day."[61] Yet despite their efforts, the 1996 election was very disappointing for the pro-life movement. Republican candidate Bob Dole's pro-life position was questionable, leading the Catholic press to speculate about how dedicated he was to fighting abortion. Dole attempted to avoid questions about his position and claimed he was unfamiliar with the Republican platform language on the abortion issue. This reduced his support from Catholic and other Christian voters.[62]

In 2000 George W. Bush encountered problems when speculation arose that he was considering the Catholic pro-choice governor of Pennsylvania, Tom Ridge, as his vice-presidential running mate. Bush's consideration of Ridge produced an angry response from Catholic leaders. Bishop Donald Trautman of Erie, Pennsylvania, reaffirmed the ban on pro-choice Catholics appearing at church-related events.[63] Like the problems that arose when Cardinal Joseph Bernardin proposed his consistent ethic of life, the bishops again found themselves publicly at odds over how to handle pro-choice Catholic politicians.

As alluded to by Kristin E. Heyer in chapter 4, in 2004 Democratic presidential candidate Senator John Kerry was placed in the hot seat by several members of the hierarchy. Angered by the fact that Kerry supported abortion rights, these bishops publicly stated that they would deny him communion. According to Kerry's Senate office, he received communion throughout the presidential election and continues to receive it.[64] Yet the mere threat to deny him communion was enough to damage his campaign. Had Kerry been able to secure the Catholic vote, he would likely have won the election. Instead, George W. Bush was able to obtain 53 percent of the Catholic vote, mainly because of his appeal to "traditional" Catholics.[65] The majority of American Catholics did not agree with denying Kerry communion, but the attention that the incident created caused Catholics to consider the notion that while Kerry was personally opposed to abortion, he did not have a problem voting to protect abortion rights.[66] The fact that a few bishops were able to sway Catholic voters away from John Kerry did not mean that the hierarchy agreed with their tactics. This time, however, they collectively attempted to develop guidelines as to when it is necessary to deny communion to a Catholic politician, but finally decided to leave it up to each individual bishop's pastoral judgment.

OTHER FORMS OF NATIONAL PARTICIPATION   The bishops' political involvement has not been limited to presidential politics. In February 2006, fifty-five Catholic House

Democrats sent a "statement of principles" to the leaders of the Catholic Church. The letter stated that the representatives did not want to see "Catholic faith defined solely by a one-issue, very narrow right-wing agenda."[67] It also stated that they would like to work with the Church on the issues of poverty, health care, and education. They said they would like to do this "under the Catholic tradition . . . that promotes the common good, expresses a consistent moral framework for life and highlights the need to provide a collective safety net for the needy."[68] The House members also agreed that abortion was undesirable and that they would work to reduce the number of unwanted pregnancies and increase alternatives to abortion. However, they did ask the Church for room to disagree on the issue of abortion rights. Cardinal Theodore McCarrick, then archbishop of Washington, D.C., and head of the task force on how to respond to dissenting politicians, said, "We know we agree on some things, we disagree on other things, but there is always room to talk."[69]

On April 18, 2007, the Supreme Court of the United States in a 5 to 4 ruling upheld the Partial Birth Abortion Ban Act in *Gonzales v. Carhart.* The decision, which did not affect the legal status of abortion, met with strong reactions from both the pro-life and the pro-choice communities. Cardinal Justin Rigali, archbishop of Philadelphia and chairman of the Committee for Pro-Life Activities of the United States Conference of Catholic Bishops (USCCB), responded to the ruling by noting that "the Court's decision does not affect the legal status of the great majority of abortions, and does not reverse past decisions claiming to find a right to abortion in the Constitution. However, it provides reasons for renewed hope and renewed effort on the part of pro-life Americans. The Court is taking a clearer and more unobstructed look at the tragic reality of abortion, and speaking about that reality more candidly, than it has in many years."[70] One reason for Rigali to be hopeful is that the decision will most likely heighten the importance of abortion in the 2008 presidential election. Democratic senator Barbara Boxer from California noted that the decision "confirms that elections have consequences."[71] The next president will appoint at least one justice to the Court, as Justice John Paul Stevens will soon be celebrating his eighty-seventh birthday and Ruth Bader Ginsberg is the next oldest justice at the age of seventy-four. The American Catholic bishops are hoping that if a Republican is elected president, there will be a significant chance that pro-life justices will be appointed and *Roe* will be overturned. It also means that the bishops will play an active role in this campaign.

Participation in State Politics

Representative Joe Pitts of Pennsylvania believes that the *Carhart* decision will "stimulate more action on the part of the state legislatures around the country to try to restrict abortion."[72] The bishops may see this as an important victory for the pro-life movement because one of the most impressive aspects of their political activity, especially in the case of abortion, is their ability to conduct a sophisticated national lobbying effort and a grassroots campaign. To give one example, the Catholic anti-abortion lobby has been particularly effective in Pennsylvania. The efforts of the Pennsylvania Catholic Conference (PCC) were a key factor in enabling the state to restrict abortion practices for over a decade. From 1965 to 1972, the PCC helped to create a political and social environment in which abortions were cast as infanticide and the moral character of the women who sought abortions was questioned. In 1967 the PCC successfully blocked the Pennsylvania General Assembly from passing Senate Bill 38, which allowed for abortions in the case of rape, incest, fetal deformity, and physical or mental threats to the health of the mother.[73]

The PCC adhered to the Vatican's definition of abortion as infanticide, therefore defining the issue in both moral and religious terms. The PCC was the only public voice against abortion until 1969, allowing it to go unchallenged by pro-choice groups for years. Perhaps the most important advantage that the PCC had, however, was the organizational and financial resources of the Catholic Church. Following the guidelines set by the Family Bureau of the USCC, the PCC established an ad hoc committee on abortion to prevent further pro-abortion changes in existing state abortion statutes.[74]

In the fall 1974 session of the Pennsylvania General Assembly, the PCC led a successful campaign to override the veto of the Abortion Control Act of 1974. Pro-choice groups were unsuccessful in sustaining the veto because the bill involved restricting access to abortion and not prohibiting it; additionally, many pro-choice groups were complacent in the belief that access to abortion was guaranteed by *Roe*. In the 1980s anti-abortion legislative initiatives began to be controlled by groups other than the PCC. Especially in Pennsylvania, the efforts to overturn abortion centered on solutions that were based largely on constitutional rather than moral grounds. As the abortion issue became nationalized, pro-life supporters turned to groups such as Americans United for Life to construct comprehensive legislation that could withstand constitutional challenges.[75] Despite the diminishment of the PCC's influence in the anti-abortion fight, it had started the fight and had fought it effectively for over a decade. Its tenacity and success showed how deep and how skillful the Church's lobbying efforts were. They were able to fight *Roe* on all levels: local, state, and national.[76]

Roe catapulted the American Catholic bishops from local politics into national politics, a position unfamiliar to them. Traditionally, the bishops had refrained from political involvement and focused on assimilating their mainly immigrant and working-class parishioners into American society. Also, fears among Protestants that the bishops would overstep the boundaries of church and state limited political activity on the part of the bishops. As a result, the bishops reserved their political involvement for issues that affected the interests of the Church, and even then they only reacted at the local level to individual cases. Soon, changes in society and within the Church would cause them to reevaluate their role as political players.[77]

By the 1950s, American Catholics were becoming an affluent part of society. They moved out of ethnic ghettoes and into middle-class neighborhoods. The 1960 election of John F. Kennedy as president signified that Catholics had become part of mainstream America. These economic and social gains forced Catholics to rethink their allegiance to the Democratic Party. The new radicalism of the left caused many Catholics to reconsider how closely the Democratic Party was aligned with their traditional moral values. In turn, the Democratic Party reevaluated its allegiance to Catholics. In 1980 the Democratic Party placed its loyalty with social liberals and endorsed legalized abortion.[78] This forced the bishops to consider whether they would stay and fight the abortion issue or allow the Republican Party to do the fighting for them. Because the bishops considered the threat to the Church so great, they vowed to put all of their energy into making abortion illegal. This meant reminding Republicans of the importance of human life and pressuring them to take the pro-life position.[79]

CONCLUSION

The bishops' decision to remain in politics is reflective of John Carroll's call to defend the interests of the Church. Once the bishops have deemed something to be a threat to the interests of the Church, they rally to fight it at the level where they can be most effective: national, state, or local. Abortion became a national issue when it was legalized by the Supreme Court in 1973. In response to *Roe v. Wade,* the hierarchy organized a sophisticated anti-abortion lobbying effort through their Conference, organized pro-life groups throughout the states, and directly addressed Catholics during Mass at the parish level. To the dismay of many abortion rights groups, the bishops have been able to focus on a single issue and devote substantial amounts of time, money, and energy in support of their ends. In response, many politicians have expended similar resources trying to obtain the support of the bishops. The enormous amount of resources that the bishops have devoted to their fight against abortion shows the skillful manner in which the hierarchy will defend the interests of the Catholic Church.

NOTES

1. Timothy A. Byrnes, *Catholic Bishops in American Politics* (Princeton, NJ: Princeton University Press, 1991), 11–14.
2. William B. Prendergast, *The Catholic Voter in American Politics* (Washington, DC: Georgetown University Press, 1999), 11.
3. A. James Reichley, "Religion and the Future of American Politics," *Political Science Quarterly* 101 (1986): 32.
4. Gene Burns, "Commitments and Non-Commitments: The Social Radicalism of U.S. Catholic Bishops," *Theory and Society* 21 (October 1992): 718.
5. Ibid.
6. Ibid., 720.
7. Thomas J. Reese, SJ, *A Flock of Shepherds* (Kansas City, MO: Sheed & Ward, 1992), vii.
8. Ibid.
9. Byrnes, *Catholic Bishops in American Politics,* 52–56.
10. Hugh J. Nolan, ed., *Pastoral Letters of the United States Catholic Bishops* (Washington, DC: United States Catholic Conference, 1983), 168.
11. Byrnes, *Catholic Bishops in American Politics,* 56.
12. Nolan, *Pastoral Letters of the United States Catholic Bishops,* 271.
13. Ibid.
14. Byrnes, *Catholic Bishops in American Politics,* 57.

15. Ibid., 58.

16. This statement of the Committee for Pro-Life Affairs, National Conference of Catholic Bishops, is reproduced in *Documentation on the Right to Life and Abortion* (Washington, DC: United States Catholic Conference, 1974), 59.

17. Ibid., 60.

18. This pastoral message of the Administrative Committee, National Conference of Catholic Bishops, is reproduced in *Documentation on the Right to Life and Abortion,* 55.

19. Ibid., 56.

20. Ibid.

21. Ibid., 58.

22. This testimony is reproduced in *Documentation on the Right to Life and Abortion,* 1.

23. Ibid., 29–30.

24. Byrnes, *Catholic Bishops in American Politics,* 58.

25. The Pastoral Plan for Pro-Life Activities is reproduced in *Documentation on Abortion and the Right to Life II* (Washington, DC: United States Catholic Conference, 1976), 45.

26. Ibid., 46.

27. Ibid.

28. Ibid., 46–57.

29. Byrnes, *Catholic Bishops in American Politics,* 59.

30. Ibid., 60.

31. Ibid.

32. Timothy A. Byrnes, "The Politics of the American Catholic Hierarchy," *Political Science Quarterly* 108 (Autumn 1993): 499.

33. Prendergast, *Catholic Voter in American Politics,* 157.

34. Byrnes, "Politics of the American Catholic Hierarchy," 500.

35. Ibid.

36. Barbara Hinkson Craig and David M. O'Brien, *Abortion and American Politics* (Chatham, NJ: Chatham House, 1993), 157–59.

37. Byrnes, "Politics of the American Catholic Hierarchy," 503.

38. Ibid., 504–5.

39. Ibid., 503–5.

40. Craig and O'Brien, *Abortion and American Politics,* 169.

41. Byrne, "Politics of the American Catholic Hierarchy," 506.

42. Ibid., 507.

43. Ibid.

44. Ibid.

45. Ibid.

46. Joseph Cardinal Bernardin, "A Consistent Ethic of Life: Continuing the Dialogue" (address delivered at Saint Louis University, William Wade Lecture Series, March 11, 1984).

47. Ibid.

48. Ibid.

49. Ibid.

50. Ibid.

51. Byrnes, "The Politics of the American Catholic Hierarchy," 508.

52. Ibid., 505.

53. Ibid., 511.

54. Byrnes, *Catholic Bishops in American Politics,* 119.

55. Ibid., 120.

56. Ibid.

57. Ibid., 121.

58. Ibid.

59. Ibid., 122.

60. The *Pastoral Plan for Pro-Life Activities* is reproduced in *Documentation on Abortion and the Right to Life II,* 46.

61. "Abortion: A Topic for November," U.S. News & World Report, April 22, 1996.

62. Prendergast, *Catholic Voter in American Politics,* 208–9.

63. Nicholas Confessore, "Ridge over Troubled Water; A Pro-Choice Catholic Could Be Just What the Bush Ticket Needs," *The American Prospect,* July 17, 2000.

64. Scott Shepard, "New Pope Was Force in Efforts to Deny Kerry Communion during 2004 Election," *Cox News Service,* April 20, 2005.

65. Ibid.

66. Melinda Henneberger, "Varia: It's about Abortion, Stupid," *Newsweek,* September 23, 2004.

67. Kevin Eckstrom, "Catholic Democrats Seek Room to Disagree with Church Teaching on Abortion," *Religion News Service,* March 1, 2006. (This article was retrieved through LexisNexis Academic.)

68. Ibid.

69. Ibid.

70. Statement from Justin Cardinal Rigali, chairman of the Committee for Pro-Life Activities, United States Conference of Catholic Bishops (USCCB), "Cardinal Welcomes Supreme Court Decision Upholding Federal Partial-Birth Abortion Ban," April 18, 2007.

71. Tom Curry, "Supreme Court Ruling Raises '08 Stakes," *MSNBC.com,* April 19, 2007, available from www.msnbc.msn.com/id/18201772/.

72. Brett Lieberman and Nancy Eshelman, "Abortion Decision's State Effect Uncertain," *Patriot News* (Harrisburg, PA), April 19, 2007.

73. Rosemary Nossif, "Pennsylvania: The Impact of Party Organization and Religious Lobbying" in *Abortion Politics in American States,* ed. Mary C. Segers and Timothy A. Byrnes (New York and London: M. E. Sharpe, 1995), 17.

74. Ibid., 24.

75. Ibid.

76. Ibid.

77. Reichley, "Religion and the Future of American Politics," 31–33.

78. Ibid., 33.

79. Ibid., 32–34.

2

POLITICAL MARRIAGE OF CONVENIENCE?

The Evolution of the Conservative Catholic–Evangelical Alliance in the Republican Party

Mark J. Rozell

I n 1995 the Reverend Pat Robertson's Christian Coalition, then the nation's leading religious conservative political organization, announced its launching of a new affiliate group called the Catholic Alliance. Christian Coalition political director Ralph Reed said that the purpose of the new group was to forge a stronger bond between conservative evangelicals and Catholics who, though perhaps unable to agree on theology, could work together in politics to promote common issues. Reed boasted that the goal of the Catholic Alliance was to recruit a million conservative Catholics into the Christian Coalition by the year 2000 and thus build a powerful pro-life force that would change the landscape of American politics.

At the same time I was working with several colleagues on a survey research project examining the religious orientations and political attitudes of delegates to Republican Party conventions in several states.[1] Although that project initially arose out of our interest in better understanding the role of the largely conservative, Protestant-led, religious right movement in the GOP, our surveys revealed a significant percentage of Catholic delegates at these conventions, many of whom identified as being a part of the religious right.

The survey findings revealed two realities about the emerging conservative Catholic–evangelical alliance in politics: first, there was little likelihood for the success of the Catholic Alliance in the Christian Coalition because, even among a population of very religiously conservative activists in the GOP, the Catholics in this

28   MARK J. ROZELL

group were distinctive on certain issues and many were not comfortable with becoming a part of conservative, Protestant-led interest group organizations; second, despite the fact that many of these Catholic Republicans were not eager to join the Christian Coalition, they were nonetheless very happy to work together with conservative evangelicals to support candidates and issue positions where these groups agreed with one another. This convergence of interests was actually not easily achieved and emerged only after many years of antipathy between these two religious groups that had kept them from working together in politics.

The Catholic Alliance ultimately failed in its effort to attract a Catholic following for the Christian Coalition. Reed obtained merely a tiny fraction of his goal of recruiting a million Catholics by year 2000, and by that time the Catholic Alliance had not only splintered away from the Christian Coalition to become an independent unit, but was being run by a Democrat. The conservative *National Review* called the hopes of recruiting Catholics into the Christian Coalition "hopelessly naïve" and continued: "Catholics weren't about to answer to Pat Robertson."[2] Nonetheless, since the mid-1990s significant strides have been made in the effort to forge an alliance in politics between conservative evangelicals and Catholics, even though this effort is not being directed by any interest group organization such as the Christian Coalition.

This chapter examines the evolution of the unlikely political alliance between Catholics and evangelicals. It will explain how two groups long steeped in opposition based on theological differences learned to put aside for the most part their debate over who will find heaven and formed the powerful alliance that has anchored the Republican Party in many parts of the country. Nonetheless, the findings here showcase the difficulties of keeping this political alliance together.

THE TRADITIONAL DIVIDE BETWEEN CATHOLICS AND EVANGELICALS

The 1960 presidential campaign of John F. Kennedy was of course the historic turning point for Catholics in U.S. politics. Questions persisted at that time over Kennedy's electability, given his religious affiliation. Much of that doubt centered on the outright hostility to his candidacy among the many prominent evangelicals who had warned their supporters of the dangers of putting a Catholic in the White House. The president of the National Association of Evangelicals (NAE) wrote to pastors that "public opinion is changing in favor of the church of Rome. We dare not sit idly by, voiceless and voteless." *Christianity Today* editorialized that the Vatican "does all in its power to control the governments of nations."[3] Kennedy famously made a speech in which he assured critics that, if elected, he would not take his directions from Rome. Although many Catholics considered the gesture demeaning, Kennedy did so to overcome fears based in anti-Catholic sentiments that were common at that time.

Although Kennedy won, antipathy between evangelicals and Catholics persisted. So deep was the contention that, prior to the landmark abortion decision of the U.S. Supreme Court in *Roe v. Wade* (1973), evangelicals and Southern Baptists often led opposition to state proposals to restrict abortion rights because Catholic-led organizations such as the National Right to Life Committee (NRTL) were promoting such legislation. For example, Marian Faux reports the interesting story of certain conservative Baptist leaders in the late 1960s who expressed discomfort with proposed anti-abortion laws mainly because of the perception that such laws reflected the religious principles of Catholics. In 1969 the Baptist General Convention of Texas went on record opposing a restrictive abortion law because it denied people "the benefit of the best medical judgment" and did not take into account such circumstances as rape, incest, and deformity. Faux traces a series of efforts by conservative Baptist leaders in Texas to thwart certain abortion restrictions out of fear that Catholic morality might become ensconced in state law. Also, evangelicals and Southern Baptists for years prominently opposed legislation providing any form of public funding to private education so that parochial schools would not reap any of the benefit.[4]

The 1970s was a decade in which there began an important shift in the intersection of politics and religion in the United States. The 1972 presidential candidacy of Senator George McGovern—dubbed by opponents as the campaign for "acid, amnesty, and abortion"—combined with the 1973 *Roe* decision caused a number of Catholics to begin to question their traditional Democratic Party loyalties. As the late William Prendergast reported in his study of Catholics in U.S. politics, for generations Catholics for the most part had comprised an immigrant working class that lived in the inner cities, joined labor unions, and voted Democratic. Newer generations of Catholics, however, were obtaining better educations and better jobs, and along with their economic success came an increased outflow from the cites to the suburbs and a willingness to vote Republican.[5] In addition, abortion through the 1960s had not been a significant issue on the national political landscape, and its emergence as a key concern in the 1970s made it, as well as economic gains, an important factor in the political shifts of some Catholics. What began in the 1970s was a gradual loosening of the Catholic habit of automatically voting Democratic; however, there was not yet any realignment toward the Republican Party.

At this time conservative evangelicals began to emerge as a major force in U.S. politics. Many prominent religious leaders, including the Reverend Jerry Falwell of Thomas Road Baptist Church in Lynchburg, Virginia, had before the *Roe* decision urged supporters not to engage the political world. But *Roe,* along with a number of state referenda on gay rights and controversies over textbooks in public schools and sex education, began to awaken evangelicals to political action. Furthermore, the 1976 presidential campaign of Jimmy Carter, a born-again Southern Baptist who proudly professed his religiosity in public, motivated many previously apolitical evangelicals to involve themselves in electoral politics. But ultimately, it was disappointment with Carter's presidency, the emergence of Falwell's Moral Majority, and 1980 GOP presidential nominee Ronald Reagan's courting of conservative evangelicals that combined to launch a powerful force in U.S. politics that became know as the religious right.

Although it was largely centered in conservative Protestantism, some political organizers saw the potential for the religious right to comprise a broad-based coalition of faithful activists. Catholics seemed the most likely potential allies in this movement. Yet in the 1980s it was the Moral Majority that overwhelmingly framed the religious right movement, and Falwell made the mistake of relying on fundamentalist pastors as the foundation of a national political organization. Few of these pastors had much political experience, and they knew little about how to reach out to nonfundamentalist groups that potentially could work in a coalition. Some observers report that beside the Moral Majority's failure to do effective ecumenical outreach, its leaders and supporters often were outright hostile to Catholics, mainline Protestants, some evangelicals, Charismatics, and Pentecostals. In a telling example, scholar Clyde Wilcox reports of attending an Ohio State Moral Majority meeting in the early 1980s, where the evening commenced with a sermon titled "Roman Catholic Church: Harlot of Rome" and continued with a political discussion in which some participants wondered why there were no pro-life Catholics and other potential allies at their gatherings.[6]

The 1970s–1980s stage of the religious right movement is widely perceived as a failure. By the end of the 1980s, Falwell's Moral Majority had gone bankrupt and disbanded, the Reverend Pat Robertson's presidential campaign had failed, several scandals involving high-profile preachers had damaged the image of the movement and hampered its fund-raising, and two terms of the Reagan presidency had delivered very little progress on the social issues agenda. Data from the General Social Survey showed that from 1978 to 1989, public opinion had become slightly more pro-choice. The 1989 Supreme Court decision in *Webster v. Reproductive Heath Services,* although it allowed the states to enact certain abortion restrictions, seemed at the time to be a hollow victory, as the political effect was to significantly recharge the abortion rights movement. As a consequence, some observers were writing the obituary for the religious right movement.

Despite all of its failings, this first wave of the movement taught a series of important lessons and built a foundation for a more successful religious right later on. Political strategists such as Paul Weyrich, Richard Viguerie, and Howard Phillips had seen the potential for a strengthened New Right if they could bring together conservative Protestants in the South and Catholics in the North and Midwest on the issue of abortion.[7] The key was to find some way to unify the different Protestant groups, and then Protestants and Catholics, around a common enemy. *Roe v. Wade* was the major impetus to awaken many of these groups into political action. Eventually, the common enemies of abortion rights, gay rights, sex education in public schools, and attacks on "family values" united a more effective political movement. The early efforts at building a broad-based movement failed, but the next wave of religious right mobilization was a different story altogether.

RELIGIOUS RIGHT GAINS WHILE CATHOLICS REMAIN AMBIVALENT

New movement organizations such as Focus on the Family and the Christian Coalition built a more successful religious right movement in the 1990s. They sought to avoid the mistakes of the first wave of the movement and to build broadly ecumenical organizations with more savvy political leaders and grassroots networks throughout the country. In an interview, Christian Coalition director Ralph Reed emphasized the diversity of his organization by pointing to the various religious affiliations of board members and state directors.[8] At its annual "Road to Victory" conferences, the Christian Coalition routinely held workshops on building bridges to Catholics and featured many Catholic speakers. It actively recruited Catholics for leadership and staff positions in the national, state, and local organizations.

There were many reasons to believe that the Christian Coalition and other Christian Right organizations could potentially attract conservative Catholics. First, there are several issues regarding which the official positions of the Catholic Church resemble those of the Christian Coalition, Family Research Council, and other religious right organizations—most notably abortion and, eventually, school vouchers. Second, there are significant numbers of Catholics in substantial agreement with certain other issue positions of the Christian Right. Third, Catholics have historically comprised a significant part of earlier right-wing movements and groups. Fourth, there had already been political cooperation in some dioceses between the Catholic Church and the Christian Coalition, particularly on school board races in some communities. Fifth and finally, some Catholics have adopted evangelical styles of religiosity, and research suggests that these Catholics are more likely to share evangelical political attitudes on issues where the Catholic Church has not staked a position.[9]

Yet Catholic teachings and tradition, particularly as articulated by the American Catholic bishops, often depart from the positions of Christian Right organizations. The Catholic Church has supported social welfare programs and expanded opportunities for women and has opposed the death penalty and nuclear weapons. The bishops have issued a critique of income inequality that is the inevitable result of unregulated capitalism. A statement by a committee of the National Conference of Catholic Bishops called for acceptance, love, and pastoral care of homosexuals. Although the Church did not abandon its traditional prohibition against homosexual activity, it recognized that a homosexual orientation is a deep-seated dimension of personality that is not in itself sinful. The statement also reiterated traditional Catholic teaching about respecting the inherent dignity of every person, and it insisted that nothing in the Bible or in Catholic teaching could be used to justify prejudicial or discriminatory attitudes and behaviors.

In an earlier research project with several colleagues, we conducted a survey of Republican Party convention delegates in several state-level nominating conventions.[10] We gathered delegates' lists from conventions in the mid-1990s in Washington, Florida, Texas, and Minnesota. For a separate project we also conducted a survey of GOP delegates in Virginia.[11] By the mid-1990s, each of these states had held nominating conventions that featured contests between moderate and religious conservative candidates. There were heavy contingents of religious conservative identifying delegates at each convention, and within this group there were large numbers of Catholics.

The survey respondents constituted an ideal group for measuring the potential for a political alliance between evangelicals and Catholics. The Catholic GOP delegates were largely conservative leaning or conservative, politically aware and active, and they had high levels of familiarity with conservative Christian organizations and leaders. They constituted the most favorable potential target group among Catholics for recruitment into Christian Right organizations. Therefore, the survey data provide some telling insights regarding the relationship between conservative Catholics and the Christian Right. A summary of our survey methods will be followed by a summary of the major findings.

Data and Methods
We surveyed random samples of delegates to the conventions. The states, years, number of cases, and return rates were as follows (all return rates exclude undeliverable mail): Florida (1996; 404 cases; 45 percent return rate); Minnesota (1995; 511 cases;

59.5 percent return rate); Texas (1995; 507 cases; 59.6 percent return rate); and Washington (1995; 506 cases; 60 percent return rate). There were no obvious response biases in any of the surveys, and the response rates were similar to those of other studies of Republican and Christian Right activists.[12]

Respondents evaluated a series of political groups on feeling thermometers. Included in the list of organizations evaluated were the Christian Coalition, Moral Majority, Concerned Women for America (CWA), and Operation Rescue. Respondents also evaluated a series of prominent Christian Right leaders and political figures. We asked respondents to indicate the types of political groups to which they belonged; one option was Christian conservative groups. The survey included measures of religious denomination, religious doctrine, religious identity, and religious practice. The survey also included a battery of questions assessing attitudes on various public policy issues.

Summary of Findings

The survey instrument asked respondents to identify their religious affiliations. Table 2.1 shows the percentages of mainline Protestants, evangelical Protestants, Catholics, Mormons, and "Other." Evangelical and mainline Protestants outnumbered Catholics in all states. Yet Catholics constituted a sizable group in each state, ranging from 9 percent in Texas to 27 percent in Minnesota.

These findings track somewhat closely with the actual percentages of Catholics in these states in the 1990s. In Minnesota, Catholics were 25 percent of the population (and 27 percent in our GOP delegate sample). Catholics were 11 percent of the Washington State population (and 13 percent in our sample). For Texas the percentage of Catholics (21 percent) was much higher than in our sample (9 percent), although the percentages would likely be closer if we excluded Latino Catholics, who are heavily Democratic. Florida was 12 percent Catholic, much smaller than the percentage in our GOP sample (21 percent), which may be explained by the large number of Latino Catholics in southern Florida who identify with the Republican Party.

Table 2.2 breaks down the membership in and support for the Christian Right by religious tradition. The data at the top half of the table show the percentages of

TABLE 2.1   Catholics, the Christian Right, and the GOP: Religious Distribution of Respondents in Each State (percent)

	FLORIDA	MINNESOTA	TEXAS	WASHINGTON
Mainline Protestants	41	31	30	29
Evangelical Protestants	30	37	56	46
Catholics	21	27	9	13
Mormons	0	0	1	4
Other	4	2	2	6
None	5	2	3	3

TABLE 2.2 Support for the Christian Right by Religious Tradition

Membership in Christian Right Organizations (percent)

	FLORIDA	MINNESOTA	TEXAS	WASHINGTON
MAINLINE PROTESTANT				
Christian conservative	29	15	26	16
pro-family	20	18	21	16
at least one	36	23	30	24
both	13	10	17	8
EVANGELICAL PROTESTANT				
Christian conservative	53	49	61	59
pro-family	40	59	58	54
at least one	57	67	71	68
both	36	41	47	45
CATHOLIC				
Christian conservative	37	26	30	40
pro-family	27	49	40	41
at least one	48	53	44	56
both	16	21	26	25

Mean Evaluations of Specific Groups

	FLORIDA	MINNESOTA	TEXAS	WASHINGTON
MAINLINE PROTESTANT				
Christian Coalition	43	40	50	40
Focus on Family	50	45	65	44
Concerned Women	37	22	57	23
Operation Rescue	24	25	39	23
EVANGELICAL PROTESTANT				
Christian Coalition	71	67	80	76
Focus on Family	76	75	87	81
Concerned Women	70	58	80	66
Operation Rescue	54	55	63	54
CATHOLIC				
Christian Coalition	55	57	67	65
Focus on Family	57	51	76	64
Concerned Women	30	35	59	29
Operation Rescue	34	45	50	46

those who claim membership in Christian conservative or pro-family groups, or both. More than half of evangelicals in the GOP are members of at least one type of group, and a sizable minority claim membership in both types. Catholics are more likely than mainline Protestants to belong to Christian Right or pro-family groups. The data show the importance of state context: in Minnesota nearly half of all Catholics are members of pro-family groups but only just over a quarter are members of a Christian conservative organization.

The bottom half of the table shows mean ratings of Christian Right groups on a "feeling thermometer" that ranges from 0 to 100, with high scores being more positive. We include the Christian Coalition, Focus on the Family, and Concerned Women for America (CWA), along with Operation Rescue, a controversial pro-life group using Christian Right rhetoric. Evangelicals in the GOP are again the most positive, with every group receiving warm ratings in each state. Catholics are generally warmer toward these groups than mainline Protestants.

Table 2.3 shows levels of support for certain Christian Right figures and political leaders. The first set of columns includes all respondents; the second set of columns includes only those respondents who are members of Christian conservative or pro-family organizations. Ratings for Robertson and especially Falwell were generally low, even among those who were members of Christian Right organizations. Catholics belonging to these organizations were even cooler toward these Christian Right leaders than evangelicals but warmer than mainline Protestants. Yet Catholic Republicans joined with evangelicals and mainline Protestants in rating Ronald Reagan highly, suggesting that candidates who make broad appeals can unify the factions of the party. The survey also examined differences in evaluations of political figures in each state (not shown). The data show that Catholic delegates were quite willing to support Christian Right–backed candidates. A similar sample of Virginia GOP delegates shows a similar general pattern: Catholic delegates were cool toward Christian Right religious leaders but very supportive of Christian Right candidates for office.[13]

The research on the Virginia Republican Party had also shown a distinctive pattern of Catholic delegates being significantly more moderate than evangelicals on the death penalty, minority rights, the role of women in society, and a host of social issues.[14] The findings of the four states survey show similar results, though the differences between Catholics and evangelicals were generally less striking (see tables 2.4 and 2.5).

TABLE 2.3 Mean Evaluations of Specific Persons

	All			Christian Right Only		
	EVANGELICAL	MAIN	CATHOLIC	EVANGELICAL	MAIN	CATHOLIC
Reagan	89	87	89	90	90	89
Robertson	60	37	46	68	57	54
Falwell	50	31	37	56	48	44
N	1123	1090	489	713	316	225

TABLE 2.4 Sources of Support for the Christian Right among Catholics—
Logistic Regression Analysis

COMBINED STATES W/ATTITUDES	Demographic Model			
	B		S.E.	
Sex	−.37	.26	−.49	.28
Education	−.05	.14	−.01	.15
Income	.08	.10	.13	.11
Born Again	2.60	1.03**	2.38	1.05*
Orthodox Religious Identities	.10	.38	.05	.39
Attendance	.29	.13**	.20	.13
Religious TV	.73	.14**	.66	.15**
Social Issue Positions			.41	.16**
Economic Issue Positions			.33	.14**
−2 log likelihood	379		337	
Predicted Correctly	68%		68%	
Of supporters	63%		61%	

B = unstandardized regression coefficient
* = <.05; ** = <.01; *** = <.10.

TABLE 2.5 Christian Right Republicans and Issue Positions

	Social Issues		Economic Issues	
	B	S.E.	B	S.E.
Sex	.15	.06**	−.09	−.07
Education	−.04	.03	.03	.04
Income	−.10	.03	.00	.03
Born Again	.13	.08	.21	.09*
Orthodox Religious Identities	.09	.03**	.07	.04***
Attendance	.12	.03**	.08	.04*
Religious TV	.05	.02*	−.03	.03
Evangelical Denomination	0.01	.08	.03	.10
Catholic Denomination	.16	.09***	.11	.11
N	1898		1875	
R²	.13		.03	

Note: All respondents in these tables are members of either "Christian conservative" or "pro-family"
groups." Data are pooled from all four state samples. * = ≤.05; ** = ≤.01; *** = ≤.10.
B = unstandardized regression coefficient.

In these four states, Catholics are more moderate than other Christian Right activists, but the specific issues differ from state to state. In three states—Minnesota, Texas, and Washington—Catholics in the GOP are less likely to favor the death penalty, but in Florida there is no significant difference. In the same three states Catholics are significantly less likely to favor regulations on pornography. In Minnesota and Texas but not Florida or Washington, Catholics are more likely to oppose cuts in services for illegal immigrants, whereas in Florida Catholics are more likely to support a higher minimum wage, to favor minimum incomes for families with children, and to favor protectionism over free trade. In Florida and Texas, Catholics are less supportive of bans on abortion and more likely to favor the Equal Rights Amendment, and in Minnesota and Washington they are less likely to support school prayer. There are twenty-three statistically significant correlations in table 2.6, and in every case Catholics are more moderate than non-Catholics.

To summarize, in the Republican Party, many Catholic activists held conservative positions on key issues emphasized by Christian Right leaders, and they said that they supported the political activities of some Christian Right organizations. More importantly from a political standpoint, they were willing to support Christian Right candidates. Yet many remained reluctant to join Christian Right groups, and many more expressed negative views toward fundamentalist groups and Protestant pastors.

Among those who were supporters of the Christian Right, Catholic delegates held policy views that were generally more conservative than mainline Protestants' but not nearly so conservative as evangelicals'. Of course, the issue differences between Catholic and evangelical Protestant delegates amounted to degrees of conservatism. Many of the Catholics attracted to the GOP were motivated primarily by moral issues, so it is no surprise that they were more agreeable to Christian Right groups and personalities than were mainline Protestants, who were largely attracted to the GOP for its economic policies.

The data report that a very small portion of all U.S. Catholics—conservative Republican Party identifiers who attend state party conventions—were favorably disposed toward Christian Right candidates and some Christian Right organizations. Although the data suggest that there was hope for those who envisioned a future political alliance between conservative Protestants and Catholics, there was very mixed evidence regarding whether Catholics were eager to accept invitations to join Christian Right organizations. That the tiny percentage of the most intensely political and conservative of potential Catholic recruits into the Christian Right was lukewarm did not send a positive message to the Christian Right about the potential for Catholic recruitment.

Politically, whether Catholics actually join the Christian Right may be less important than whether they work for its candidates. Catholics in the GOP were happy to support conservative, evangelical-backed candidates who shared a common viewpoint on certain moral issues. In personal interviews with delegates, some Catholic activists said they were reluctant to join predominantly evangelical organizations but were willing to support candidates and to lend their support on issues. Indeed, some activists said that the very process of working for non-Catholic Christian conservative GOP candidates helped to bridge some of the Catholic–evangelical divide.

TABLE 2.6 Differences in Issue Positions between Catholics and Non-Catholics in the Christian Right

	FLORIDA	MINNESOTA	TEXAS	WASHINGTON
ECONOMIC ISSUES				
Tax cut	.04	.02	.13*	.13*
Unemployment worse than inflation	.10	.01	.01	.03
Cut services for illegal immigrants	−.04	.16*	.20**	.05
Minimum income for families with children	.29**	.07	.05	.05
Free trade even if costs jobs	.18*	−.12	.01	.02
Raise minimum wage	.27**	.12	.02	.03
Gold Standard	−.07	.06	.11	.15*
SOCIAL ISSUES				
Government ban on abortion	.21**	−.06	.25**	−.07
Homosexuals allowed to teach	.02	.03	−.01	.10
ERA needed to secure women's rights	.19*	.07	.13*	.01
Government should regulate pornography	.00	.21**	.22**	.21**
Government has gone too far helping blacks and women	.04	.01	.19**	.03
Return prayer to public schools	.12	.17**	.11	.23**
Government should reduce violent TV	−.05	.03	.03	.10
Parental notification	.02	.20**	.09	−.01
Encourage women to be homemakers	.17*	.08	.02	.01
OTHER				
Tax credits for private school tuition	.18*	−.03	.13*	.05
Death penalty	.03	.26**	.14*	.25**

Note: Correlation between Catholic religious affiliation and issue positions, among all GOP activists in each state. * = ≤.05; ** = ≤.01

Bridging the Divide
While political operatives such as Reed were working hard to promote an evangelical–Catholic alliance, religious leaders were also making important efforts to bring these two groups together. But again, the results initially were mixed. In 1995 a group of evangelical and Catholic leaders—mostly theologians and scholars—issued a document titled "Evangelicals and Catholics Together: The Christian Mission in the Third Millennium" (ECT). The initial inspiration for the document came from Father Richard John Neuhaus, a prominent Catholic priest and scholar, and Chuck Colson,

the former Watergate co-conspirator and now a leading born-again Christian. Numerous major figures in the evangelical and Catholic communities signed the twenty-eight-page document that, although largely theological in context, made specific pledges to work together in politics on such issues as abortion and government aid to religious schools.

The early reactions to the document highlighted the challenges of forging a working coalition between evangelicals and Catholics. A group of one hundred evangelical leaders signed a letter denouncing ECT. Largely, these dissenters protested that ECT offered a "false unity" based on worldly political goals while undermining the true purpose of faith—eternal salvation. They objected to the document's appeal to evangelical and Catholic leaders not to engage in "sheep stealing," or proselytizing members of other faiths. Signatories of the protest letter maintained that the major error of ECT was the implied acceptance of Catholic doctrine by prominent evangelicals. Colson reported that over a million dollars in donations to his Prison Fellowship Ministries were withdrawn after the ECT document was issued, and that he received numerous angry letters from evangelicals.[15] Several evangelical signers of ECT removed their names from the document after the protest, and some kept their names on it but issued clarifications of their views on Catholic doctrine. There was not a similar organized protest to ECT by leading Catholics, although some warned that evangelical signers' real motivation was to open a door to efforts to convert Catholics. Indeed, some evangelical signers defended themselves from criticism within their community by stating that they supported ECT exactly for that reason.

Nonetheless, evangelical and Catholic leaders report that the protests eventually faded and that the impact of ECT was far more positive in the long run toward fostering a dialogue and political cooperation. Common enemies, particularly abortion, the decline of "traditional values," and the strengthening of the gay rights movement had a good deal to do with making such cooperation possible. Also, savvy GOP leaders have played an important role in fostering cooperation among religious conservatives.

As Wheaton College scholar Mark Noll puts it, "Catholics and evangelicals who advocate conservative convictions on chastity, family, and community have found each other as co-belligerents, and this co-belligerency has eased much of the hostility that once separated the two movements. President [George W.] Bush, himself a born-again Christian, has worked hard at nurturing cooperation with conservative Catholic leadership." Noll acknowledges that some Catholics and evangelicals still exchange condemnations, "but over the past few decades the once isolated worlds of Catholic and evangelical Christianity have experienced unprecedented interchange, overlap, and cross-fertilization." In addition to ECT, Noll cites as especially important to this development the commitment to interreligious dialogue of Pope John Paul II, who attracted the admiration of evangelicals for his past resistance to communism and his steadfast commitment to the "culture of life." Many younger generation evangelicals in particular became strong admirers of the pope and undertook efforts to learn more about Catholic theology.[16]

President George W. Bush also stands as a key figure in the evolution of a conservative Catholic–evangelical political alliance. Bush made outreach to conservative Catholics a centerpiece of his strategy to build a broad base of support among the faithful. He purposefully weaved familiar Catholic discourse into many of his speeches and thus showcased his support for much of what traditional Catholics believe.

Conservative Catholics and evangelicals now comprise the core support of the Republican Party. In 2004 President Bush won 80 percent of the evangelical vote and 52 percent of the Catholic vote against a Catholic candidate, Senator John Kerry. Catholics and evangelicals delivered about thirty-six million votes for Bush, significantly more than one-half of his nearly sixty-million-vote total.

Considering that Catholics were once a reliable part of the old New Deal coalition that anchored the Democratic Party, and that for generations Catholics and evangelicals stood in strong opposition in theology and politics, this development is remarkable. That conservative Catholics shied away from joining conservative, Protestant-led political organizations such as the Christian Coalition turned out to be not very important to the quest to bring these two religious groups together in politics. The 1990s research surveys discussed above make it clear that Catholic activists in the GOP were still quite distinctive in their views on a number of issues and that they were not favorably inclined to support certain religious right leaders or organizations. But the survey data also made it clear that on certain moral issues, these religious groups could easily come together and work for causes and candidates who supported their common views. In electoral politics, that is far more important than coming together in an interest group.

CONCLUSION

That conservative Catholics and evangelicals did eventually come together in politics was due to several factors, primarily opposition to the cultural challenges to "traditional values." Common enemies can do far more to unite once-opposing groups than proactive attempts to bring those groups together. Common interests also united these groups somewhat as well. For example, for generations evangelicals stood for a strict separation of church and state and strongly opposed government aid to parochial schools. Now, with many Christian academies for evangelicals, that sentiment has been reversed as evangelicals and Catholics have joined to support government aid to religious schools through vouchers.

Leaders admired within the evangelical and Catholic communities also played a key role. For Catholics, the call by John Paul II for active interreligious dialogue had a significant impact, and many evangelicals also came to admire a pope who, they felt, spoke more forcefully on "life issues" than many of their own leaders. In some quarters there even were references to "the evangelical pope." David Kuo, the former director of the Office of Faith-Based Initiatives, wrote that: "The union of Catholics and evangelicals wouldn't have been possible without John Paul II. His encyclicals on abortion were well-known in evangelical Christian intellectual circles. . . . He made evangelicals feel right at home."[17] For traditional Catholics, the outreach by certain evangelical leaders and by President Bush, as well as the increased interest among many younger evangelicals in learning Catholic theology, all contributed to an increased comfort level or of feeling "right at home."

Yet the case for a continued political alliance can be made only with caution, because divisions persist between these religious groups. Evangelicals were among the strongest supporters of the U.S. war in Iraq. The Vatican opposed the war. A study by Jeremy Mayer shows that conservative Protestant and Catholic attitudes on Israel and on the Palestinian issue diverge significantly, with the former far more pro-Israel and anti-Palestinian than the latter.[18] Many Catholics retain their sentiments on social and economic justice issues that once attracted most of them to the Democratic Party. Even the small population of Catholics who were GOP delegates identified with more moderate positions on all issues than did the conservative Protestant delegates.

The 2006 elections also offer a hint of caution to those who foresee a long-term alliance between Catholics and evangelicals in the GOP. In the congressional elections the Democrats matched Bush's 2004 showing among Catholic voters at 52 percent. The Democrats also improved significantly among evangelicals, although unfortunately data comparisons nationally are not possible because many states' exit polls lacked a question that would have identified the evangelical vote. In some key states featuring pro-choice Democratic candidates against Christian Right–backed Republicans, the outcomes were quite telling. In Ohio, for example, the GOP ran a leading Christian Right figure for governor who lost the Catholic vote by a 20 percent margin to his victorious Democratic opponent. In this same state in 2004, Bush had won a commanding margin among Catholics, 55 percent to 44 percent for Kerry. The GOP gubernatorial candidate probably won the evangelical vote, though pre-election polls showed a close margin even there. In the Senate race in Ohio, the Democratic candidate won the election and carried the Catholic vote 54 percent to 46 percent. The gubernatorial race in Michigan saw 56 percent of Catholics voting for the Democratic incumbent, again a significant improvement over Bush's showing in 2004, when he won 50 percent of the Catholic votes in the state. Only a slight majority of evangelicals favored the GOP candidate, a more than 30 percent swing from Bush's showing among evangelicals in that state in 2004.[19]

Of course, 2006 was an unusual election year in which the failing war in Iraq, Bush's declining popularity, a lobbying scandal, and the egregious personal misconduct of GOP congressman Mark Foley, who resigned in disgrace, had dominated political discourse and undercut the prominence of issues that normally would have brought conservative evangelicals and Catholics together as a GOP voting bloc. Even so, that the much-touted alliance between these groups largely faltered in a single election cycle reveals its fragility. Proponents of this alliance had hoped that these voters would stand firmly together on the so-called life issues in each election cycle, regardless of the political context, and would propel the GOP into permanent majority status.

Scholar Mary Segers explains that the fragility of the alliance is due more to Catholic than to evangelical wavering, given the conflicting partisan sentiments of American Catholics generally. "They tend to support simultaneously an activist government in economic matters (a Democratic tendency) and in moral matters (a Republican tendency). A Catholic citizen may vote Republican on the issue of abortion and Democratic" on social justice issues, she observed.[20] And very noticeably, almost all of the organized, political-based effort to date to bring evangelicals and Catholics together has been initiated by conservative, Protestant-led groups, with Catholics being the often-ambivalent receptors of these appeals for cooperation.

Thus, there appear to be reasons both for cooperation and conflict between evangelicals and Catholics. Within the conservative GOP community, cooperation is strong but not always certain. Given the enduring differences between these groups, the emergence of a conservative evangelical and Catholic alliance gives meaning to the old adage that "politics makes for strange bedfellows." Of course, sometimes strange bedfellows end up in a marriage of convenience when they see that they can benefit together. But many of the differences that preceded their marriage remain and could make for a bumpy long-term relationship.

NOTES

1. Mark J. Rozell, John C. Green, and Clyde Wilcox, "The Christian Right in the 1990s," *Social Science Quarterly* 79, no. 4 (December 1998): 815–20; Mary E. Bendyna, RSM, John C. Green, Mark J. Rozell, and Clyde Wilcox, "Catholics and the Christian Right: A View from Four States," *Journal for the Scientific Study of Religion* 39, no. 3 (September 2000): 321–32; Mark J. Rozell and Clyde Wilcox, *Second Coming: The New Christian Right in Virginia Politics* (Baltimore, MD: The Johns Hopkins University Press, 1996).

2. Kathryn Jean Lopez, "Religious Fight," *National Review,* May 18, 1998, 42–43.

3. Laurie Goodstein, "The 'Hypermodern' Foe: How Evangelicals and Catholics Joined Forces," *New York Times,* May 30, 2004, available from www.yucareport.com/Dominionism/HowCatholicsJoinedEvangelicals.html (accessed January 29, 2007).

4. Marian Faux, *Roe v. Wade: The Untold Story of the Landmark Supreme Court Decision That Made Abortion Legal* (New York: Macmillan, 1988).

5. William B. Prendergast, *The Catholic Voter in American Politics* (Washington, DC: Georgetown University Press, 1999). See chapter 1 on demographic and political shifts of U.S. Catholics.

6. Clyde Wilcox, *God's Warriors: The Christian Right in Twentieth-Century America* (Baltimore, MD: The Johns Hopkins University Press, 1992), 130.

7. A. James Reichley, *Religion in American Public Life* (Washington, DC: Brookings Institution, 1985).

8. Rozell and Wilcox, *Second Coming,* 61.

9. Michael R. Welch and David C. Leege, "Dual Reference Groups and Political Orientations: An Examination of Evangelically Oriented Catholics," *American Journal of Political Science* 35 (1991): 28–35.

10. Bendyna et al., "Catholics and the Christian Right," 321–32.

11. Rozell and Wilcox, *Second Coming;* Mary E. Bendyna, RSM, John C. Green, Mark J. Rozell, and Clyde Wilcox, "Uneasy Alliance: Conservative Catholics and the Christian Right," *Sociology of Religion* 62, no. 1 (Spring 2001): 51–64.

12. Wilcox, *God's Warriors;* Rozell, Green, and Wilcox, "The Christian Right in the 1990s," 815–20; Rozell and Wilcox, *Second Coming.*

13. Bendyna, Green, Rozell, and Wilcox, "Uneasy Alliance," 51–64.

14. Ibid.

15. Laurie Goodstein, "The 'Hypermodern' Foe."

16. Mark Noll, "The Evangelical Pope?" *Boston Globe,* April 10, 2005, available from http://boston.com/news/globe/ideas/articles/2005/04/10/the_evangelical_pope?mode... (accessed January 29, 2007).

17. David Kuo, "Crossing the Thresholds of Faith, Hope, and Politics," 2006, available from www.beliefnet.com/story/164/story_16446.html (accessed February 7, 2007).

18. Jeremy Mayer, "Christian Fundamentalists and Public Opinion toward the Middle East: Israel's New Best Friends?" *Social Science Quarterly* 85, no. 3 (September 2004): 695–712.

19. Amy Sullivan, "Catholics and Evangelicals Are Now Voting for Democrats," *The New Republic Online,* November 8, 2006, available from http://magazines.enews.com/doc.mhtml?i=w061106&s=sullivan110806 (accessed on February 7, 2007).

20. Mary Segers, "Catholics and the 2000 Presidential Election: Bob Jones University and the Catholic Vote," in *Piety, Politics, and Pluralism: Religion, the Courts, and the 2000 Election,* ed. Mary Segers (Lanham, MD: Rowman & Littlefield, 2000), 89.

3

ONE CHURCH, MANY MESSAGES

The Politics of the U.S. Catholic Clergy

GREGORY A. SMITH

ROUGHLY ONE IN FOUR ADULTS in the United States is Catholic, making this group a vitally important segment of the American electorate. Accordingly, an important part of the burgeoning research on religion and politics has focused on understanding the political attitudes and voting decisions of American Catholics, which has shed a great deal of light on the religion-politics connection within this group. But while much has been learned in recent years about how their Catholicism shapes the politics of American Catholics, one topic that has been somewhat underexplored is the question of the role played by Catholic religious leaders in influencing the politics of the American Catholic laity.

There are several potential sources of religious authority within the Church that might plausibly be expected to wield political influence with American Catholics. Most obviously, the Church hierarchy might be looked to as a source of political guidance. Surveys show, however, that many Catholics hold political opinions that diverge from Church teaching on a number of important issues. And the influence of the institutional Church is also limited by the fact that its political positions do not map well onto American politics. The argument here is that parish priests, by contrast, represent a more promising source of Church authority to which to look for evidence of political influence wielded by religious elites. Given their potential influence with such a large segment of the American electorate, it is vitally important to examine the nature and the tone of the political messages emanating from parish priests. Drawing on structured interviews with a sample of nine Catholic pastors conducted during the 2004 election season, this chapter demonstrates that the political messages emanating from religious leaders to which Catholics are exposed vary considerably from parish to parish. Priests at some parishes consistently deliver homilies with politically liberal overtones, while priests at other parishes regularly deliver sermons with politically conservative overtones, and still other pastors fall somewhere in between. The varying content and tone of these priestly messages have potentially large implications for American politics and electoral outcomes.

BACKGROUND AND THEORY

As mentioned, much research in recent years has focused on the changing politics of American Catholics. Since the 1960s the Catholic vote has become less monolithically Democratic, and a substantial amount of evidence indicates that this change is due in part to simple changes in Catholic demographics.[1] Earlier in the twentieth century, Catholics were poorer, less educated, and more recently immigrants as compared to the rest of the population, and as such were much more likely to vote Democratic. Over time, however, as Catholics caught up with the rest of the population in terms of wealth and education, so too did Catholic voting patterns come to resemble more closely those of the rest of the country.

But Catholic politics cannot be explained solely by reference to the sociodemographics of the group. For Catholics, much as for Americans of other religious traditions, religious identity, beliefs, and behavior each play an important role in forming and shaping political attitudes. Clyde Wilcox, Ted G. Jelen, and David C. Leege, for example, determined that knowing the "specific identity of a Catholic" (for example, whether one is a traditional, ethnic, charismatic, or post–Vatican II Catholic) can provide important additional insight into Catholics' political attitudes over and above that gained from simply knowing whether one is Catholic.[2]

Just as religious identity is important for shaping the religion and politics connection among Catholics, so too is religious behavior. Kenneth D. Wald, Lyman A. Kellstedt, and Leege, for instance, determined that for Catholics, as with those of other religions, involvement in church activities was a key predictor of certain political attitudes. Specifically, they found that although Catholics "were significantly more prochoice than the nonreligious," they "turned against liberal abortion laws as a consequence of high levels of church involvement," confirming that "the message transmitted by the church was apparently perceived and internalized by the strongly involved congregant."[3] In addition to involvement in Church activities, evangelicalism has been shown to play an important role in shaping Catholic politics. According to Michael R. Welch and Leege, "Catholics who practice evangelical-style patterns of devotion take more 'conservative' positions on issues relating to abortion, premarital cohabitation, and the male's role as sole 'breadwinner' for the family."[4]

Finally, religious beliefs play an important role in forming Catholics' approach to politics.[5] Kellstedt and Smidt, for instance, demonstrate that, among Catholics, views of the Bible are related to attitudes about abortion; those who considered the Bible to be the actual word of God were significantly more opposed to abortion than were those Catholics who considered the Bible to be only the inspired word of God.[6] And in another study, Leege used respondents' answers to questions about the fundamental problem of human existence, their views about how religion responds to that problem, and their thoughts on possible solutions to the problem to classify Catholics along an individualist-communitarian continuum. The findings show that, for Catholics, religious individualists were more conservative than were religious communitarians with regard to "women's rights, male-female family roles, the threat of secular humanism, and sexuality."[7]

Much important research thus demonstrates the important role that religion plays in shaping Catholic politics in the United States. But one topic that has been largely underexplored in the research on Catholic politics (and in the religion and politics literature more generally) is the question of the role of religious elites in helping to shape the political attitudes of religious adherents.[8] Within the Catholic tradition, perhaps the most obvious source of elite guidance to which Catholics might turn for political direction is the hierarchy of the institutional Church. This is especially so since the Church hierarchy has staked out very clear positions on a number of contemporary sociopolitical issues; the Church advocates a "consistent ethic of life" by taking a very (politically) conservative position with respect to many social issues such as abortion and sexual morality and adopting a much more (politically) liberal approach to capital punishment, social justice issues, and foreign affairs.

But if one thing is clear about Catholic politics, it is that most American Catholics do not subscribe to a consistent ethic of life.[9] Indeed, recent polling conducted by the Pew Research Center reveals that roughly four in ten Catholics (and half of white, non-Hispanic Catholics) believe that abortion should either be generally available or legal with more limitations than are currently in place; fewer than one in five Catholics, by contrast, say that abortion should never be permitted.[10] And though large majorities of Catholics favor providing more generous government assistance to the poor, a majority also favors the death penalty for persons convicted of murder.[11] Of course, it is not entirely surprising that American Catholics do not march in lockstep with the political directives of the Church hierarchy. High-level Church leaders, such as the pope, cardinals, and bishops, may be rather distant from the American laity, which may or may not be aware of Church teachings and pronouncements on social and political issues. Additionally, as other scholars have pointed out, official Catholic social and political thought does not align well with the American political context; while both the Republican and the Democratic Parties share the Church's convictions on certain political issues, neither party espouses positions consistent with Catholic teaching across the spectrum of political issues, leaving any American who hopes to pursue a completely Catholic politics with few options in the electoral arena.[12] Should a faithful Catholic vote for the Republican Party on the basis of its conservative positions on abortion and sexual morality, or for the Democratic Party because of its relatively liberal positions on social justice issues?

Parish priests, in contrast to the Church hierarchy, might be in a better position from which to influence Catholic politics.[13] Priests are closer and more accessible to the laity than is the Church hierarchy. And while Church leaders are constrained to consistently and forcefully advance the Church's teachings across the full spectrum of sociopolitical topics, priests are not so constrained. Though priests may not be able to openly dissent from official Church teaching, they may choose, in their preaching, to emphasize particular issues while downplaying others. Because the size of the Catholic population in the United States makes Catholics a highly important segment of the American electorate, because it is known that that the laity's Catholicism helps to shape its politics, and because parish priests (and not simply the Church hierarchy) represent a potentially important link in shaping the religion and politics connection among American Catholics, it is vitally important to consider the political messages to which Catholics are exposed from their local priests.

METHODS AND RESULTS

Of course, the assertion that priests represent a potentially important source of independent influence in American politics—and do not simply serve as conduits of official Church positions—necessarily implies that there is variance in the priestly messages to which parishioners are exposed. And while it would be surprising, given the hierarchical nature of the Church, to find that priests publicly express opinions (such as support for legalized abortion or opposition to efforts, governmental and otherwise, to help the poor and disadvantaged) that clearly conflict with official Church teaching, the hypothesis here is that substantial variance exists in the priestly messages to which Catholic parishioners are exposed.

To attempt to understand the nature and degree of variance in priestly messages heard by Catholic parishioners, case studies have been conducted at nine Catholic parishes. These studies were conducted during the summer and fall of 2004, while the presidential campaign was well under way, as part of a broader consideration of Catholic politics. Of the nine Catholic parishes, three were randomly chosen from each of three Catholic dioceses located in the mid-Atlantic region.[14] The Diocese of Arlington encompasses Catholic parishes in the northern part of Virginia; the Diocese of Richmond comprises the rest of the state of Virginia; and the Archdiocese of Washington encompasses Catholic parishes in Washington, D.C., and in part of central and southern Maryland. Pseudonyms for the parishes and priests that participated in the project (used to protect the anonymity of the parishes and the priests) are provided in table 3.1.

TABLE 3.1   Parish and Pastor Information (pseudonyms)

Diocese of Arlington		Diocese of Richmond		Archdiocese of Washington	
PARISH	PASTOR	PARISH	PASTOR	PARISH	PASTOR
St. Anastasia	Fr. Alexander	St. Margaret	Fr. McCormick	St. Winifred	Fr. Williams
St. Barnabas	Fr. Boyd	St. Leon	Fr. Lewis	St. Yolanda	Fr. Yardley
St. Cyrus	Fr. Cook	St. Norbert	Fr. Nolan	St. Zachary	Fr. Zimmerman

At each parish, in-depth, structured interviews with the pastor were conducted, designed primarily to learn about his approach to preaching. Each pastor was asked about the frequency and manner with which he addresses each of a number of different topics. These interviews provided strong support for the hypothesis outlined above. Though there were certain similarities that most of these pastors shared (nearly all of them indicated that they enjoy preaching and indicated that their homilies consist of a combination of a reflection on the day's scripture reading and an application of the material contained therein to everyday life, and there was little variance in the manner with which they reported addressing foreign affairs), there was remarkable variance in the number and tone of political messages that the pastors who were interviewed report delivering to their parishioners. During the course of the interviews with them, important differences emerged in the pastors' various approaches to addressing aid to the poor, abortion, homosexuality, and birth control. In addition, the interviews revealed that there are substantial differences among pastors as to which issue or issues receive paramount attention in their preaching and public messages.

Specifically, three pastors can be described as "social justice priests," in that they speak often about the need to provide aid to the poor and disadvantaged while rarely addressing abortion, homosexuality, or contraception in their sermons. Three other pastors can be classified as "personal morality priests"; though they do not shy away from preaching about aid to the poor, they do dedicate substantially more attention to abortion and sexual morality in their preaching than do other priests, and they tend to place special emphasis on abortion (as opposed to other sociopolitical issues) in their public statements. Finally, three pastors can be classified as "mixed-emphasis priests," in that they fall somewhere in between.

The political messages emanating from parish priests to which Catholic parishioners are exposed thus vary considerably from parish to parish. We turn now to a more complete description of these varying approaches to political preaching.

Social Justice Priests

Three of the pastors who participated in this project—Father Williams and Father Yardley from the Archdiocese of Washington and Father McCormick from the Diocese of Richmond—can be described as social justice priests. All three indicated that they regularly address the Church's teachings on the necessity of providing aid and assistance to the poor and disadvantaged. And, importantly, their comments suggest that when they address this subject, they do so not only in the context of urging individuals to be sensitive to the needs of the less fortunate, but also in the context of highlighting a governmental or political responsibility to care for the poor. Father Williams, for instance, when asked whether he preaches on aid to the poor in primarily an individual or governmental context, responded by saying, "I think, both . . . you know, if the gospel lends it to talk about the hungry in the world, for instance, I might talk about bread for the world . . . [and] how that helps people directly financially but also through lobbying groups. And . . . I talk about the government responsibility, although I think one [area] where people can be more responsive nowadays is they read the paper where the government's cutting back on programs and so the churches have to pick up the slack."

Father McCormick, in a similar vein, reported that his own preaching on this issue is "a combination of both [individual and governmental context]. To awaken the individual parishioner, but the parish as a community, as a group working together toward these issues and alleviating those issues. . . . It would be on the occasion . . . that the Diocese itself comes out with an issue as regards the Virginia legislature, or the Bishops of the United States do as regards a national motion towards something." And though Father Yardley initially indicated that he typically preaches about aid to the poor in terms of individual responsibility, the examples he cited suggest that he, too, might frequently address governmental policy toward the poor. He indicated, for instance, that though he does not think aid to the poor "has much to do with public policy," it is true that

> Every once in a while we will alert people, we have a social concerns table in our gathering space. And there may be something that comes across my desk from the social concerns committee, that will say something like this is what . . . [Walmart] is doing . . . this is how it affects the local economy. Or it has to do with living wage. So there will come things, we have a legislative network here so that people can be tied into that so that they can get announcements about how to respond to their politicians from the Maryland Catholic Conference. . . . I don't preach about it very much, but it's something that they become aware of those things.

Though Father Yardley, then, refrains from frequently structuring his homilies around the topic of governmental responsibility to provide aid to the poor, his comments make clear that he takes steps to publicize political issues on this topic with his parishioners as the issues arise.

While Father Williams, Father Yardley, and Father McCormick thus speak freely about aid to the poor, and do so even in the context of highlighting the government's role in this arena, they are much more circumspect in the frequency with which, and the manner in which, they preach about the Church's (conservative) position on abortion. Each of them indicated that they publicly address the abortion issue only on rare occasions, most typically on special Sundays (such as the weekend of the March for Life, in January, or on Respect Life Sunday, in October) set aside by the Church as days on which to focus on abortion, or life issues in general. When asked how often the subject of abortion arises in his homilies, Father Yardley told me that "it comes up maybe, I think I might talk about it twice a year. At the anniversary of *Roe v. Wade,* and October is Respect Life Month . . . it's probably only those things that prompt me to bring it up. Otherwise it doesn't come up very often." For Father Williams, abortion may arise even more infrequently. When asked how often he speaks about abortion in his homilies, he replied by saying, "Usually in the month of January, we're encouraged to talk about this issue, so usually I do once a year." He went on to elaborate, explaining that "it's hard to bring a new slant to it [the abortion issue], and I find the people in front of you have not had abortions, so you have to treat it in a sense of education but not indict the people that are sitting in front of you, because the people who have abortions don't go to Church, so by talking about people who don't go to Church on Sunday, the people in front of you are there, so why talk about those who aren't there?" Similarly, Father McCormick indicated that he, too, publicly addresses abortion on only a couple of occasions throughout the year. He told me, "I preach on it on the anniversary of the Supreme Court decision. . . . And then I'll have a special Mass during the week of whenever March 25 occurs, which is the Catholic Feast of the Annunciation. So when Jesus' life began in the womb of Mary. . . . And so, it would be the occasion of the Roe decision and then March 25, so they'd be deliberate times when the thing would be on abortion."

While Father Yardley, Father Williams, and Father McCormick report similar frequency in publicly addressing abortion, there is important variance in the context in which they report doing so. Father Yardley indicated that he addresses abortion in the dual context of individual morality and government policy. He told me that in his congregation, "There are not many people who are out having abortions. There are a number of people out there I'm aware who believe that it should be legalized. And so when I speak about it, I speak about . . . how can it be that we even can come to a conclusion that . . . having an abortion is something that we can choose to do? Because it's the taking of a life, and it's denying a fact, a reality, a person."

Father Williams and Father McCormick take different approaches to their preaching on abortion. When asked whether he focuses on individual morality or politics and public policy with regard to abortion, Father Williams said simply, "Usually that issue is more individual responsibility." And Father McCormick adopts an approach unique among all of the pastors who were interviewed. He explained to me that, under canon law, the fetus is not considered a person. Abortion, therefore, despite the claims made by so many priests and other pro-life activists, is not murder under canon law. Most importantly, Father McCormick emphasized that he makes this point clear to his parishioners whenever he discusses abortion, telling them that "you cannot ever say it's murder." None of this is to imply that Father McCormick is not just as pro-life as the other pastors interviewed, for he is clearly opposed to abortion. Nevertheless, it seems safe to conclude that parishioners who hear Father McCormick claim explicitly that abortion is not murder are hearing a message that is quite different than that heard by parishioners at other parishes in this study who, as will be shown below, hear that in abortion, "we're dealing with authentic human life."

While these three social justice priests only rarely preach about abortion, they address other issues on which the Church takes a conservative stand—contraception and homosexuality—with even less regularity. All three priests reported that contraception, for instance, is a topic that rarely or never arises in their homilies. Father Yardley explained, "I guess I haven't publicly said anything about it [birth control] . . . I mean I totally accept and agree with everything the Church teaches. But I also don't feel like these are issues that I'm trying to force on people." Father Williams was even more explicit and forceful when asked whether or not he addresses contraception in his homilies. He said, "I think that's something that's been decided by the people. I think that issue . . . that's a non-issue. That issue's over . . . I don't see a need to [discuss contraception] because I don't think it's an issue." Finally, Father McCormick suggested that this is a topic that does not arise in his own homilies, but hinted that when it does, he may imply that the prohibition on birth control might not be so clear-cut. He explained, "I don't use the term birth control . . . or contraception. . . . When this does come up, I say people have the responsibility to plan their families reasonably.

And they should do so according to how the Church teaches. But I said there's a lot of things that aren't clear in this area. It doesn't come up." For this group of pastors, then, contraception is not a key, or even a peripheral, focus of their preaching.

Father Williams and Father Yardley adopt a similar approach to preaching about homosexuality, which is a topic they largely avoid. Father McCormick indicated that homosexuality is a topic that arises in his homilies and in his public prayers on occasion. Importantly, he indicated that when homosexuality does arise in his public comments, he is careful to balance the Church's teaching about the sinfulness of homosexual behavior with the need to have compassion for individuals of homosexual orientation. When I asked him whether he tended to emphasize the sinfulness of homosexual behavior or the need to be compassionate toward homosexuals, he said, "I would think it's a combined thrust." This is in stark contrast to the approach adopted by personal morality priests, as will be shown below.

Finally, I asked each pastor whether he tends to place special emphasis on any sociopolitical issue or set of issues. Many of the pastors I spoke with—including Father McCormick and Father Williams—indicated that they attempt to place equal emphasis on all of the sociopolitical issues on which the Church has taken a stand. Only one, Father Yardley, indicated that he tends to emphasize aid to the poor (on which the Church espouses relatively liberal teachings) over other issues. He said, "I mention abortion, or life issues, that happens twice a year, January and October. Unless there's something else that happens that it's right in our faces that we should bring something up. . . . But I think that, of those, the fact that we do talk about helping others does come up probably more than anything else . . . through Haiti, through other projects that we do, the Cardinal's appeal, and saying to people and talking to them about stewardship and tithing, where are they putting their treasure." While there is reason to suspect that many Catholic priests share Father Yardley's tendency to emphasize aid to the poor and social justice issues in their preaching, he was the only pastor participating in this study who explicitly acknowledged that pattern.

Father Yardley, Father Williams, and Father McCormick, then, exhibit what might safely be described as a social justice–focused approach to preaching. They preach often about the Church's teachings on aid to the poor, and do so even in the context of pointing out the role of government in addressing the needs of the disadvantaged. They speak much less frequently about other issues on which the Church takes a more politically conservative stand (abortion, contraception, and homosexuality), and even when these issues are addressed, the conservative thrust of the Church's teachings on these issues may be mitigated by the context in which they are discussed.

Mixed-Emphasis Priests

Three priests, Father Alexander and Father Cook from the Diocese of Arlington and Father Nolan from the Diocese of Richmond, exhibited a more middle-of-the-road approach to their preaching on political issues. Like social justice priests, all three mixed-emphasis pastors indicated a willingness to address the Church's teachings on aid to the poor. And the comments of one mixed-emphasis pastor, Father Alexander, suggest that he, too, like the social justice priests, occasionally highlights the government's responsibility to assist in alleviating poverty.

All three mixed-emphasis priests indicate that they tend to place equal emphasis on a variety of sociopolitical issues rather than highlight any single issue as the paramount political topic with which Catholics should be concerned. Father Cook, for instance, explicitly invoked the example of Cardinal Bernardin's consistent ethic of life:

> I guess I would have to say, what guides me is, in my own personal preaching and spiritual life and pastoral leadership, I think I have a pretty strong conviction that Cardinal Bernardin had a point with his consistent ethic of life. So if I had one theme that's important to me, it's that all human life is sacred. And that means one thing, that principle means one thing when it's applied to war and peace, when it's applied to abortion and euthanasia and capital punishment, when it's applied to issues of poverty, health care, housing. I guess that's what I try to do. I don't have a hierarchy. . . . If I'm pro-life, that means I'm against abortion, against capital punishment, I'm for providing healthcare to the greatest number of people, and adequate housing, and food and clothing to the greatest number of people. And I'm against war. You know, that war should be a last resort, a real last resort. So that's how I would look at it. That's the value to me that's paramount. Are we consistently pro-life.

The primary difference between mixed-emphasis priests and social justice priests consists in the relative willingness of the mixed-emphasis priests publicly to address abortion in their preaching; both Father Alexander and Father Cook indicated that abortion is a topic they discuss occasionally, whereas the social justice priests indicated that they publicly preach about abortion only rarely. Father Alexander said that his homilies during the week of the March for Life (in January) and on Respect Life Sunday (in October) "might be totally devoted to life." Otherwise, abortion might come up "as part of" a homily "four or five times a year." Father Cook told me that he does not

> shy away from speaking about abortion, but it's not something that comes up that frequently, but I would suppose it comes up, maybe, four to six times a year, in a special way I would say at least once a year at the March For Life in January. And in October, which is a special month that the Church designates as a month for respecting life. And then on other occasions, when it seems to be appropriate based on [the scripture] readings, or I try to be aware of what is . . . in people's attention, especially media attention to issues. So I wouldn't come up on a particular Sunday and think I haven't talked about abortion in three months, maybe I should remind people about that. I would be more looking at the fact that, since I read the newspaper everyday and I watch the news every night, . . . and if the issue is in the forefront of what the media is addressing, . . . then I would think the Church needs to share its vision or its message.

While Father Alexander and Father Cook thus publicly discuss abortion on an occasional basis, the frequency with which Father Nolan preaches about abortion was less clear. Unlike the social justice priests, however, Father Nolan did not indicate that he restricts his comments on abortion to one or a few Sundays each year. He did make clear that he scrupulously avoids discussing public policy as it relates to abortion. Indeed, Father Nolan made this point emphatically, stating, "I have never once said from the pulpit the words 'Roe v. Wade.' Never." He went on to explain that he thinks it is the duty of the Catholic and Christian communities to hold their members accountable on these types of issues, and that relying on politicians or public officials for moral guidance is futile. He said that he has "more trust and faith in them [his parishioners], and they should in me, because we both are trying to follow the Lord Jesus in all that we do, and I don't sit down there looking at eleven people on that dais in city council and think that any of them are trying to follow Jesus necessarily. Or Mohammed, or any of the rest of the guys."

The approach to preaching adopted by mixed-emphasis priests is similar, in many ways, to that adopted by social justice priests. Both groups preach openly about the Church's teachings on aid to the poor and tend to avoid focusing much attention on homosexuality or birth control. Mixed-emphasis priests are, however, comparatively more willing publicly to address the Church's teachings on abortion and indicated that they place equal emphasis across the spectrum of sociopolitical issues.

Personal Morality Priests

Finally, the comments of three priests—Father Boyd from the Diocese of Arlington, Father Lewis from the Diocese of Richmond, and Father Zimmerman from the Archdiocese of Washington—suggest that they might best be described as personal morality priests. All three, like the social justice and mixed-emphasis priests, indicated a willingness to address the Church's teachings on aid to the poor. When they address this issue, however, these priests do so primarily with reference to the responsibility of individuals to come to the aid of the poor and disadvantaged and tend to avoid focusing on public policy regarding these matters. Father Boyd, for instance, when asked specifically whether he emphasizes individual responsibility for helping the poor, public policy, or some combination thereof, responded by saying, "It's the first [individual responsibility]." He went on to tell me that he, personally, greatly admires the work of Mother Theresa, who sought "out the poorest of the poor." He pointed out, however, that "mostly, Mother Theresa, not that she didn't believe in government programs, but she, her main pitch was we do our own, and so, subsidiarity, the lowest level possible." Father Zimmerman stated

> I'm more of the bent that we should try and help those we can see. I'm not fond of the anonymous institutions that you give to [such as the government] and somehow feel gratified. See, I want you to go visit a poor person, sit in their home, eat with them, just as Jesus would. See what their problems are, and how you can assist them. It's not always money. You've got people who sometimes just need companionship. And money as the solution to problems, I think, as Paul tells Timothy, money is the root of all evil ... in that bent I'm more toward the individual thing.

Perhaps Father Lewis was the most blunt of the pastors who indicated that they encouraged individuals to become involved in providing assistance to those in need while refraining from encouraging parishioners to support government programs designed to do the same:

> I would say that Catholics have a moral responsibility from the very aspect of what faith is to follow out Christ's call to practice the corporal and spiritual works of

mercy. These are not options, they are obligations that are placed upon us. . . .
And I always emphasize that we have to be personally involved, not remotely involved. And so the individual charities that we might be involved in, these are
things that have direct impact in a personal way. I also believe that because of our
faith we have to have a clear and consistent voice in the political domain.

Despite this need for a clear political voice, however, Father Lewis went on by
claiming, "I would also say that many times, church sponsored agencies do a much
better job of assisting the poor than government initiated enterprises. I would for example support the whole idea of faith based initiatives. They have a proven track
record. Government controlled agencies are inefficient and expensive and often inef-
fective." In short, while they do not shy away from addressing the Church's teaching
regarding aid to the poor, this group of priests adopts quite a different approach than
that employed by social justice priests, in that their preaching on this issue focuses almost exclusively on the need for individual parishioners and citizens, in their private
capacities, to become involved in these kinds of activities.

While there are important differences in the context within which personal
morality priests and social justice priests report addressing Church teachings on aid
to the poor, there are even more dramatic contrasts in the frequency and tone with
which the two groups report preaching on abortion and sexual morality. Whereas the
three social justice priests indicated that abortion is a subject only rarely addressed
in their homilies, all three personal morality priests indicated that they regularly address abortion in their public statements and that the Church's opposition to abortion is a frequently recurring theme in their preaching. Father Zimmerman, for instance, when asked how often he addresses abortion in his homilies, said "Once a
month . . . once or twice a month." Similarly, Father Lewis stated, "I have given many
homilies about the problems of our declining culture and how so many of these problems are directly connected to each other. So abortion and all those threats against
the defenseless are certainly things that I raise on a regular basis." Finally, Father Boyd
indicated that he delivers homilies that focus directly and perhaps exclusively on
abortion a couple of times a year, but that "it comes up often in the course of a homily as an example of something a person could do, or a listing of evils." For these three
pastors, then, abortion is a common theme that regularly arises in their preaching.

It is also important to point out that personal morality priests tend not to restrict their comments on abortion to a discussion of its implications for individuals,
but in addition, two of them indicate that they often address the political and policy
implications of the Church's teachings on this issue. Father Boyd, for instance, refrains
from giving his parishioners specific instructions, and has not "given a sermon on passing a constitutional amendment, but you could surmise" from his homilies that he
would support such an amendment. Perhaps Father Lewis was most blunt in emphasizing his attention to public policy as it relates to abortion in stating, "I try to express
the idea that we're dealing with human life here, we're not dealing with potential human life, we're dealing with authentic human life. And I would say that our goal
should be to work at minimizing the possibility of having abortions done under the
mantle of law."

Just as they are more likely than their social justice and mixed-emphasis counterparts to preach often about abortion, so the personal morality priests are more likely publicly to address concerns about sexual morality, including homosexuality and contraception, as well. While most priests reported that they rarely (if ever) preach about homosexuality, Father Lewis and Father Boyd indicated that they occasionally address homosexuality and related issues in their sermons. Father Lewis reported having spoken specifically about homosexual marriage "on several occasions," and he indicated that when (in the spring and early summer of 2004) various localities in California, New York, and Massachusetts experimented with permitting gay marriages, the topic arose in his homilies "as things began to percolate on the west coast and also up north." Father Boyd, when asked how often homosexuality is discussed in his sermons, said that it comes up "in passing," and that when "listing . . . sins and problems today, homosexuality" comes up. He also mentioned that at times he attempts to discuss the issue in a way that gets a message across to adults in a format suitable for discussion in front of children. He has, for instance, on occasion recounted the stories of famous individuals who (as the adults in the congregation know) were homosexuals but who eventually repented and renounced that lifestyle.

The relatively conservative nature (politically speaking) of the preaching of this group of priests is further attested to by the context within which homosexuality is discussed. It may be recalled that Father McCormick, one of the social justice priests described above, shared this group's proclivity for preaching occasionally about homosexuality. When he does so, Father McCormick balances the Church's condemnation of homosexual behavior with the need to have compassion and understanding for those of homosexual orientation. Father Boyd and Father Lewis, by contrast, concentrate more exclusively on the sinfulness of homosexual behavior and the impermissibility of gay marriage. Father Boyd, for instance, while reiterating the mercy of Jesus and the possibility for active homosexuals to repent and reform, said that in his own preaching he focuses primarily on "the need to repent of it [homosexuality]," as opposed to the need to have compassion for those of homosexual orientation. He also explained, "I mention [in homilies] same sex marriage as one of the problems today. I did talk on it one Sunday. That it was a danger and that, I did say we must do everything we can to support marriage, and that means opposing homosexual marriage." Similarly, Father Lewis said that

> I have on several occasions deplored how the court system is trying to legislate on a very clearly understood, historically defined meaning of marriage. It's one thing to recognize that in our society today there are people who are living in what they call a union of members between the same sex. We've also mentioned that people have rights to be respected though we disagree with how they're living. We recognize that they're still human beings made in the image and likeness of God. But I have very clearly denounced the idea that the institution of marriage should be compromised by any kind of recognition.

All three personal morality priests report preaching about the Church's teachings on contraception with a comparatively high degree of regularity. Father Zimmerman, for instance, stated, "Oh yeah, I'll bring that [birth control] up. Because it's a form of abortion, you're aborting the natural process God has. You may not be aborting a baby, but you're aborting a possible conception. Or, you may be aborting a conceived child, you don't know. Some of these artificial contraceptions abort a conceived child rather than prevent conception. But those would be . . . in that context, we may not like to hear what the Church teaches, that artificial contraception is not the way, that responsible parenthood requires natural family planning. That sort of thing."

Father Boyd, as well, indicated that contraception arises as a topic in his homilies from time to time. When asked how often he speaks about it, he replied, "Whenever I talk on marriage. When I talk on slavery, I give a sermon on slavery, I connect it with birth control. Because the Church's teaching on slavery has been consistent despite what the media says," as has the Church's teaching on birth control. Finally, Father Lewis explained,

> I have brought that [contraception] up, I have heard one of the [assistant parish] priests talk about it too. That the widespread acceptance of this has contributed to a host of social problems and that it is certainly a direct, has a direct impact on the instability of marriage and family life. Those who practice contraception have a much higher probability of having problems in their marriage, and also of having their marriage come to an end. I promote natural family planning in this parish. And I also encourage people who have formed the habit of contraception to have the courage to deal with that in the confessional.

In the homilies of Father Boyd, Father Zimmerman, and Father Lewis, then, the Church's teaching regarding artificial contraception is regularly reinforced. This is in stark contrast with the homilies of some of the other pastors spoken to.

Finally, this group of priests stands out in that Father Boyd, Father Lewis, and Father Zimmerman each indicated that in their preaching, they emphasize the unique importance of abortion and related issues as compared to other issues on which the Church espouses a more politically liberal stance. Father Boyd, for instance, when asked which political issues he emphasizes, reiterated that he addresses all of these issues, but claimed, "The intensity of course would be abortion." Father Lewis was perhaps even more direct and explicit during the course of our conversation. When asked whether he preaches about abortion, he replied, "Absolutely. To me, it is the preeminent issue that we cannot ignore. Because we're dealing with the fundamental right to life here. If you cannot uphold the rights of the unborn, then you have begun to challenge if not destroy the foundation for everyone else's rights." When I asked Father Lewis whether or not he places particular emphasis on one issue in his sermons, he said, "Well . . . the most foundational issue is whether or not we're going to protect the young who've been brought forth into creation. If we're not going to do that, then all the other things aren't going to be able to work out. So in other words there is a bottom line that I believe we have to deal with." Finally, Father Zimmerman indicated that he shares the general approach adopted by Father Boyd and Father Lewis, saying "if I stress things more often than other things it would be premarital sex and abortion. Again I think they're becoming so commonplace."

In sum, Father Boyd, Father Lewis, and Father Zimmerman can be described as personal morality priests. Like all of the priests I spoke with, they exhibit a willingness to preach about the Church's (relatively politically liberal) teachings on aid to the poor, though they do so primarily in the context of promoting individual (not governmental) action. And unlike many of the other priests who participated in the study, this group reported being quite willing to address—and even to place special emphasis upon—abortion and issues of sexual morality, on which the Church has adopted more politically conservative positions.

CONCLUSION

At the conclusion of the first interview, which happened to be with Father Williams, he made a statement that proved quite prescient. He said, "As you talk to more and more people [pastors], I think just one thing to keep in mind [is] you're going to get a *very* big diversity of answers. And it depends what diocese you're in and what priest you're talking to. So what I say today may be totally contradicted by what you hear tomorrow. . . . You cannot categorize priests, they're uncontrollable and unorganizable." And indeed, these interviews revealed that despite the hierarchical nature and clearly established teachings of the institutional Church, parish priests retain and exercise considerable autonomy in their preaching. And even though the nine Catholic priests who participated in this project share certain similarities in their backgrounds and their approaches to preaching, they exhibited a remarkably wide range of preaching styles. Three pastors have adopted what might be called a social justice approach to preaching, in that they often preach about the Church's teachings on aid to the poor and about governmental responsibility to provide for the disadvantaged, while only rarely addressing issues like abortion and sexual morality. Three other pastors can be described as personal morality homilists; though they also speak freely about aid to the poor, they are much more willing than other priests publicly to expound upon and emphasize the Church's conservative approach to abortion and sexual morality. Finally, three priests can be described as mixed-emphasis priests, in that they fall somewhere in between.

These findings have several important implications for political observers and scholars studying the sociology of religion or the link between religion and politics. First, much care should be exercised before describing the political positions or public statements of the Catholic Church in monolithic terms. Even when the Church hierarchy adopts a particular approach to a policy issue or political event—such as abortion, aid to the poor, immigration, or any of the other host of issues about which Church leaders make public statements—it should be kept in mind that the messages emanating from parish priests, who are the representatives of the Church with whom practicing Catholics have the most frequent and direct contact, may or may not echo the volume and context of the statements emanating from Church leaders.

Second, these findings suggest that, to the maximum extent possible, the nature of the local religious context should be accounted for when analyzing the connection between religion and politics. Social scientific research demonstrates that there is much that serves to differentiate Catholics, politically speaking, from members of other religious traditions. But the findings presented here suggest that even within Catholicism, the political context of the local religious environment varies from parish to parish. This variance in the political contexts of Catholic parishes has potentially important implications for Catholic politics.

Third, and finally, these findings suggest that Catholic priests may, indeed, represent a source of potential political influence. It may be that personal morality priests, by focusing much attention on the Church's conservative stands on abortion and issues relating to sexual morality, help to make their parishioners more politically conservative than they otherwise might be. Similarly, social justice priests may exercise a politically liberalizing influence with their parishioners. But there are a host of additional factors (such as homily quality, length of a pastor's tenure, length of a parishioner's parish membership, and so on) that have the potential to mediate the relationship between priestly preaching and parishioners' political attitudes. More research designed to investigate the effects of this substantial variance in priestly messages is clearly warranted.

NOTES

1. See, for instance, George Gerner, "Catholics & the Religious Right: We Are Being Wooed," *Commonweal*, May 1995, 15–20; David C. Leege, Kenneth D. Wald, Brian S. Krueger, and Paul D. Mueller, *The Politics of Cultural Differences: Social Change and Voter Mobilization Strategies in the Post–New Deal Period* (Princeton, NJ: Princeton University Press, 2002); William B. Prendergast, *The Catholic Voter in American Politics: The Passing of the Democratic Monolith* (Washington, DC: Georgetown University Press, 1999); James A. Reichley, "Religion and the Future of American Politics," *Political Science Quarterly* 101 (1986): 23–47. But also see Mark D. Brewer, *Relevant No More? The Catholic/Protestant Divide in American Politics* (Lanham, MD: Lexington Books, 2003); James M. Penning, "Changing Partisanship and Issue Stands among American Catholics," *Sociological Analysis* 47 (1986): 29–49.

2. Clyde Wilcox, Ted G. Jelen, and David C. Leege, "Religious Group Identifications: Toward a Cognitive Theory of Religious Mobilization," in *Rediscovering the Religious Factor in American Politics,* ed. David C. Leege and Lyman A. Kellstedt (Armonk, NY: M. E. Sharpe, 1993).

3. Kenneth D. Wald, Lyman A. Kellstedt, and David C. Leege, "Church Involvement and Political Behavior," in *Rediscovering the Religious Factor.*

4. Michael R. Welch and David C. Leege, "Dual Reference Groups and Political Orientations: An Examination of Evangelically Oriented Catholics," *American Journal of Political Science* 35 (1991): 28–56.

5. See, for instance, David C. Leege, "Catholics and the Civic Order: Parish Participation, Politics, and Civic Participation," *Review of Politics* 50 (1988): 704–36; David C. Leege and Lyman A. Kellstedt, "Religious Worldviews and Political Philosophies: Capturing Theory in the Grand Manner through Empirical Data," in *Rediscovering the Religious Factor;* David C. Leege and Michael R. Welch, "Religious Roots of Political Orientations: Variations among American Catholic Parishioners," *Journal of Politics* 51 (1989): 137–62; Michael R. Welch and David C. Leege, "Religious Predictors of Catholic Parishioners' Sociopolitical Attitudes: Devotional Style, Closeness to God, Imagery, and Agentic/Communal Religious Identity," *Journal for the Scientific Study of Religion* 27 (1988): 536–52.

6. Lyman A. Kellstadt and Corwin E. Smidt, "Doctrinal Beliefs and Political Behavior: Views on the Bible," in *Rediscovering the Religious Factor*.

7. David C. Leege, "Catholics and the Civic Order."

8. See, for instance, Joel S. Fetzer, "Shaping Pacificism: The Role of the Local Anabaptist Pastor," in *Christian Clergy in American Politics*, eds. Sue E. S. Crawford and Laura R. Olson (Baltimore: The Johns Hopkins University Press, 2001); James L. Guth, "Reflections on the Status of Research on Clergy in Politics," in *Christian Clergy in American Politics;* Ted G. Jelen, "Notes for a Theory of Clergy as Political Leaders," in *Christian Clergy in American Politics*. Also, see Thoroddur Bjarnason and Michael R. Welch, "Father Knows Best: Parishes, Priests, and American Catholic Parishioners' Attitudes toward Capital Punishment," *Journal for the Scientific Study of Religion* 43 (2004): 103–18; Paul A. Djupe and Christopher P. Gilbert, "The Construction of Political Mobilization in Churches" (paper presented at the annual meeting of the Society for the Scientific Study of Religion, Salt Lake City, UT, 2002); Paul A. Djupe and Christopher P. Gilbert, "The Nature of Religious Influence on Political Behavior: Perception and Reception" (paper presented at the annual meeting of the Midwest Political Science Association, Chicago, 2002); Paul A. Djupe and Christopher P. Gilbert, *The Prophetic Pulpit: Clergy, Churches, and Communities in American Politics* (Lanham, MD: Rowman & Littlefield, 2003); Gregory A. Smith, "The Influence of Priests on the Political Attitudes of Roman Catholics," *Journal for the Scientific Study of Religion* 44 (2005): 291–306.

9. But see Paul Perl and Jamie S. McClintock, "The Catholic 'Consistent Life Ethic' and Attitudes toward Capital Punishment and Welfare Reform," *Sociology of Religion* 62 (2001): 275–99.

10. Pew Research Center for the People and the Press, "Pragmatic Americans Liberal and Conservative on Social Issues: Most Want Middle Ground on Abortion," August 3, 2006, available from http://people-press.org/reports/display.php3?ReportID=283: (accessed January 18, 2007).

11. Pew Research Center for the People and the Press and Pew Forum on Religion & Public Life, "Religion a Strength and a Weakness for Both Parties: Public Divided on Origins of Life," August 30, 2005, available from http://people-press.org/reports/display.php3?ReportID=254 (accessed January 18, 2007); Pew Research Center for the People & the Press, "Strong Public Support for Right to Die: Most Americans Discussing—and Planning—End of Life Treatment," January 5, 2006, available from http://people-press.org/reports/display.php3?ReportID=266 (accessed January 18, 2007).

12. Timothy A. Byrnes, *Catholic Bishops in American Politics* (Princeton, NJ: Princeton University Press, 1991).

13. Bjarnason and Welch, "Father Knows Best," 103–18; Djupe and Gilbert, "Construction of Political Mobilization in Churches"; Djupe and Gilbert, "Nature of Religious Influence on Political Behavior"; Djupe and Gilbert, *Prophetic Pulpit;* Smith, "Influence of Priests on the Political Attitudes of Roman Catholics," 291–306.

14. In several instances, pastors of parishes that were randomly selected to be included in this study refused the invitation to participate. The most typical reason given for such refusals was an inability to commit to the time necessary for participation. In these instances, alternative parishes were randomly selected for participation in the project. In one instance, the pastor of a parish that had been randomly selected to be included in the project was transferred to a different parish while the study was ongoing. As a result, this pastor's new parish was included in the study, and his previous parish was dropped from the project.

The leadership of the Diocese of Arlington expressed concern about which of their parishes would be participating in this project. Due to institutional review board constraints and the desire to preserve the integrity of the project by protecting the anonymity of the participating priests, I was unable to inform the diocesan leadership of the identity of the parishes I randomly selected to participate. Instead, I randomly selected three parishes, plus seventeen others. I gave the diocese the resulting list of twenty parishes, informed them that the three parishes that were randomly selected for participation were included in the list, and asked which, if any, of the twenty parishes they desired for me to refrain from including in the study. They indicated that I should avoid seven of the twenty parishes, though none of the three parishes I originally selected were among the parishes I was told to avoid. However, one of the original three parishes I selected declined to participate, necessitating the selection of a new parish. I randomly selected this new parish from the reduced list that had been approved by the diocese.

4

CATHOLICS IN THE POLITICAL ARENA

How Faith Should Inform Catholic Voters and Politicians

Kristin E. Heyer

SPECULATION ABOUT how the "faith factor" will transform the American political landscape in the 2008 presidential election began nearly two years in advance, in a race that included Catholic hopefuls as diverse as Sam Brownback, Joe Biden, Christopher Dodd, Dennis Kucinich, and Rudy Giuliani. We recall 2004, however, as the presidential election that reportedly turned on "moral values" and was marked by well-publicized threats to deny Communion to John Kerry and other Catholic politicians whose voting records conflicted with church teaching. These sanctions generated extensive debate over the precise obligations of Catholic politicians and voters, the appropriate role of the Church vis à vis politics, and the relative significance of various political issues with moral dimensions. On the one hand, the stance denoted by what has come to be known as the "Cuomo doctrine," which says, "I am personally opposed but," justifies too airtight a compartmentalization between personal and public morality. On the other hand, Eucharistic sanctions based on single- or select-issue politics risks inappropriate politicization. Helping politicians navigate between each inadequate extreme is the larger Church's task, yet what will be suggested here is that fostering moral formation and genuine dialogue offers more promising means of equipping Catholic politicians for prophetic and conscientious leadership.

Ordinary Catholic citizens also encountered threats of excommunication depending on how they cast their ballots and came upon competing "voter guides," each trumpeting the authentically Catholic platform. This chapter suggests that the fullness and depth of the Catholic tradition oblige believers to promote the comprehensive range of issues on which the tradition touches, as challenging at that may be, given the contemporary state of American politics and culture. This chapter begins by briefly articulating the core elements of Catholic communitarian personalism; it next argues that the consequences of this vision demand attention to a broad and interconnected range of social issues; and, finally, it concludes with directives for Catholic voters' and politicians' prudential discernment.

CATHOLIC COMMUNITARIAN PERSONALISM

Broadly understood, Catholic social thought and action are grounded in a theology of the fundamental goodness of creation, the mediation of the divine through the human, and an insistence on the universality of God's concern. The Catholic tradition affirms the link between faith and civic responsibility and the moral function of government in protecting human rights and securing basic justice for all citizens. The gospel imperative to defend human dignity requires the Church to relate positively to the political order and engage social and economic institutions, "since social injustice and the denial of human rights can often be remedied only through governmental action."[1]

More fundamentally, the Catholic social tradition grounds its essential commitment to human life and dignity in a vision of the human person as created in God's image, social and political by nature, and endowed with inviolable dignity and human rights. This notion is rooted in "a philosophical anthropology that regards human beings as naturally embodied, intelligent, free and social," grounded, in turn, in a "theological anthropology of human beings as created in God's image, wounded by sin, and redeemed by grace."[2] Catholic beliefs about Creation and Incarnation ground the tenet that every human life is sacred from conception to natural death, yielding a commitment to protecting life at its vulnerable stages and promoting universal human rights. The Catholic articulation of human rights encompasses not only civil and political liberties, but also "thicker" social and economic rights such as housing, health care, education, and employment.

The social anthropology grounding Catholic thought indicates that human rights are primarily realized in community, and rights are matched by corresponding duties to contribute to the common good. This social emphasis is theologically grounded in the Christian belief in a Trinitarian God, for humans created in the image of that God are thus inherently social; to be a person is to be in relationship with other persons. Catholics also stress the mutual implication of mutuality and relationality: God is love, and to the degree that humans actualize their capacity for love, mutual communion, and solidarity, their goodness becomes more like God's.[3] Thus, the marginalization of persons from participation in the life of community becomes the ultimate injustice. The significance of human interdependence is expressed in teachings on the most intimate sphere of family life outward to Catholic calls for institutional solidarity amid globalization. In this context, human rights are not absolute claims made by radically autonomous individuals, but rather, claims to goods "necessary for the person to participate with dignity in the communal life of a society."[4]

The resulting composite perspective may be summarized as one of Catholic personalist communitarianism: "'Personalism' affirms the dignity of each human being as made in the image of God, morally free and accountable, and bearing intrinsic rights and duties. Personalism is 'communitarian' when it acknowledges each individual as a 'person in relation' who is only able to flourish as a member of a community that makes available the whole array of goods necessary for human life. . . . Finally, communitarian personalism is 'Catholic' when its motivation, character, and ultimate term are informed by the sacramental, incarnational imagination that is generated by active participation in the life of the church."[5] According to Stephen Pope, "If this kind of Catholic communitarian personalism were to play a role in American public life, we ought to expect it to generate in Catholic citizens both greater degrees of civic responsibility and capacities to criticize radical individualism and the social 'atomism' that underlies it."[6] Many have noted, however, that Catholic communitarian values necessarily encounter a difficult reception in a democracy based on individual liberty. While the Catholic vision shares certain commitments of a democracy like the United States, it radically challenges a culture that prioritizes economic efficiency over solidarity with the weak and marginalized, or narrow national interest over global concern.

PRIORITY OF ADDRESSING A COMPREHENSIVE RANGE OF ISSUES

Catholic personalist communitarianism yields a stance that is at once pro-life, pro-poor, pro-family, pro-immigrant, pro-environmental, and pro-racial justice. In myriad ways, Catholics work to relate theological principles to social issues in attempts to directly influence policy and culture from local to national to international levels. While more specialized advocacy groups will appropriately persist, and at times, the starkness of certain issues or overwhelming injustices will require a special focus, addressing a comprehensive range of social issues should constitute a central goal for the institutional Church's social mission and for Catholics in public life.

Given the reach of personalist communitarianism, no single issue should serve as a litmus test for political behavior, but rather the larger texture of many issues rightly constitutes the context for political discernment and participation. Inattention to the full range of issues risks a reductionistic understanding of the Church's social mission and entanglement in interest group politics, given the temptation to skew the rest of an agenda to ensure allies' support on a single issue.[7] The latter is perhaps a particularly dangerous temptation for U.S. Catholics, since a comprehensive scope defies typical partisan configurations. Voters and politicians across the spectrum can become equally vulnerable to single- or narrow-issue politics and the distortion that ensues. Single-issue agendas of any stripe can blind Catholics to the tradition's call articulated by Cardinal Joseph Bernardin both to protect human life and foster its development at every stage and ensure that social institutions foster such development.

The multivocal nature of the fullness of the Christian tradition and church–state boundaries in the U.S. context compel a nonpartisan approach.[8] If Christians are "in the world but not of it," they should remain uncomfortable within either political party and institutionally independent from any. It remains especially important for church officials to avoid overtly ideological tendencies, particularly when advising Catholic politicians. Serving as a community of conscience in the U.S. context, the Church will inevitably be poised and obliged to critique the Right and the Left alike to promote human life and dignity across the spectrum. Furthermore, the great importance of the Church witnessing to transcendent values and remaining independent demands its nonpartisanship in intent as well as in effect.[9]

Thus, in contrast to litmus-test approaches allowing single issues to trump all others, it is helpful to recall that the Congregation for the Doctrine of the Faith's 2003 "Doctrinal Note on Some Questions Regarding the Participation of Catholics in Political Life" explicitly asserts, "The Christian faith is an integral unity, and thus it is incoherent to isolate some particular element to the detriment of the whole of Catholic doctrine. A political commitment to a single isolated aspect of the Church's social doctrine does not exhaust one's responsibility toward the common good."[10] A narrow perspective of any "hue" fails to do justice to the tradition's catholic scope, leaving pivotal moral values unattended and weakening the Church's credibility.

Comprehensiveness need not entail dilution of prophetic witness on fundamental life issues or capitulation to accommodationist approaches. For as Cardinal Joseph Bernardin once put it, "a Church standing forth on the entire range of issues which the logic of our moral vision bids us to confront, will be a Church in the style of both Vatican II's *Gaudium et spes* and in the style of Pope John Paul II's consistent witness to life."[11] Cardinal Theodore McCarrick has recently highlighted the intrinsic connection between "life" and "justice" issues, even while acknowledging the logical priority of the former.[12] McCarrick cites John Paul II standing up, in various speeches during visits to the United States, for the unborn and the world's poor, condemning the death penalty, and underscoring his support for peace and human rights in Iraq and the Holy Land during his final visit with President Bush, making it impossible to conclude, in McCarrick's words, that we are a single-issue church.[13]

Opposing "life" and "dignity" agendas weakens each cause and further divides the Church, also compromising persuasive force. As Richard Doerflinger rightly points out, the pro-life message and pro-justice message deeply need one another: "Without a firm foundation in the radical value of each and every human life, efforts for justice are blind; without compassionate service to help those struggling to lead lives of dignity, the defense of life will be empty."[14] Hence, rather than opposing the two, emphasizing the interrelatedness of life and justice issues would enhance Catholic integrity and credibility. Thus, for example, more explicitly linking opposition to abortion to concrete policy issues (regarding prenatal care, infant feeding programs, health care, and education) than is typically embraced by either political party would help Catholics guard against partisanship and attend to the full range of issues on which the tradition touches.[15] Likewise, a Catholic commitment to the oft-cited "culture of life" challenges American values not only with respect to issues of abortion or euthanasia, but prompts us to consider how respect for a culture of life should shape policy around Iraq, immigration, torture of prisoners, the death penalty, and health care reform.[16]

Hence, being a good Catholic voter or politician may not be simply boiled down to one's positions on select wedge issues or "nonnegotiables" alone. Catholic political practices must embrace this comprehensive scope not because it is politically prudent of late to pander to "values voters" or to identify more than a few social issues as religiously relevant, but because it is theologically sound. In addition to the breadth and depth of the Catholic moral tradition and the ecclesiological significance of a multi-issue approach, the Church's character as a sacrament of the reign of God also demands that it witness to the entire range of values that reflects that reign.[17]

TASK FOR CATHOLIC VOTERS

Given the American political landscape, this comprehensive scope of social issues does not provide voters with easy answers at the ballot box. For citizens in particular, then, the tasks of informing their consciences and applying prudence are critical. Whereas freedom remains a necessary element for genuinely moral actions, the inviolability of the conscience is not an excuse for failing to adequately inform one's conscience in light of the wisdom of the tradition. In order to bring values at the core of the Catholic social tradition to bear on candidates' platforms, voters should first familiarize themselves with its central principles. Following from the tradition's commitment to human rights realized in community with others, the tradition makes an option for those on society's margins, promotes the rights of workers, pursues global solidarity and environmental stewardship, and frames social priorities in terms of the common good. Researching candidates' positions on the range of policy issues that touch upon these values constitutes a key next step in discerning which candidates or initiatives are most closely "in sync" with Catholic values. Voters should decipher which issues in a given race bear directly on the life and dignity of human beings and therefore demand urgent attention. Nevertheless, a simplistic calculus for determining the "faithful vote" in a particular race is no substitute for conscientious and prudential discernment, given the complexity of applying core values to complex practical contexts.

Examining a candidate's record of action, where possible, is also a critical step in discerning who will actually deliver on the protection of values promised in a given campaign season. Recent findings on the relationship between rhetoric and action resulting from a study by Harvard economists on politicians' use of "strategic extremism" are instructive for this task. The study found that, with respect to religious values, "one can usually determine whether conviction or strategy motivates a politician to take a particular extreme policy stance. If the stance arises from personal conviction ('nonstrategic extremism'), then actions taken in support of it will typically be more extreme than the rhetoric of the campaign. If a stance arises from strategy, though, the campaign message will be more extreme than the policy actions ultimately taken."[18] For example, theologians and political analysts alike have suggested that the current impasse on abortion serves politicians whose rhetoric or appearance of working toward a solution advances political interests without delivering results.[19] Hence, attending more closely to proven record than selective rhetoric constitutes an important responsibility for any voter.

Catholic teaching holds that the faithful may not, in good conscience, disagree with the Church on fundamental questions of morality. Catholics *may* disagree in good conscience, however, on the question of how to do the right thing in a concrete situation. The virtue of prudence is what helps guide the conscience in such moral decisions, including how citizens should vote. Prudence carefully considers human experience, others' counsel, anticipated consequences, and the discernment of God's invitation to reach a decision that best fits the complexities of a given situation.[20] The tasks of conscience formation and prudential discernment should be communal acts, wherein Catholics work together to integrate the wisdom of communities of reflection, past and present. Finally, just as the institutional church must guard against cooptation in the political sphere, so must individual Catholic voters guard against manipulation by either empty campaign promises, the misuse of religious rhetoric, or a culture of relativism that reduces conscience to lightly donned personal preference.

CHALLENGES FACING CATHOLIC POLITICIANS

How can Catholic politicians responsibly balance fidelity to tradition and conscience with service to a pluralistic base in a secular democracy? The much-publicized Communion controversy during the 2004 presidential campaign thrust the challenges Catholic politicians face into the national spotlight. Amid a climate of diatribes against "errant politicians" ranging from charges of "cafeteria Catholicism" to calls for excommunication, there was little sustained attention to alternate explanations for the diversity evidenced in Catholic politicians' platforms and voting records. Rather than indicating open defiance of the tradition to incur scandal, such politicians' illiteracy in the Catholic social tradition, their disagreements over the most prudent strategies to protect values, and the limits of the existing party system may signal the complexity of relating the fullness of the tradition to ever-changing signs of the times.

The first possibility is that Catholic politicians do not fully appreciate the depth and reach of the tradition with respect to social issues. If public officials remain unschooled in the social doctrine of the Church—indeed its "best kept secret status" among the laity more broadly has been widely lamented—then moral formation and effective education are called for. With renewed attention to quality formation, Catholic politicians' exercise of prudential discernment and conscientious leadership would not necessarily pose serious risk of scandal. In the months surrounding the 2004 election, some aptly suggested that abandoning strategies of education and persuasive collaboration in favor of sanctions would be to acknowledge the Church's failure in effective moral transformation. In his June 2006 task force report, Cardinal McCarrick proposed meetings between bishops and Catholic members of Congress to help develop "vital, principled, candid and respectful relationships between a bishop and Catholic public officials."[21] Structuring such exchanges among and between bishops, theologians, activists, coalition partners, elected officials, and citizens themselves offers a promising step forward.

Once properly formed and informed, however, Catholic politicians may yet differ on the best way practically to protect and promote core principles. The moral status of such disagreement was at issue in the debates surrounding the appropriate pastoral treatment of pro-choice Catholics in the 2004 election. Those favoring the denial of communion to certain politicians and voters drew upon the aforementioned "Doctrinal Note," which recognizes that the political sphere possesses a certain autonomy yet also reminds Catholic legislators that, in light of the obligation to truth underlying all social systems, they are under grave obligation to oppose "any law that attacks human life."[22] Yet in line with traditional Catholic teaching on such matters, then-Cardinal Joseph Ratzinger's response to the U.S. bishops indicated "there is a difference between voting for someone specifically because of their pro-abortion position and voting for someone for other reasons and in spite of his or her position on abortion or euthanasia." Ratzinger explained that the latter could be acceptable provided "proportionate reasons" exist.[23]

The "Doctrinal Note" elaborates on the "duty to be morally coherent," since the conscience is indivisible. This concept of moral integrity demands that once public officials reach a conscientious conclusion about a particular social issue, their participation in politics should conform to that judgment of conscience.[24] The document asserts that the way in which politicians strive to end attacks on human life or promote justice is complex, however, and there exist "a variety of strategies available for accomplishing or guaranteeing the same fundamental value."[25] In fact it specifically states that the Church's efforts to illuminate Catholics' consciences do not reflect a desire on the part of the Church "to exercise political power or eliminate freedom of opinion of Catholics regarding contingent questions."[26] Thus, at this level of practical strategy, Catholic politicians may differ over what "sort of political-legal response will actually reduce the numbers of abortions [or state executions or war casualties] in the United States in the face of current constitutional and social realities."[27]

The distinctions made by John Courtney Murray, SJ, between morality and legality are instructive at this level of prudential strategy. Frequently, the most dominant positions in public debate about Catholicism and politics either call for objective religious morality to be translated directly into law or deem morality and law completely separate, understanding the former as necessarily privatized amid pluralism. From the perspective of the Murray tradition, both of these approaches fail.[28] Rather, as Murray has carefully delineated, morality and law are related yet differentiated. Murray distinguishes between the character and end of the common good and public order in relating law and morality. These categories follow from his differentiation of society from state, with the common good involving all social goods the human person seeks in society, and public order entailing only justice, public peace, and public morality, the end and purpose of the state.

Thus, state intervention with the coercive power of law is restricted to the protection and promotion of certain minimum standards that impact these limited goods of public order. According to Murray's position on the subtle and complex relationship between law and morality, the connection must be judged in light of four principles: "the presumption in favor of as much freedom as possible and as little restraint as necessary, the demands of public order, questions of enforceability and equitableness, and the feasible and prudential aspects of lawmaking."[29] Thus, by delineating a more limited sphere of public order and highlighting prudential facets of legislation such as enforceability and relative promise for eradicating social vice, Murray's insights remain instructive in considering how the Church can best support and challenge politicians. Disagreement, of course, persists over which contemporary policies properly constitute issues of public morality or justice, yet Murray's distinctions serve as reminders that ecclesial and political leaders' goals should remain less sweeping than enacting a full religious vision of the good life via legal coercion. That said, his underlying commitment to the truths we hold in common should nonetheless call Catholic politicians to prophetic leadership on fundamental issues.

Again, determining how long-standing and new social questions fit into these frameworks that weigh religious freedom against questions of public morality, justice, and the public order will be better accomplished by dialogue and persuasion than sanctions that shut down such exchange. Facilitating deliberative dialogue regarding tensions between unacceptable moral compromise and the incremental changes and pragmatism intrinsic to our imperfect systems, amid situations of not only reasonable pluralism but conscientious pluralism, would better serve public figures. Politicians could then be engaged on questions such as which factors they consider when balancing their own duties to their conscience and to their constituents, or at what point (or on which issues) they believe advocating policies consistent with Catholic values becomes an attempt to impose a particular religious morality on a pluralistic society.[30] Such dialogue would enable greater attention to nuance and creativity alongside fidelity to the tradition. Differing in prudential judgments about how to best enact values amid shifting social and cultural contexts need not betray moral flaccidness. There has remained space for faithful disagreement on the best judicial, legislative, and cultural strategies to protect fundamental values within the Catholic tradition, and such space invites and demands ongoing dialogue toward more adequate understandings and applications.[31]

Finally, once robust formation and dialogue yield public officials steeped in the fullness of the Catholic tradition with pragmatic ideas about promoting human life and the common good legislatively, Catholic politicians may well find such strategies politically unviable. Due to partisan divides and related campaign funding constraints, few individual politicians' platforms reflect the catholic scope of priorities articulated above.[32] The reality of the political landscape hence calls Catholic politicians to avoid prioritizing partisan loyalties to their moral commitments and to work prophetically for change within their respective parties.

A few officials on both sides of the aisle have attempted to prod their parties out of a Catholic integrity. For example, Timothy Roemer, a six-term former Democratic representative from Indiana, faced pro-choice opposition to his candidacy over the years, yet he attempted to advocate "strongly and consistently for the rights of the unborn child and support programs which directly assist the mother" during his tenure.[33] It remains to be seen whether newly elected senator Bob Casey Jr. of Pennsylvania will fare better in influencing his party from within than his father did.[34] On the Republican side, Chris Smith of New Jersey, not only coleader of the House Pro-Life Caucus but also one of the few Republicans to vote for the recent minimum wage increase, opposes the death penalty, is active on matters of international human rights abuses such as human trafficking, and has shown some willingness to disagree with

President Bush on the issue of torture, voting to reaffirm the U.S. commitment to the Geneva Conventions. Smith is a cosponsor of the Pregnant Women Support Act, a bill introduced in September 2006 that aims to reduce the abortion rate by 95 percent over ten years by addressing the root causes of abortion—poverty, lack of affordable health care, and job security. The bill is a promising example of legislation that reflects a comprehensive and integrated approach to life and dignity issues.

CONCLUSION

Regardless of whether Catholics serve in public life as elected officials or informed voters, they would do well to allow their mode of engagement to be infused by the same values they promote. In advocating for justice and charity, Catholics must practice these very virtues in public life as well, which requires a nuanced attitude toward wider society, and an epistemological humility that forbids impugning motives.

It is also important to bear in mind that the task of Catholic political witness far exceeds the votes cast at the ballot box or on the floor of the House. In order to alter public opinion on policies affecting human dignity or to reduce the existing distance between current law and Catholic morality, it is essential to begin with measures other than the law and itself.[35] Intermediate institutions (including the Church itself) may provide a better vehicle for minimizing this distance. Turning attention to how the Church can embody the reign of God in its own ministries and outreach does not conflict with efforts to influence law or policy, but it is a "concrete precondition for bringing morality and law closer together."[36] Thus, the Church's political witness includes its robust community organizing efforts, hospice care, relief work, educational efforts, and even its ecclesial practices. Focused attention upon the Church's own internal embodiment of the values it advances will not only enhance its integrity, but may ultimately prove a more persuasive and effective means of American Catholic political advocacy.

NOTES

I wish to express gratitude to Charles Bergman for research assistance with this chapter.

1. United States Catholic Conference Administrative Board, "USCC Statement on Political Responsibility," *Origins* 25, no. 22 (November 16, 1995): 375.

2. Stephen J. Pope, "Catholic Social Thought and the American Experience," in *American Catholics & Civic Engagement: A Distinctive Voice,* ed. Margaret O'Brien Steinfels (Lanham, MD: Rowman & Littlefield, 2004), 27.

3. See David Hollenbach, SJ, *The Common Good and Christian Ethics* (New York: Cambridge University Press, 2002), 130–31.

4. Michael J. Himes and Kenneth R. Himes, OFM, *Fullness of Faith: The Public Significance of Theology* (New York: Paulist Press, 1993), 46.

5. Pope, "Catholic Social Thought," 31.

6. Ibid.

7. Kenneth R. Himes, O.F.M., "Vatican II and Contemporary Politics," in *The Catholic Church and the Nation State*, ed. Paul Christopher Manuel, Lawrence C. Reardon, and Clyde Wilcox (Washington, DC: Georgetown University Press, 2006), 27.

8. See also Kristin E. Heyer, *Prophetic and Public: The Social Witness of U.S. Catholicism* (Washington, DC: Georgetown University Press, 2006), especially chapter 2, on the multivocal nature of fullness of Christian tradition that yields problematic methodological tensions in contemporary Catholic social ethics.

9. For instance, in the singling out of dissenting politicians, prominent pro-choice Catholic Republicans like Rudolph Giuliani, Tom Ridge, and Arnold Schwarzenegger were not treated with the same severity as pro-choice Democrats like John Kerry and David Obey.

10. "Doctrinal Note," *Origins* 32, no. 30 (January 30, 2003): 537–43 at para. no. 21.

11. Cardinal Joseph Bernardin, "A Consistent Ethic of Life: Continuing the Dialogue," *Consistent Ethic of Life*, ed. Thomas G. Fuechtmann (Kansas City, MO: Sheed & Ward, 1988), 18.

12. "Surely, all of us must remember that the right to life is essential, and that without it there is no subject to whom rights can be ascribed. *Primum est vivere* (To live is foremost) is the active and necessary phrase. Without life, we do not survive. And so we must begin always with great priority about the right to life, but we may not stop there. If someone says, 'I believe in life and am opposed to any attacks against it,' we are in solidarity with that person; but you must go beyond that since Jesus himself came to preach 'good news to the poor, liberty to captives and to set the downtrodden free.' The church calls on all of us to embrace this preferential option for the poor and vulnerable, to embody it in our own lives and to work to have it shape policies and priorities" (Cardinal Theodore McCarrick, "The Call to Serve in a Divided Society," inaugural address of the Canisius Lecture Series, sponsored by the Jesuit Institute at Boston College, March 3, 2005, *Origins* 34, no. 40 [March 24, 2005], 638).

13. See "Interim Reflections of the Task Force on Catholic Bishops and Catholic Politicians," June 15, 2004, available from www.usccb.org/bishops/taskforce.shtml (accessed February 7, 2007).

14. Richard Doerflinger, "The Pro-Life Message and Catholic Social Teaching: Problems of Reception," in *American Catholics, American Culture: Tradition and Resistance*, ed. Margaret O'Brien Steinfels (Lanham, MD: Rowman & Littlefield, 2004), 49–50.

15. Pax Christi USA provides a particularly useful example of such an approach in formulating its opposition to abortion. They connect their "unwavering reverence for human life" and rejection of "the claim of any individual, organization, or nation to the 'right' to destroy human life, whether singly or as entire populations," to a concern for the well-being of children, social conditions that limit women's options, and the treatment of women who undergo abortions. They also link this reverence to their stance on the spectrum of life issues, including the death penalty, war, and the nuclear arms race. See www.paxchristiusa .org/news_events_more.asp?id=71 for Pax Christi USA's 2001 statement (accessed February 7, 2007).

16. Paul Lauritzen, "Holy Alliance? The Danger of Mixing Politics and Religion," *Commonweal*, March 24, 2006, 16–17.

17. Himes, "Vatican II and Contemporary Politics," 26–27.

18. Daniel Finn, "Hello, Catholics: Republicans & the Targeting of Religious Voters," *Commonweal*, November 4, 2005, 16.

19. Ibid., 17. According to ibid., 16, "The number of abortions has remained about the same under Democratic and Republican presidents, even apparently rising somewhat since George W. Bush's election. Republicans remain perennially the champions of Christians opposed to abortions—without actually bringing about any change. (Even partial-birth legislation doesn't reduce the number of abortions; it just requires another method be used.)"

20. See Richard Gula, *Reason Informed by Faith: Foundations of Catholic Morality* (Mahwah, NJ: Paulist Press, 1989), 316.

21. See Cardinal Theodore McCarrick, "Task Force on Catholic Bishops and Catholic Politicians" (oral report to U.S. Bishops' Conference, June 15, 2006), available from www.usccb.org/bishops/mccarrickrpt6-06.shtml (accessed February 7, 2007).

22. Some bishops, such as Archbishop Raymond Burke and Archbishop Alfred Hughes, also cited the authority of canon law (canon 915) and Pope John Paul II's *Evangelium vitae*. The Note continues, "For them, as for every Catholic, it is impossible to promote such laws or to vote for them" ("Doctrinal Note," no. 4). On the other hand, "[a] Catholic would be guilty of formal cooperation in evil, and so unworthy to present himself for holy Communion, if he were to deliberately vote for a candidate precisely because of the candidate's permissive stand on abortion and/or euthanasia. When a Catholic does not share a candidate's stand in favor of abortion and/or euthanasia, but votes for that candidate for other reasons, it is considered remote material cooperation, which can be permitted in the presence of proportionate reasons" (Ratzinger, *Denver Catholic Register,* July 21, 2004, 13).

23. Ratzinger, *Denver Catholic Register,* July 21, 2004, 13.

24. In *Evangelium Vitae* John Paul II considers the possible liceity of legislators voting for measures on abortion and euthanasia that would aim at limiting the harm done by abortion and euthanasia, especially in cases where it is not possible to overturn a law that is not pro-life: "This does not in fact represent an illicit cooperation with an unjust law, but rather a legitimate and proper attempt to limit its evil aspects. "Public authorities could support and administer such laws as long as they publicized their opposition to the principle of abortion." See also Thomas Massaro, SJ, "Catholic Bishops and Politicians: Concerns about Recent Developments," *Josephinum Journal of Theology,* 12, no. 2 (Summer/Fall 2005): 268–87, at 286–87.

25. "Doctrinal Note," no. 6.

26. Ibid. See also Gregory A. Kalscheur, "American Catholics and the State: John Courtney Murray on Catholics in a Pluralistic Democratic Society," *America,* August 2–9, 2004, 17.

27. Kalscheur aptly asks, "Have we listened to the voices of women who have felt compelled to make the choice for abortion, and are we working to establish a set of social policies that might provide women with the support needed to make the decision to carry their baby to term? In short, are we working to build a legal system that as a whole supports and promotes the virtues necessary to protect human dignity and sustain a culture of life?" (ibid., 18).

28. See Todd David Whitmore, writing on the public debate about abortion, in particular, in "What Would John Courtney Murray Say?" *Commonweal,* October 7, 1994, 19.

29. Charles Curran, *Catholic Social Teaching, 1891–Present: A Historical, Theological, and Ethical Analysis* (Washington, DC: Georgetown University Press, 2002), 238.

30. John Huebscher, "Questions Bishops and Catholic Politicians Ask," address at the University of San Francisco's annual Archbishop Quinn Colloquium on Catholic Social Teaching,

March 12, 2005, *Origins* 35, no. 4 (June 9, 2005): 62. Huebscher serves as executive director of the Wisconsin Catholic Conference.

31. See *Evangelium vitae*, no. 73, and "Doctrinal Note," no. 4, for their explicit provisions permitting Catholics to act so as to engage unjust laws in a manner that seeks to limit the harm done under their provisions. For a lengthier elaboration of the need for dialogue and the duties facing bishops and Catholic politicians, see Kristin E. Heyer, "Prophetic and Conscientious Leadership: Advising U.S. Catholics in Political Life," *Journal of Peace and Justice Studies* 15, no. 2 (Summer 2006): 18–36.

32. Many Catholics in public life "believe they can't win on a platform that includes a consistent life ethic" (Huebscher, "Questions Bishops and Catholic Politicians Ask," 63).

33. Timothy Roemer, "A Catholic in the Public Square," *Origins* 34, no. 40 (March 24, 2005): 643. Roemer adds that he believes there is an opportunity to change the debate on abortion in the Democratic Party for the first time in thirty years. He recommends a goal of reducing abortions by 70 percent in the next decade by (1) dramatically reducing unwanted pregnancies by supporting teen pregnancy prevention programs, abstinence and family planning programs, contraception, and appropriate sex education; (2) providing mothers with economic and personal security by, for example, opposing proposed cuts in the budget to the Woman, Infants, and Children health program or providing adoption tax credits; and (3) finding agreement on wider Democratic support for banning late-term abortions and supporting parental notification for young teenagers. He also urges Democrats to support and fund pro-life candidates, reflecting on pro-choice opposition to his own candidacy over the years (ibid., 645).

34. Governor Bob Casey was prevented from speaking at the 1992 Democratic Convention because of his pro-life views. In a lecture on September 14, 2006, his son took both parties to task for their inadequate positions, noting, "We can't realistically expect to tackle the difficult question of abortion without embracing the 'radical solidarity' with women who face a pregnancy that Pope John Paul II spoke of many years ago. If we are going to be pro-life, we cannot say we are against abortion of unborn children and then let our children suffer in degraded inner city schools and broken homes. We can't claim to be pro-life at the same time as we are cutting support for Medicaid, Head Start, and the Women Infant's and Children's program. I believe we need policies that provide maximum feasible protection for the unborn and maximum feasible care and support for pregnant women, mothers, and children. The right to life means the right to a life with dignity" (Bob Casey Jr., Pope John XXIII Lecture, "Restoring America's Moral Compass: Leadership and the Common Good," available from http://inquirer.philly.com/rss/news/091406casey remarks.pdf (accessed February 7, 2007).

35. Whitmore, "What Would John Courtney Murray Say?," 19.

36. Whitmore identifies as "the most neglected requirement of the Catholic community" its "obligation to exemplify through its own practice the kind of community where official teaching on abortion and assisted suicide is plausible. It is only in this way that there can be any hope that other persons, communities, and constituencies will reshape their beliefs on these two fundamental issues. Aiding and joining women in the care of the children for the full eighteen years that is required, and providing hospice care for the duration needed are not only ways to exemplify 'the true visage of the Church of God's kingdom'; they also constitute the most prudent way to proceed if we are concerned about the common good of the earthly city" (ibid., 22).

PART II
The Catholic Public

5

BETWEEN CHURCH, PARTY, AND CONSCIENCE

Protecting Life and Promoting Social Justice among U.S. Catholics

MARK M. GRAY AND MARY E. BENDYNA

A Catholic moral framework does not easily fit the ideologies of "right" or "left," or the platforms of any party. Our values are often not "politically correct." Believers are called to be a community of conscience within the larger society and to test public life by the values of Scripture and the principles of Catholic social teaching. Our responsibility is to measure all candidates, policies, parties, and platforms by how they protect or undermine the life, dignity, and rights of the human person, whether they protect the poor and vulnerable and advance the common good.

—United States Conference of Catholic Bishops

AS THE STATEMENT by the U.S. Catholic bishops above indicates, the teachings of the Catholic Church as well as pronouncements made by its leaders are often at odds with the partisan and ideological organization of the U.S. political system. The Church is opposed to abortion, euthanasia, cloning, embryonic stem cell research, and the death penalty and supports immigration and immigrant rights, social welfare programs for the poor, and programs to provide affordable and accessible health care and housing.[1] This combination of issue stances cuts across the official platforms of both the Democratic and Republican Parties as well as the more general ideological distribution of issue positions in the U.S. political discourse between conservatives and liberals. If a Catholic wishes to cast a ballot that is entirely consistent with Church teachings, there is nearly always no valid choice.

At the same time, for nearly a century the Church has encouraged Catholics to participate in electoral politics and vote their conscience. For only a short time in the late nineteenth century, after the emergence of mass democracy, the Church officially opposed the political participation of Catholic Italians due to the Vatican's own conflicts with the newly created Italian state and asked that citizens become "neither elected nor electors."[2] With the 1922 papal encyclical *Urbi arcano Dei*, a role for lay Catholic organizations in the political process, which would eventually evolve into European Christian Democratic Parties, began to emerge.[3] As the Vatican began to encourage Italian and other European Catholics to vote, often in opposition to Communist Parties, the Vatican began to take a more vocal role as a supporter of citizen politics.

The inspiration for civic responsibility in the Catholic faith is often derived from Scripture in two commonly related New Testament passages that highlight the duty of citizenship.[4] The first is the response Jesus gives to the Pharisees when asked if it is lawful to pay the census tax to Caesar and Rome. In Matthew 22:1, Jesus asks to see a coin and then asks, "Whose image is this and whose inscription?" and they reply, "Caesar's," and he then instructs, "Then repay to Caesar what belongs to Caesar and to God what belongs to God." The second is by Paul, who in Romans 13:6–7 instructs Christians to "pay taxes, for the authorities are ministers of God, devoting themselves to this very thing. Pay to all their dues, taxes to whom taxes are due, toll to whom toll is due, respect to whom respect is due, honor to whom honor is due."

Prior to every U.S. presidential election since 1976, the United States Conference of Catholic Bishops (USCCB) has released a statement encouraging Catholics to vote and outlining Church teachings that are important to the political issues being debated. The 1999 statement, *Faithful Citizenship: Civic Responsibility for a New Millennium*, acknowledged the constrained choices of the U.S. political system, stating that "sometimes it seems few candidates and no party fully reflect our values. But now is not a time for retreat. The new millennium should be an opportunity for renewed participation. We must challenge all parties and every candidate to defend human life and dignity, to pursue greater justice and peace, to uphold family life, and to advance the common good."[5]

The Vatican has provided instruction that constrains choices further. The Congregation for the Doctrine of the Faith's 2002 doctrinal note, *The Participation of Catholics in Political Life*, observes that a "well-formed Christian conscience does not permit one to vote for a political program or an individual law which contradicts the fundamental contents of faith and morals."[6] In many political systems, including that of the United States, this edict alone would limit the ability of Catholics to vote at all, as ballots typically represent parties or candidates and not line-item options to select actual policies, programs, or legislation.

Perhaps with this complication in mind, the Congregation for the Doctrine of the Faith defends the tradition of requiring civic participation by noting that "a political commitment to a single isolated aspect of the Church's social doctrine does not exhaust one's responsibility towards the common good. Nor can a Catholic think of delegating his Christian responsibility to others."[7] Thus, Catholics are instructed to participate in the political process but are still prohibited from supporting a candidate specifically for a policy position that is inconsistent with Church teachings. In the U.S. political system, this often requires the faithful to choose between the lesser of two "evils," as few if any candidates have policy proposals and platforms that are entirely consistent with Church teachings on life, social justice, and peace issues. Catholics must base their support for a candidate at least in part on the fact that the candidate has expressed policy positions that are consistent with Church teachings.

The tensions created by the interplay of Church teachings and the party system in the United States have had an important role in the electoral process. With Catholics making up nearly one-quarter of the electorate, Bendyna argues that they have introduced a "Goldilocks effect" into the system, ensuring that the overall political discourse in the United States is moderated, never reaching either too far left or right in the political spectrum.[8] Bendyna and colleagues have shown that Catholic Republicans express more liberal attitudes than their non-Catholic counterparts on issues of social welfare and that Catholic Democrats are more conservative than non-Catholic counterparts on many cultural issues.[9] The implication of this research is that Catholics have played a moderating role in the U.S. political discourse, constraining extremism in either direction.

The potential influence of Catholic teachings and statements by Church leaders on the attitudes and preferences of the Catholic electorate remains an issue of debate among social scientists.[10] Direct evidence of influence is rarely documented, and only then for a few issues. One well-known example is the reaction to the U.S. Catholic Bishops' Pastoral Letter, *The Challenge of Peace: God's Promise and Our Response* (1983), where the percentage of Catholic respondents in the General Social Survey who felt that the U.S. spent too much on weapons increased.[11] Yet this shift was short lived. During the past few decades some evidence has also emerged that the most committed Catholics, especially those who are anti-abortion, are also more opposed to the death penalty than other Catholics.[12] There is also some evidence that parishioners may be influenced by their pastors, in particular, on the issue of capital punishment.[13] However, there is less evidence that pastors can influence their parishioners on abortion.[14]

CATHOLIC SURVEY DATA: SOCIAL AND POLITICAL ISSUES

In this chapter we explore the potential interconnections between Catholic partisanship, issue stances, and the influence of Church teachings using a unique collection of data from 2002 and 2006. The Center for Applied Research in the Apostolate (CARA) at Georgetown University conducted surveys in each of these years to study the attitudes of Catholics regarding international relief and global social justice. These studies were funded by Catholic Relief Services (CRS) and were based on nationally representative samples of self-identified adult Catholics using the Knowledge Networks panel. Knowledge Networks is a polling organization that conducts Internet surveys using a large panel of U.S. households matched against the U.S. Census. Sample sizes for each poll exceed 1,200 and margins of error are ±2.5 percentage points or less.[15] All the questions used here were identically worded in the 2002 and 2006 surveys. In neither poll were respondents queried about voting, voter registration, or citizenship; thus, the sample reflects the U.S. Catholic population and not some approximation of the Catholic electorate or likely Catholic voters.

In table 5.1 we show the consistency in issue preferences among Catholics in 2002 and 2006. Differences between the percentages of Catholics agreeing ("somewhat" or "strongly") with each statement between these two years exceed the margin of error for four items: immigration; use of military force; tax increases; and consideration of statements made by Church leaders. For each of these changes there are reasonable explanations.

TABLE 5.1 The Stability of U.S. Catholics' Attitudes on Social, Political, and Moral Issues, 2002 and 2006

(percentage agreeing "Somewhat" or "Strongly")

	2006	2002	DIFFERENCE
I support the death penalty for people convicted of premeditated murder.	67	67	–
A woman should have the right to choose whether or not to abort an unwanted pregnancy.	58	55	+3
All human life, from conception to natural death, is sacred. For this reason, the taking of life—whether through abortion, the death penalty or assisted suicide—is wrong.	41	45	−4
The number of immigrants who are permitted to come to the United States should be decreased.	54	60	−6
The United States should be willing to use military force to overthrow governments that support terrorism against the U.S., even if it means losing lives of U.S. service members.	43	63	−20
Affirmative action programs that give minorities preferences in hiring and promotion should be ended.	53	56	−3
Regardless of cost, the U.S. government should guarantee basic health care for all citizens.	78	75	+3
There should be a tax increase for the wealthiest Americans.	65	52	+13
Some people say the U.S. government should do everything possible to improve the standard of living of all poor Americans. Other people think it's not the government's responsibility, and that people should take care of themselves.[a]	63	60	+3
Workers have a right to a living wage and the right to form and join labor unions.	82	83	−1
An equitable society can be achieved only if special attention is given to the needs of the poor	54	50	+4
I seriously consider the Church's statements, such as those of the pope or the U.S. bishops, on social, political, and moral issues.	37	42	−5
In deciding what is morally acceptable, I believe my own conscience is more important than Church teachings.	59	57	+2

[a] Percentage "somewhat" or "strongly" favoring the government improving living standards of poor people.

Catholics expressed opinions more favorable of immigration in 2006 following the emergence of this issue in political debate, in which many bishops have been active in supporting the Church's stance to allow for a fair and socially just immigration policy. The 2002 survey was conducted after U.S. military forces were sent to Afghanistan but before they had been sent into Iraq. In 2002, 63 percent of Catholics agreed with the use of military force to overthrow governments that support terrorism against the United States. Following more than three years of conflict and casualties in Iraq, Catholic opinion had changed substantially in 2006 to where a minority, 43 percent, agreed with the use of military force for this end.

Catholics have become more supportive of tax increases for the wealthiest Americans. Only 52 percent supported such increases in 2002. However, in the wake of news of growing deficits and national debt, in part caused by military commitments and tax cuts in 2001 and 2003, 65 percent of Catholics were supportive of such a tax increase in 2006. Finally, in the four years between the polls, Catholics became slightly less likely to agree that they seriously consider the Church's statements, such as those of the pope or the U.S. bishops, on social, political, or moral issues. However, this shift only slightly exceeds the margins of error for the polls. This change could represent some Catholics' reactions to allegations of clergy sex abuse that began to emerge in the media in 2002 and the Church's response to these cases.

Catholics responded similarly in 2006 as they did in 2002 for all other statements in table 5.1. This represents some stability in attitudes about the death penalty, abortion, affirmative action, health care, labor issues, and programs for the poor.

Comparing Catholic responses to these questions to the U.S. Catholic Bishops' 2003 *Faithful Citizenship* document, which outlines the Church's positions on important political issues, there are a number of noticeable inconsistencies on life issues.[16] In opposition to Church teachings described in this document and elsewhere, majorities of Catholics in 2006 agreed with the use of the death penalty for people convicted of premeditated murder (67 percent) and with a woman's right to choose to abort an unwanted pregnancy (58 percent). A minority of Catholics, 41 percent, either "somewhat" or "strongly" agreed with the Church's stance that "all human life, from conception to natural death, is sacred. For this reason, the taking of life—whether through abortion, the death penalty or assisted suicide is wrong."

In 2006, majorities of Catholics expressed agreement with statements that are consistent with Church teachings regarding social justice, including guaranteed health care for all citizens (78 percent), government responsibility for improving standards of living for the poor (63 percent), and workers' rights to organize and earn a living wage (82 percent).[17]

Support for social justice issues and a woman's right to abortion are consistent with the platform of the Democratic Party, with which a majority of Catholics identify. In 2006, 58 percent of Catholics noted some affiliation as Democrats (including "leaners"), compared to 38 percent Republican (including "leaners"). Four percent of respondents described themselves as entirely undecided, independents, or affiliates of some other party.[18] This distribution is similar to the vote of Catholics as measured in exit polls in the 2006 congressional elections, with 55 percent selecting a Democrat and 44 percent selecting a Republican.[19]

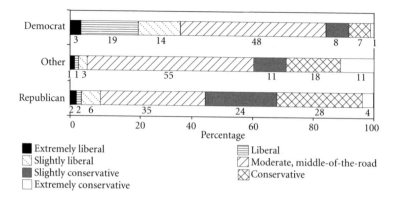

FIGURE 5.1   *Party Identification and Ideology of U.S. Catholics, 2006*

Many researchers, as well as political consultants, have preferred to disaggregate Catholics by race and ethnicity.[20] In terms of party identification, some 43 percent of non-Hispanic white Catholics identify as Republicans and 53 percent as Democrats. By comparison, only 27 percent of Hispanic Catholics identify as Republicans, with 68 percent identifying themselves as Democrats.

Political ideology is, as expected, correlated with partisanship (see figure 5.1). Republican Catholics are less likely than Catholic Democrats and others to describe themselves as moderates. Just over one-third does so, with a majority (56 percent) identifying as slightly to extremely conservative. Catholic Democrats, as well as those who identify with a third party or no party at all, are more likely to describe themselves as moderates. Only 22 percent of Catholic Democrats self-identify as being liberal or extremely liberal.

Religious service attendance can be an important predictor of many political attitudes and behaviors (see figure 5.2). This is somewhat the case for Catholics and

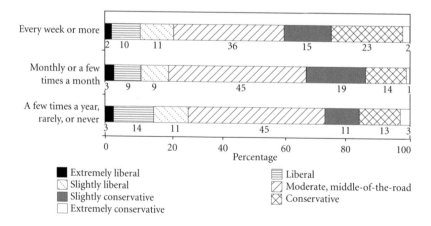

FIGURE 5.2   *Church Attendance and Ideology of U.S. Catholics, 2006*

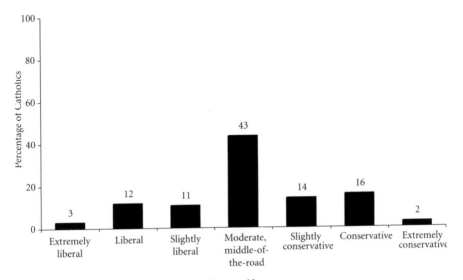

FIGURE 5.3   *In general do you think of yourself as . . .*

political ideology, with those who attend mass at least once a week being less likely than more infrequent attendees to describe themselves as ideologically moderate. Four in ten weekly attendees describe themselves as conservative.

Catholics who go to church with less frequency, perhaps only at Christmas and Easter or less often, are most likely to be moderates (45 percent), with nearly equal percentages within this group placing themselves at either end of the spectrum (28 percent liberal and 27 percent conservative). Thus, as in figure 5.3, a plurality of all Catholics describe themselves as moderates (43 percent), with similar-sized proportions describing themselves as liberal or conservative. There are slightly more conservatives than liberals (32 percent compared to 26 percent).[21]

CHOICE OF PARTY IDENTIFICATION

The discovery of the tendency of U.S. voters to have long-standing attachments to a political party was one of the most important findings of early voting studies.[22] This phenomenon was found to be rooted in parental socialization as well as socioeconomic status. It was long thought that party identification was primarily a stable core element of one's political psychology, which in turn shaped ideology, issue stances, and vote choices.

However, more recent research, as well as classical and more recent rational choice models, have highlighted the malleability of these partisan attachments due to more short-term, specific election factors and the influence of single-issue attitudes.[23] Carol J. Uhlaner and Chris Garcia provide perhaps the most concise definition of partisanship, calling it "the cumulative product of political experiences."[24] This revisionist perspective is also described well by Charles H. Franklin and John E.

Jackson, who note that "each campaign leaves its imprint, or residue, on individual identifications."[25] It is also noted that the tendency for citizens to develop partisan attachments has waned since the 1980s in the United States as well as other advanced industrial democracies.[26]

Although newer perspectives have introduced instability into the study of party identification, the methods used to measure party identification among U.S. voters have not changed significantly. The standard seven-point scale created with responses to three questions creates a typology from strong Democrat and not strong Democrat (i.e., "weak") to leaning Democrat, nonidentifier, leaning Republican, not strong Republican, and strong Republican. Although this scale is often used in voting research, it is not clear that the numerical differences between scale categories are representative of real differences in attachment. For example, the scale treats the difference between a strong and weak identifier as identical to differences between a weak identifier and a leaner. Although it is often used as an interval or ratio measure, the seven-point scale is best used as an ordinal-level measure.

Uhlaner and Garcia argue that the scale can be used to measure two separate but related concepts.[27] They cite Warren E. Miller in naming these with the term *party identification* to denote choice of affiliation as Democrat or Republican and the term *partisanship* to represent the strength of attachment to the party with which one identifies.[28] In the absence of a question measuring vote preference in the data used here, the analysis below focuses on party identification rather than partisanship, and does so including leaners. As Bruce E. Keith, David B. Magleby, Candice J. Nelson, Elizabeth Orr, Mark C. Westlye, and Raymond E. Wolfinger have shown, leaners have attitudes and behaviors that are consistent with weak identifiers, whereas those not leaning or identifying are distinguishably different.[29] Also, with the surveys used here conducted just two months before a national election, the inclusion of leaners offers a good approximation of the most current party choice of Catholics in terms of long-standing attachment and in terms of those strongly affected by the short-term forces of the election cycle.

Much is already known about the party choices of Catholics who have traditionally favored the Democratic Party.[30] Whether because of the aid the Democratic Party and its leaders provided many Catholic immigrants, or the historical working-class roots of the Catholic population, or the presidential campaigns of Democratic Catholic candidates Al Smith and John F. Kennedy, Catholics have traditionally been more likely to identify as Democrats. However, they have not always voted en masse for Democrats in presidential elections or for Catholic candidates.[31] Some have argued for an emerging Catholic shift to conservatism and Republican identification since the 1980s, spurred by suburban migration or changing socioeconomic status; however, this shift appears to fall short of any realignment.[32]

Overall, as can be seen in table 5.2, 59 percent of U.S. Catholics at least "somewhat" agree with the statement, "In deciding what is morally acceptable, I believe that my own conscience is more important than Church teachings." Fewer, 37 percent, show the same level of agreement with the statement, "I seriously consider the Church's statements, such as those of the pope or the U.S. bishops, on social, political, and moral issues." Thus, few say they seriously consider the Church's statements on social, political, and moral issues and many say they rely more on their own conscience for deciding what is morally acceptable. Just 9 percent of Catholics indicate

TABLE 5.2   Consideration of Church Statements and the Importance of One's Own Conscience

(percentage of U.S. Catholics by agreement with each statement, 2006)

In deciding what is morally acceptable, I believe that my own conscience is more important than Church teachings	I seriously consider the Church's statements, such as those of the Pope or the U.S. bishops, on social, political, and moral issues.					
	STRONGLY AGREE	SOME-WHAT AGREE	NEITHER AGREE NOR DISAGREE	SOME-WHAT DISAGREE	STRONGLY DISAGREE	
Strongly Agree	3	6	10	4	7	30
Somewhat Agree	2	10	12	5	1	29
Neither Agree nor Disagree	2	5	16	2	0	25
Somewhat Disagree	2	3	3	1	0	10
Strongly Disagree	3	1	1	0	1	6
	12	25	42	12	9	100

Note: Totals may sum to 99 or 101 due to rounding error.

both disagreement that their "own conscience is more important" and agreement that they "seriously consider the Church's statements." These results indicate that the Catholic Church has rather weak influence on U.S. Catholics' political decisions. Partisanship and ideology are likely to be more important factors.

ANALYSIS

Table 5.3 shows the results of a factor analysis evaluating the connections between responses to questions and statements regarding issues in the U.S. political system and how Catholics say they use Church teachings on social, political, and moral issues. Any loading of .5 or higher is considered to be significant.

The first factor to emerge focused on responses to questions about social welfare programs and policies. Specifically, these were support for universal health care provided by the government, a tax increase on the wealthiest Americans, government action for improving the standard of living for the poor, the right of workers to form unions and earn a living wage, and a belief that an equitable society can only be achieved if special attention is given to the needs of the poor.

The second factor focused on abortion, the sanctity of human life, and the degree to which the respondent follows Church teachings and statements. The strongest loadings are for opposition to abortion as a legal right, support for the belief that all human life from conception to natural death is sacred. Also important was the degree to which one seriously considers Church leaders' statements on social, political, and moral issues, as well as the degree to which one does not put the importance of

TABLE 5.3   Factor Analysis

Rotated Component Matrix

	SOCIAL WELFARE	PRO-LIFE	DIVERSITY
Opposes death penalty	−0.001	0.430	0.581
Opposes abortion	−0.209	0.755	0.038
Believes all human life from conception to natural death is sacred	0.154	0.776	0.077
Supports immigration	−0.081	0.055	0.745
Supports affirmative action programs	0.175	0.019	0.684
Opposes use of military force to overthrow governments supporting terrorism	0.185	−0.121	0.609
Supports universal government health care	0.760	−0.135	0.096
Supports tax increase for wealthiest	0.674	−0.181	−0.005
Supports government improving standard of living for poor	0.652	−0.041	0.320
Supports workers' right to form unions and a living wage	0.649	0.068	−0.096
Believes an equitable society can only be achieved if special attention is given to needs of the poor	0.708	0.194	0.193
Seriously considers Church's statements on social, political, and moral issues	0.117	0.704	−0.117
Does not believe their own conscience is more important than Church teachings	−0.163	0.598	0.083
Eigenvalue (% of variance)	2.834 (21.8%)	2.455 (18.9%)	1.512 (11.6%)

Note: **Bold** entries represent items with higher loadings (greater than .50) and underlined entries represent items with moderately high loadings (.30 to .49). Rotation Method: Varimax with Kaiser Normalization.

one's conscience before Church teachings. Although opposition to the death penalty did not load above .5, it was nearly this strong, and conceptually it fit partially in this factor.

However, opposition to the death penalty loaded higher on the third factor than on the second. This third factor included what may seem to be a disconnected set of issues but which on closer examination reveals an underlying structure. Clustering items on this third factor included support for immigration, support for affirmative action programs, and opposition to the use of U.S. military force for regime change in countries supporting terrorism. Collectively, these items all share a common thread of being issue stances held by many minority and immigrant groups in the United States who support affirmative action and immigration and who feel that the death penalty and the burdens of military service have disproportionately affected minority communities. Although not loading above the threshold, respondents with high scores on this factor are also somewhat likely to support a government role for improving the standard of living for the poor.

That abortion and the death penalty do not align as well as other issues represents a challenge to the Catholic Church's opposition to each on the grounds that these violate the sanctity of all human life from conception to natural death. The percentage of Catholics who state opposition to both abortion and the death penalty is small. If one factors in those who oppose each and who support social justice and welfare issues consistent with Church teachings, the number of Catholics in agreement with Church teachings and statements on these issues diminishes even further.

Only 8 percent of adult Catholics "somewhat" or "strongly" disagree with both of the following statements: "A woman should have the right to choose whether or not to abort an unwanted pregnancy" and "I support the death penalty for people convicted of premeditated murder." Only 6 percent of adult Catholics disagree with these two statements and also "somewhat" or "strongly" agree with the generic social justice statement, "An equitable society can be achieved only if special attention is given to the needs of the poor."

Although collectively many Catholics appear not to follow Church teachings and statements on many issues, these clearly exert some influence. For example, among Republicans who "strongly agree" with the statement, "In deciding what is morally acceptable, I believe that my own conscience is more important than Church teachings," 87 percent "somewhat" or "strongly agree" that "I support the death penalty for people convicted of premeditated murder." By comparison, among Republicans who "strongly *disagree*" that their own conscience is more important than Church teachings, 58 percent "somewhat" or "strongly" agree that the death penalty should be used for those convicted of premeditated murder. Among Democrats who "strongly agree" with the statement, "In deciding what is morally acceptable, I believe that my own conscience is more important than Church teachings," 83 percent "somewhat" or "strongly agree" that "A woman should have the right to choose whether or not to abort an unwanted pregnancy." By comparison, among Democrats who "strongly *disagree*" that their own conscience is more important than Church teachings, only 34 percent "somewhat" or "strongly" agree that women should have a right to have an abortion. Thus, within each party affiliation group, there are some Catholics who place Church teachings ahead of their personal conscience in opposition to their party.

Although the Church instructs Catholics to choose the lesser evil in voting when faced with a choice that cannot be consistent with all the Church's teachings, which is almost always the case in the United States, the Church does not support Catholics themselves holding viewpoints in opposition to Church teachings. Yet the results presented here provide evidence of widespread selective adherence to Church teachings in the attitudes of U.S. Catholics that seems to be at least in part linked to the party divide in U.S. politics.

Table 5.4 presents models of party affiliation among Catholics. Because few Catholics in 2006 did not identify with or at least "lean" toward one party or the other,

TABLE 5.4 Regression Models

	Model 1		Model 2		Model 3	
	ESTIMATE	SIG.	ESTIMATE	SIG.	ESTIMATE	SIG.
Constant	−1.050*	0.000	−1.287*	0.000	−0.857*	0.000
Education						
High school or less	REF		REF		REF	
Some college or A.A.	−0.209	0.089	−0.324*	0.018	−0.284	0.059
College degree	−0.238	0.099	−0.299	0.069	−0.314	0.089
Graduate school	−0.346	0.073	−0.505*	0.024	−0.826*	0.001
Sex						
Female	0.312*	0.002	0.129	0.247	−0.131	0.290
Male	REF		REF		REF	
Household Income						
Less than $40,000	REF		REF		REF	
$40,000–$84,999	−0.408*	0.000	−0.435*	0.001	−0.297*	0.032
$85,000 or more	−0.565*	0.000	−0.667*	0.000	−0.470*	0.016
Race and Ethnicity						
Non-Hispanic white	−0.580*	0.000	−0.460*	0.001	0.052	0.732
Hispanic	REF		REF		REF	
Other race or ethnicity	−0.128	0.560	0.043	0.925	0.334	0.220
Political Ideology						
Conservative			−1.723*	0.000	−1.211*	0.000
Slightly Conservative			−1.319*	0.000	−0.978*	0.000
Moderate, middle of the road			REF		REF	
Slightly liberal			0.496*	0.010	0.316	0.127
Liberal			1.582*	0.000	0.802*	0.001
Mass Attendance						
Rarely or never			REF		REF	
Once or twice a year			0.190	0.204	0.118	0.471
Once or few times a month			0.107	0.506	0.401*	0.029
Weekly or more			0.326*	0.043	0.800*	0.000
Issue Factors						
1: Social Welfare					0.984*	0.000
2: Pro-Life					−0.480*	0.000
3: Diversity					0.620*	0.000
Pseudo R-Square (Nagelkerke)	6.6%		29.6%		44.0%	
Number of Respondents	1,810		1,802		1,780	

*p < .05.

REF = excluded reference category.

we use logit to predict whether a respondent identifies or leans Democrat (1) or Republican (0). Negative coefficient numbers indicate a variable is associated with a decreased likelihood of identifying as a Democrat (and thus increased likelihood of identifying as a Republican) and positive numbers indicate a greater likelihood of identifying as a Democrat.

In model 1, a baseline sociodemographic model of party choice is presented. This model's pseudo r-square is weak and indicates that Catholic women are significantly more likely than men to be Democrats and that non-Hispanic whites are more likely than Hispanics to be Republicans. Catholics residing in households with annual incomes of $40,000 or more are more likely than those in homes with lower incomes to identify as a Republican.

In model 2, political ideology and mass attendance were added. This addition increased the explained variance.[33] As expected, conservatives are more likely than moderates to identify as Republicans and those who are liberal are more likely than moderates to be Democrats. Only weekly mass attendees can be distinguished from those who rarely or never attend mass. The direction of the effect runs counter to some widely held assumptions about emerging patterns of party identification and vote choices among Catholics and evangelical Christians. Weekly attendees are more likely to be Democrats than those who rarely or never attend. With these additions, differences between male and female Catholics in party choice disappear.

In model 3, the issue factors scores derived from the factor analysis presented in table 5.3 were introduced. The coefficients for the issue factors were in the expected directions, with those who score highly on the social welfare and diversity factors being more likely to be Democrats and those scoring highly on the pro-life factor being more likely to be Republicans. Catholics who describe themselves as "slightly liberal" became undistinguishable from moderates ideologically. The inclusion of the factor scores increased the pseudo r-square to 44 percent.[34] Additionally, those who attend mass once a month or more became distinguishable from those attending less often. All other things being equal, Catholics who attend mass at least once a month are more likely than those attending rarely or never to be Democrats.

With the introduction of information about issue attitudes, racial and ethnic differences could no longer be distinguished. Thus, there are no differences in party affiliation between Hispanic and non-Hispanic white Catholics or that of other racial and ethnic identities, once one includes information about specific issue preferences. Differences in party affiliation among Catholics are not a direct function of ethnic identities or cultures but instead flow more directly through attitudes about important social, political, and moral issues.

In an additional model (not shown in table 5.4), we explored the impact of measuring responses to the thirteen individual questions used in the factor analysis rather than the three factor scores.[35] This increased the explained variance slightly and led to the disappearance of income differences. Results for specific life and social justice issue questions are noted below.

On life issues, Catholics who "strongly agree" with the statement "I support the death penalty for people convicted of premeditated murder" are more likely than those who "strongly disagree" with this statement to identify as a Republican. Those with intermediate responses (that is, somewhat agree or disagree or neither agree nor disagree) cannot be distinguished from those who "strongly disagree." Those who "strongly disagree" with the statement, "A woman should have the right to choose whether or not to abort an unwanted pregnancy," are more likely to be Republican than those responding in any other way to that question. Thus, as expected, and in opposition to Church teachings, those who specifically strongly support the death penalty and strongly oppose abortion are likely to affiliate with the Republican Party. Those who "strongly disagree" with a statement that most closely approximates Church teachings on life issues, namely that "all human life, from conception to natural death, is sacred. For this reason, the taking of life—whether through abortion, the death penalty or assisted suicide is wrong," are more likely than those who "strongly agree" with this statement to be Democrats.

Turning to social welfare and justice issues, in a linear manner, the less respondents agree with the statement, "Regardless of cost, the U.S. government should guarantee basic health care for all citizens," the more likely they are to identify as Republicans. A similar distribution is evident for the statement, "There should be a tax increase for the wealthiest Americans." Catholics who "strongly" agree with this statement are most likely to identify as Democrats, with those exhibiting less agreement being less likely to identify as such. Those who "strongly favor" the U.S. government doing "everything possible to improve the standard of living of all poor Americans" are most likely to identify as Democrats, with those who instead favor the statement that "people should take care of themselves" being less likely to identify as Democrats. Those who "strongly disagree" that "workers have a right to a living wage and the right to form and join unions" are more likely than those who "strongly agree" with that statement to be Republicans.

CONCLUSION

For Catholic Church leaders, voting one's conscience is acceptable in an electoral system that has no party or candidate which aligns with the Catholic Church ideologically. Speaking one's mind on specific issues is another matter. As Pope John Paul II said, "It is sometimes claimed that dissent from the Magisterium is totally compatible with being a 'good Catholic,' and poses no obstacle to the reception of the Sacraments. This is a grave error that challenges the teaching of the Bishops in the United States and elsewhere."[36] Even as this is the case, many American Catholics are unfazed in making such an error for at least a few issues when asked about them in a survey.

In the data explored here, a representative sample of the U.S. Catholic population, a majority of respondents expresses attitudes about life issues that run counter to Church teachings, while many Catholics' attitudes regarding social justice are more consistent with those expressed by Church leaders. Overall, the attitudes of Catholics on many issues show much greater consistency with their party affiliation than with their religious affiliation. With the majority of the Catholic population identifying as Democrats, even if at levels lower than in decades past, the overall distribution of the majority of Catholic opinion is consistent with the Democratic Party platform—pro-social justice and pro-abortion rights.

Yet there clearly is tension between life and social justice issues among Catholics in the United States. However, as shown here, this is not primarily a microlevel internal conflict. Instead, this is occurring more at the macrolevel, where differences are primarily defined by party identification among U.S. Catholics.

APPENDIX: DATA AND METHODOLOGY

In 2002 and 2006, CARA surveyed self-identified adult Catholics using the Knowledge Networks panel. Knowledge Networks, a leading Internet survey research firm, has created a large panel of randomly sampled residents of the United States who are invited take part in regular online polls for a variety of government, academic, and commercial purposes. This panel is refreshed on a quarterly basis. Households are recruited into the panel through standard random digit dialing telephone research methods. Those who agree to participate have their Internet costs provided by Knowledge Networks in exchange for participating in an online survey three to four times a month. Households without computers are given an Internet appliance that turns a television into a web browser. Panel members are sent e-mails informing them that they have been selected for a particular survey. The e-mails contain links that take them to the questionnaire, and responses are made by clicking buttons (for close-ended questions) or typing in information in boxes (for open-ended questions).

These methods ensure that the Knowledge Networks panel is as reflective as possible of the national population and the research is not biased toward those who have preexisting access to the Internet or who own a computer. Several studies have found that the Knowledge Networks panel and samples drawn from it are as representative of the U.S. population as samples obtained from high-quality traditional telephone polls, and Knowledge Networks has been used in other published voting studies.[37]

In the 2002 CARA survey, Knowledge Networks polls were conducted only in English. However, since that time it has become possible for those who prefer Spanish to receive a Spanish version of the Knowledge Network polls. Accordingly, the 2006 questionnaire was translated into Spanish by a Knowledge Networks staff member. A total of twenty-five respondents chose to take the survey in Spanish rather than English (1.5 percent of all respondents, or 4.7 percent of self-identified Hispanic/Latino respondents).

All results presented here have been calculated using statistical weights. The weights, calculated by Knowledge Networks, adjust for aspects of panel design and survey methodology that depart from true random sampling. More importantly for current purposes, the weights also adjust results to better reflect estimated demographic characteristics taken from the Census.

For the 2006 survey, panel members previously identified as Catholic were e-mailed the survey on September 20, 2006. The poll was closed on September 28. Responses were received from 1,892 individuals, an overall response rate of 77 percent. Following standard assumptions of statistical inference, this provides a margin of sampling error of ±2.3 percent. For the 2002 survey, panel members previously identified as Catholic were e-mailed the survey on September 6, 2002. The poll was closed on September 20. Responses were received from 1,488 individuals, an overall response rate of 66 percent. However, 13 percent of these respondents indicated in the initial screening question that they do not currently consider themselves Catholic. While this 13 percent of respondents probably includes some individuals who have disaffiliated from Catholicism in months or years previous to the poll, the great majority were probably misclassified in the Knowledge Networks panel. Analyses presented here include the 1,299 self-identified Catholics who completed the 2002 survey. Following standard assumptions of statistical inference, this provides a margin of sampling error of ±2.7 percent.

In comparing basic demographics for the two polls, all differences between polls were within the margins of sampling error.

NOTES

1. United States Conference of Catholic Bishops, *Faithful Citizenship: A Catholic Call to Political Responsibility* (Washington, DC: USCCB, 2003), 4.
2. Stathis Kalyvas, *The Rise of Christian Democracy in Europe* (Ithaca, NY: Cornell University Press, 1996), 180.
3. Ibid., 183.
4. Titus Cranny, *The Moral Obligation of Voting* (Washington, DC: Catholic University of America Press, 1952), 34.
5. United States Conference of Catholic Bishops, *Faithful Citizenship: Civic Responsibility for a New Millennium* (Washington, DC: USCCB, 1999), 3.
6. Congregation for the Doctrine of the Faith, *The Participation of Catholics in Political Life* (Rome: Congregation for the Doctrine of the Faith, 2002).
7. Ibid.
8. Mary E. Bendyna, "The Catholic Ethic in American Politics: Evidence from Survey Research" (PhD diss., Georgetown University, 2000).
9. Ibid.; Mary E. Bendyna, John C. Green, Mark J. Rozell, and Clyde Wilcox. "Uneasy Alliance: Conservative Catholics and the Christian Right," *Sociology of Religion* 62 (2001): 51–64.
10. Michael R. Welch, David C. Leege, Kenneth D. Wald, and Lyman Kellstedt, "Are the Sheep Hearing the Shepherds? Cue Perceptions, Congregational Responses, and Political Communication Processes," in *Rediscovering the Religious Factor in American Politics,* ed. David C. Leege and Lyman Kellstedt (New York: M. E. Sharp, 1993).
11. Kenneth Wald, "Religious Elites and Public Opinion: The Impact of the Bishops' Peace Pastoral," *The Review of Politics* 54 (1992): 112–43.
12. David C. Leege and Paul D. Mueller, "American Catholics at the Catholic Moment: An Analysis of Catholic Political Patterns, 1952–1996" (address, annual meeting, American Political Science Association, Washington, DC, 2000); James R. Kelly and Christopher Kudlac, "Pro-Life, Anti-Death Penalty?" *America,* April 1, 2000; Paul Perl and James S. McClintock, "The Catholic 'Consistent Life Ethic' and Attitudes toward Capital Punishment and Welfare Reform," *Sociology of Religion* 62 (2001): 275–99.
13. Thoroddur Bjarnason and Michale R. Welch, "Father Knows Best: Parishes, Priests, and American Catholics and the Christian Right," *Sociology of Religion* 62 (2003): 51–64.
14. Welch et al., "Are the Sheep Hearing the Shepherds?"
15. For more information, see the appendix in this chapter.
17. United States Conference of Catholic Bishops, *Faithful Citizenship: A Catholic Call to Political Responsibility.*
17. A majority of respondents express support for ending affirmative action programs (53 percent) in opposition to the U.S. bishops' stance on this issue.
18. About one-third of respondents, 32 percent, place themselves in the "leaner" groups (15 percent Republican and 17 percent Democrat). Some 11 percent identify themselves as

"strong Republicans" and another 11 percent identify as "not strong Republicans." Some 21 percent identify themselves as "strong Democrats" and 20 percent say they are "not strong Democrats."

19. CNN, CNN.com Election Results: Exit Polls, 2004, available from www.cnn.com/ ELECTION/2004/pages/results/states/US/P/00/epolls.0.html.

20. Following John Kerry's loss in the 2004 presidential election, Stan Greenberg and Matt Hogan of Democracy Corps authored a widely circulated memo and statistical analysis titled "Reclaiming the White Catholic Vote" (2005).

21. Non-Hispanic white Catholics are slightly more likely than those who self-identify as Hispanic to describe themselves as conservatives. More than one-third of non-Hispanic whites say they are conservative, compared to 26 percent of Hispanics.

22. Paul F. Lazarsfeld, Bernard Berelson, and Hazel Gaudet, *The People's Choice* (New York: Columbia University Press, 1948); Bernard Berelson, Paul Lazarsfeld, and William McPhee, *Voting: A Study of Opinion Formation in a Presidential Election* (Chicago: University of Chicago Press, 1954); Angus Campbell, Philip E. Converse, Warren E. Miller, and Donald E. Stokes, *The American Voter* (New York: Wiley, 1960).

23. Anthony Downs, *An Economic Theory of Democracy* (New York: Harper and Row, 1957); John E. Jackson, "Issues, Party Choices, and Presidential Votes," *American Journal of Political Science* 19 (1975): 161–86; Samuel Popkin, John W. Gorman, Charles Phillips, and Jeffrey A. Smith, "Comment: What Have You Done for Me Lately? Toward An Investment Theory of Voting," *American Political Science Review* 70 (1976): 779–805; Morris P. Fiorina, "An Outline for a Model of Party Choice," *American Journal of Political Science* 21 (1977): 618; Morris P. Fiorina, *Retrospective Voting in American National Elections* (New Haven, CT: Yale University Press, 1981); Benjamin I. Page and Calvin Jones, "Reciprocal Effects of Policy Preferences, Party Loyalties, and the Vote," *American Political Science Review* 73 (1979): 1071–89; Carol A. Cassel, "Predicting Party Identification, 1956–80: Who Are the Republicans and Who Are the Democrats?" *Political Behavior* 4 (1982): 265–82; Charles H. Franklin and John E. Jackson, "The Dynamics of Party Identification," *American Political Science Review* 77 (1983): 957–73; Michael MacKuen, Robert Erikson, and James A Stimson, "Macropartisanship," *American Political Science Review* 83 (1989): 1125–42.

24. Carole J. Uhlaner and F. Chris Garcia, "Foundations of Latino Party Identification: Learning, Ethnicity, and Demographic Factors among Mexicans, Puerto Ricans, Cubans, and Anglos in the United States" (paper 98-06, Irvine: Center for the Study of Democracy, University of California, Irvine, 1966), 6.

25. Franklin and Jackson, "Dynamics of Party Identification," 968.

26. Martin P. Wattenberg, *The Decline of American Political Parties 1952–1994* (Cambridge, MA: Harvard University Press, 1996); Russell J. Dalton and Martin P. Wattenberg, *Parties without Partisans: Political Change in Advanced Industrial Democracies* (Oxford: Oxford University Press, 2002).

27. Uhlaner and Garcia, "Foundations of Latino Party Identification," 10.

28. Warren E. Miller, "Party Identification, Realignment, and Party Voting: Back to the Basics," *American Political Science Review* 85 (1991): 557–68.

29. Bruce E. Keith, David B. Magleby, Candice J. Nelson, Elizabeth Orr, Mark C. Westlye, and Raymond E. Wolfinger et al., *The Myth of the Independent Voter* (Berkeley: University of California Press, 1992).

30. David J. O'Brien, *The Renewal of American Catholicism* (New York: Doubleday Anchor, 1972); Joan L. Fee, "Political Continuity and Change," in *Catholic Schools in a Declining Church*, ed. Andrew Greeley, William McReady, and Kathleen McCourt (Kansas City, MO: Sheed and Ward, 1976), 76–102; Andrew M. Greeley, "How Conservative Are American Catholics?" *Political Science Quarterly* 92 (1977): 199–218; Mary T. Hanna, *Catholics and American Politics* (Cambridge, MA: Harvard University Press, 1979).

31. Mark M. Gray, Paul M. Perl, and Mary E. Bendyna, "Camelot Only Comes But Once? John F. Kerry and the Catholic Vote," *Presidential Studies Quarterly* 36 (2006): 203–22.

32. Scott Greer, "Catholic Voters and the Democratic Party," *Public Opinion Quarterly* 25 (1961): 611–25; Kevin Phillips, *The Emerging Republican Majority* (New York: Doubleday Anchor, 1969); James Penning, "Changing Partisanship and Issue Stands among American Catholics," *Sociological Analysis* 47 (1986): 29–49.

33. The influence of measures for income and race and ethnicity is unaffected; however, education emerges as an important factor. Catholics who attended some college but did not earn a four-year degree, as well as those who did get a degree and attended graduate school, are more likely than those with high school educations or less to identify as a Republican.

34. Results are consistent with Cassel's findings regarding issues stances as predictors of party choices. As she notes, "when demographic and socialization variables are controlled, policy attitudes not only make a difference in predicting party identification but are some of the best predictors of partisanship" (Cassel, "Predicting Party Identification, 1956–80").

35. Results omitted due to space limitations. Available upon request. When this model is applied to a modified dependent variable, a more traditional measure of party identification excluding leaners, few important differences emerge. The latter does achieve the highest pseudo r-square of all models, but no new issues emerge. Rather, when one excludes leaners, the influence of attitudes about the death penalty all but disappears in the direct question about premeditated murder as well as in the indirect measure regarding the general sanctity of life.

36. As quoted in an article by Pat Windsor, "The Pope in America: Dialogue with Diversity," *St. Anthony Messenger*, December 1987, available from www.americancatholic.org/Features/JohnPaulII/6-USA-1987.asp.

37. Krosnick, John A., and Lin Chiat Chang, "A Comparison of the Random Digit Dialing Telephone Survey Methodology with Internet Survey Methodology as Implemented by Knowledge Networks and Harris Interactive," available from http://communication.stanford.edu/faculty/Krosnick (accessed April 9, 2009). Laurance Baker et al., "Use of the Internet and E-mail for Health Care Information," *Journal of the American Medical Association* 289 (2003): 2400–06; Hillygus, D. Sunshine, and Simon Jackman, "Voter Decision Making in Election 2000: Campaign Effects, Partisan Activation, and the Clinton Legacy," *American Journal of Political Science* 47 (2003): 583–96; Jennifer L. Lawless, "Women, War, and Winning Elections: Gender Stereotyping in the Post-September 11th Era," *Political Research Quarterly* 57 (2004): 479–90.

6

THE MYTH OF A DISTINCT CATHOLIC VOTE

Matthew J. Streb and Brian Frederick

*I*N A JUNE 2006 article in *Sojourners* magazine, Maurice Timothy Reidy asks the question, "Who owns the 'Catholic vote'?"[1] "Roughly 40 percent of Catholics are reliable Republicans, and 40 percent are reliable Democrats," writes Reidy. "The rest could go either way. That makes Catholics the ultimate swing voters."[2] Reidy certainly is not alone in his assessment that American elections could ultimately hinge on how Catholics vote.[3] It is not entirely clear, however, that Catholics are indeed swing voters, even if candidates and campaign strategists treat them this way. In fact, it is not obvious that a "Catholic vote" still exists. Several scholars argue that "religiosity" has replaced denomination when it comes to measuring the Catholic vote.[4]

This chapter examines whether Catholics are a unique political group by comparing Catholics and non-Catholics in terms of voting, party identification, and attitudes toward the Democratic and Republican Parties. While it largely avoids weighing in on the religiosity versus denomination debate, the evidence seems to indicate that Catholics are no longer different politically. We find that while Catholics were a distinct group in the 1950s and 1960s, today they are quite similar to non-Catholics in their political behavior and partisanship. It appears that Catholics have not been immune to the broader changes that have occurred among the American electorate as a whole.

The chapter begins by discussing the difficulties in studying the "Catholic vote." It then looks at the fact that Catholics appear to be a group without a partisan home. From there, we review the literature that questions the distinctiveness of a Catholic vote. Finally, we conduct a few tests of our own to determine whether Catholics are different politically from non-Catholics and conclude with a brief discussion of what the findings (and the findings of others) mean for American elections in the future.

STUDYING THE CATHOLIC VOTE AND PARTY AFFILIATION

On the face of it, analyzing how Catholics vote or what party Catholics identify with seems to be incredibly simple. All one has to do is look at surveys that ask for a person's religious affiliation and vote choice for a certain office or party identification. What seemingly is so simple, however, really is quite complex. As David C. Leege and Paul D. Mueller aptly write, "Despite a veritable cottage industry of scholars who have studied religion and politics among American Catholics, a single theory that explains the dynamics of Catholic political behavior has eluded their grasp."[5]

The reason for the difficulty in studying Catholic political behavior is that, like most groups, Catholics are not a monolith. "[Catholics] are a mosaic difficult to capture," Leege and Mueller continue, "composed of diverse ethnic groups with varied histories of separatism, persecution, or acceptance, and assimilation."[6] The American Catholic population has been primarily an immigrant population—Irish, German, Italian, French—and certainly there have been tensions between different ethnic Catholics in the past. Furthermore, while the Catholic immigration of the early twentieth century came primarily from European countries, the Catholic immigration of the early twenty-first century is primarily of Mexican descent. Because of issues like immigration and bilingual education, Mexican Catholics have divergent political concerns from those held by most of today's second- and third-generation European Catholics.

The ethnic diversity of the population is not the only variable that makes it difficult to study Catholic political behavior; the fact that some people identify more strongly as Catholics than others matters as well. There are Catholics who attend mass weekly (or even more often than that) whose Catholicism is a major aspect of their identity, which, in turn, influences them politically. There are also Catholics who have not attended church in thirty years. When asked their religion on surveys, these people may reply "Catholic" but do not identify as being Catholic. In other words, the fact that they are Catholic does not influence them politically; the views of the Church have little impact on their positions on issues. This discussion barely begins to tap into the rich diversity in the Catholic community, but it illustrates why it is so difficult to get a clear grasp on Catholic political behavior. What makes this behavior even more complicated to study is that Catholics—even practicing Catholics—seem to be a group without an obvious partisan affiliation. We turn to this issue now.

A GROUP WITHOUT A PARTISAN HOME

One of the first schools of thought on voting—the Columbia School—emerged in the 1940s and 1950s.[7] Adherents to the Columbia School held that people made their voting decisions primarily based on the groups to which they belonged. According to the Columbia School, sociological variables create common group interests that define which party is most attuned to the needs of various types of people. For example, African Americans may vote Democratic because of the party's position on civil rights, while the wealthy may vote Republican because of the party's support of free markets and tax cuts. At the time of the writing of the original Columbia School works, this theory seemed to make sense regarding Catholic voters. Catholics were an instrumental part of the New Deal coalition that helped put—and keep—Franklin Roosevelt in office. Furthermore, even with the defection of two prominent Catholics in 1936—Al Smith and Father Charles E. Coughlin—from the Democrats, there was little division in the Catholic vote.[8] According to one analysis, Roosevelt carried approximately 80 percent of the Catholic vote in both 1932 and 1936.[9] Although the Catholic population of the 1930s was ethnically quite diverse, the vast support for the Democratic Party made perfect sense. The Catholic population as a whole was not well-off financially, and cultural issues like abortion and same-sex marriage were nowhere near anyone's radar.

While the Catholic voter fit nicely into the Columbia theory during the 1930s and 1940s, there no longer appears to be a Catholic vote. Catholic support for the Democratic Party in presidential elections began to crack with the group's backing of Republican Dwight Eisenhower in 1952 and 1956. With a Catholic on the ticket in 1960, the Democratic Party rebounded with the Catholic vote and maintained it in 1964 when just about every group of voters supported President Lyndon Johnson over Republican Barry Goldwater. However, as Leege and Mueller note, by 1968 it seemed clear that Catholics "would not be permanently anchored in the Democratic party after the Kennedy election."[10] Indeed, empirical studies find that Catholics have become increasingly independent or Republican in both their voting and party identification.[11] Geoffrey Layman writes that although the number of Catholic independents grew in the 1970s, the 1980s witnessed a substantial increase in Catholic Republicans among both committed and less committed Catholics.[12]

Scholars generally cite two reasons for the split in Catholic voters: the first is an economic explanation, the second is a cultural one. As has been noted, since Catholics have been primarily an immigrant community, they often were financially disadvantaged, thus making the Democratic Party—because of its positions on social welfare issues—the most palatable option. However, in the decades after World War II, the economic status of many Catholics improved greatly.[13] As a result, the Republican Party became a viable alternative. Ted Jelen argues that the socioeconomic status (SES) hypothesis is certainly plausible, since Republican Party identification is increasing not only among churchgoing Catholics, but among non-churchgoing Catholics as well.[14]

Other scholars are not as convinced by the SES explanation and claim that the Catholic movement to the Republican Party has been sparked by the increasing importance of cultural issues over the last thirty years.[15] According to Layman, this movement is most prominent in presidential elections. He states that "the combination of Catholic cultural conservatism and cultural issue salience in president elections may have led committed Catholics to be increasingly likely to support Republican presidential candidates."[16] "Meanwhile," he writes, "the Catholic Church's continued liberalism on other matters of public policy may account for the failure of committed Catholics to move their basic partisan ties much closer to the GOP."[17]

Layman's words illustrate why, although greater numbers of Catholics support the Republican Party today than during the 1960s, there has not been a complete Catholic realignment to the Republican Party. Catholics are really a group without a political home; as Kristin E. Heyer points out in chapter 4 of this volume, neither political party is fully consistent with the teachings of the Catholic Church. On the one hand, the rising economic status of many Catholics and the Church's stance on issues such as abortion, same-sex marriage, and prayer in school make the Republican Party a logical option for Catholic voters. On the other hand, after the Second Vatican Council, or Vatican II, held in 1962, church leaders called on Catholics "to apply their Christian values to the problems of the world."[18] These values included fighting poverty and social injustice. Shortly thereafter, liberation theology—the notion that the church should side with the poor in the fight against large landowners—became a prominent view of church leaders. As Kenneth D. Wald states, "liberation theology imparted a willingness to challenge the power of the state in pursuit of the prophetic mission of the church."[19] "This example stimulated many American Catholics (and Protestants) similarly to reconsider the role of their church in struggles between rich and poor," Wald asserted, and makes the Democratic Party the more viable choice.[20]

Furthermore, on life and death issues, major inconsistencies exist between Church doctrine and party platforms. The Republican Party celebrates life in some instances—namely, opposition to abortion and to the use of human embryos in stem cell research—while the Democratic Party defends the sanctity of life in others—namely, opposition to the death penalty and advocacy of limited use of military force. As columnist E. J. Dionne aptly puts it, "On so many of the issues in American politics, being a Catholic liberal or a Catholic conservative inevitably means having a bad conscience about something."[21]

IS THERE A DISTINCTIVE CATHOLIC VOTE?

The previous discussion leads one to believe that there remains a "Catholic vote" today. Although it may not be as united as it once was because of the conflict between Catholics and the Democratic Party on values issues and between Catholics and the Republican Party on social welfare issues, the discussion above implies that Catholics are still voting as Catholics. However, not everyone is convinced that Catholics still constitute a distinct voting bloc.[22] According to these scholars, denomination has faded in importance but "religiosity" has not.[23] For example, Morris P. Fiorina finds that Catholics and Baptists who attend church regularly are more alike in their voting than are Catholics who attend church regularly and those who do not.[24] In 2004, 55 percent of Baptist "attenders" voted for Bush, as did 53 percent of Catholic "attenders." On the flip side, only 34 percent of Baptist "nonattenders" and 33 percent of Catholic "nonattenders" voted for Bush.[25]

Leege also questions whether a Catholic vote exists.[26] He notes that there are significant differences between younger and older Catholics as well as young male and female Catholics. In fact, Leege claims that the "largest gender gap among any religious group opened up in the 1990s among younger Catholics."[27] Young female Catholics, for example, are slightly more liberal on both economic and cultural issues than young male Catholics and are also more likely to attend mass. Younger Catholics of both sexes are less likely to attend church than their older counterparts (although church attendance has declined for all groups).

Leege's research, like Fiorina's, indicates that religiosity is more important than denomination. He finds that Catholics who never attend mass are more comparable to seculars in their political thinking than they are to regular-attending Catholics. Furthermore, the difference in political views between never-attending and regular-attending Catholics is the greatest among the religious traditions.[28]

Other scholars argue that ideology plays a greater role in determining partisanship than does group membership status. According to Alan I. Abramowitz and Kyle L. Saunders, most of the decaying support for the Democratic Party among Catholics in the past generation has come as a result of conservative Catholics shifting to the Republican Party at a much higher rate than have liberal Catholics.[29] This pattern is one that mirrors the transformation that has materialized among all groups of white voters over the past generation.

Perhaps most simply, Catholics as a whole have become like most Americans. Partisanship matters more than group affiliation. Mark M. Gray, Paul M. Perl, and Mary E. Bendyna certainly subscribe to this view.[30] "For Catholics, partisanship is substantially more important than religion now than it was in 1960," they conclude in their recent study on Catholic voting behavior in presidential elections.[31] The following section investigates further the distinctiveness (or lack thereof) of Catholic voting and party identification. Using data from the American National Elections Studies (ANES) and the National Annenberg Election Survey (NAES), we come to similar conclusions as the scholars cited in this section: while Catholics once were a distinct political group, in recent years they have become virtually indistinguishable from the American public as a whole.

FURTHER TESTS OF THE DISTINCTIVENESS OF CATHOLIC VOTERS HYPOTHESIS

Before presenting the findings on patterns of Catholic political behavior, it may be instructive to look at the proportion of Catholics in the U.S. electorate over time. Figure 6.1 plots this percentage from 1956 to 2004 as reported by the ANES. It reveals that the percentage of Catholics in the electorate has remained relatively stable over time. Although there are year-to-year fluctuations, Catholics have typically made up about one-quarter of the electorate over this period. This number never falls below 20 percent and tops out at around 28 percent in 1998. In 1960, when Catholic candidate John F. Kennedy ran for president, Catholics were about 22.6 percent of the electorate, close to the 24.4 percent figure when Catholic candidate John Kerry ran for president in 2004. In sum, Catholics have constituted a considerable proportion of the electorate, and so it is certainly understandable why campaign strategists think that the Catholic vote is an important part of building an electoral coalition. The question now becomes whether this large group of voters is distinctive from non-Catholics in the electorate.

The analysis of Catholic voting behavior begins by focusing on the Catholic vote for president over time. Most studies have examined the Catholic presidential vote exclusively, without a direct comparison to non-Catholic voters.[32] Figure 6.2 displays the percentage of the vote received by Democratic presidential candidates from both Catholics and non-Catholics from 1952 through 2004. It reveals that since the 1964

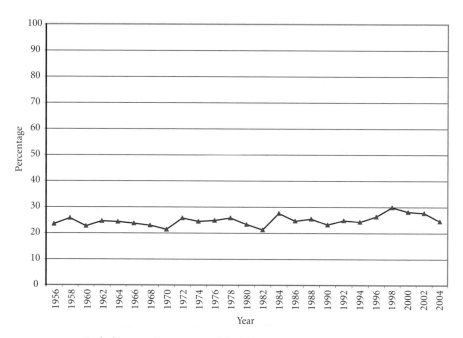

FIGURE 6.1 *Catholics as a Percentage of the Electorate, 1956–2004*

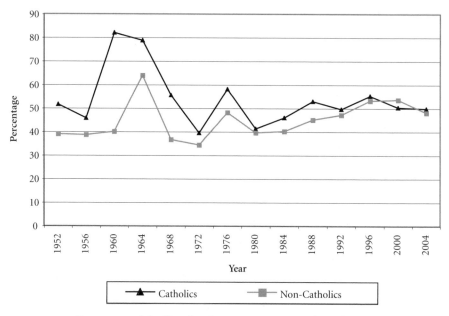

FIGURE 6.2 *Percentage of the Vote for the Democratic Presidential Candidate among Catholics and Non-Catholics, 1952–2004*

election, there has been a precipitous decline in the proportion of Catholics casting ballots for the Democratic ticket. In 1960 Kennedy garnered 82 percent of the vote, and in 1964 Johnson received 79 percent. The allegiance of Catholics to Democratic presidential candidates started to wane in 1968, when Hubert Humphrey received 57 percent of the Catholic vote. Four years later, George McGovern carried only 39 percent of the Catholic vote. The Catholic support for Humphrey and McGovern was far cries from the staggering percentages Kennedy and Johnson had racked up just a few years earlier.

Despite the drop-off in Democratic support from Catholics, they gave a higher percentage of their votes to Democrats compared to non-Catholics in every election until 2000; Al Gore performed about three points better among non-Catholics than Catholics. However, the gap between the groups began to narrow noticeably in 1972, when McGovern did only five points better with Catholics, a stark contrast to Kennedy's forty-two-percentage-point gap between the two groups. Examining the 1976 and 1996 elections also illustrates this trend. In 1976 Jimmy Carter received 10 percent more votes among Catholics, as opposed to 1996, when Bill Clinton's gap between Catholics and non-Catholics was only two percentage points (the same gap that existed in 2004 with Catholic John Kerry heading the Democratic ticket). The basic conclusion that can be drawn from the data in figure 6.2 is that Catholics no longer vote as a distinctive bloc for president. Sometimes they are more supportive of Democrats, but not to the extent they were in previous eras. At a macro level, Catholics and non-Catholics have become almost indistinguishable in their voting behavior for the office of the presidency.

Figure 6.3 plots the percentage of the vote given to Democratic candidates for the U.S. House of Representatives from 1956 to 2004. It tells a slightly different story.

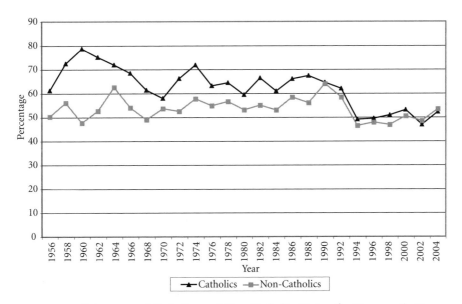

FIGURE 6.3   *Percentage of Catholics and Non-Catholics Voting for Democratic House Candidates, 1956–2004*

Catholic voters supported House Democratic candidates by healthy margins from 1956 through 1992; in only one election cycle over this period did the vote share dip below 60 percent. Part of that support is attributable to the incumbency advantage that Democrats maintained over this period as the majority party in the House. Nevertheless, non-Catholics were clearly less inclined to back Democratic candidates at the same rate. Over this same time period, in only one election cycle did the non-Catholic vote for Democratic House candidates surpass the 60 percent mark. However, beginning in the 1990s there is a clear convergence between the two groups. In the six House elections between the years 1994 and 2004, the percentage of Catholic votes going to Democrats was about 1.3 percent higher than for non-Catholics. Equally noteworthy is that in 2002 and 2004 Democratic House candidates fared marginally better with non-Catholics than they did with Catholics. These data are more compelling evidence that Catholics have faded as a distinctive group of voters more loyal to candidates who carry the Democratic banner.

Scrutinizing the trends in party identification among Catholics and non-Catholics paints a portrait congruent with the previous results. Figures 6.4 and 6.5 present the percentage of Catholics and non-Catholics who reported identifying with the Democratic and Republican Parties from 1952 through 2004 (including leaners). Figure 6.4 displays the percentage of Democratic identifiers, and it shows that there was clearly a noticeable gap between the two groups early in this time series. Catholics were much more willing to cite a preference for the Democratic Party than was the rest of the electorate. This preference reached its zenith in 1960, with about 73 percent of Catholics professing to identify with the Democratic Party. In that same year,

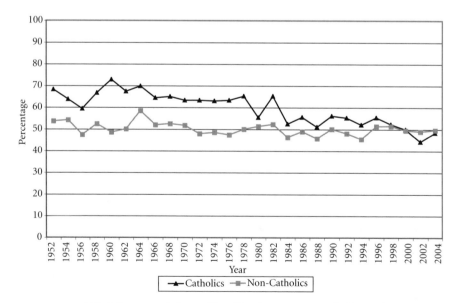

FIGURE 6.4   *ANES Democratic Party Identification among Catholics and Non-Catholics, 1952–2004*

just below 49 percent of non-Catholics identified with the Democratic Party, a difference of twenty-four percentage points. This gap narrowed in the following two decades but remained fairly substantial. However, as it did with non-Catholics, the Democrats' edge in party identification eroded dramatically in the 1980s. By 1988, only 51 percent of Catholics identified with the Democratic Party, compared to approximately 46 percent of non-Catholics. In the first decade of the twenty-first century, the Catholic defection from the Democratic Party has only heightened, as in 2002 and 2004 the percentage of Democratic identifiers was a few points higher among non-Catholics than Catholics.

The Democratic Party's loss among Catholics and non-Catholics has been the Republican Party's gain. From 1952 through 1982, Republican identification among Catholics never passed the 30 percent threshold (see figure 6.5). Since 1984 it has stayed above that benchmark, and in 2000, for the first time in the ANES series, more Catholics than non-Catholics identified with the Republican Party. In 2002, the number of Catholics identifying as Republicans also exceeded the number of Catholics identifying as Democrats. Though the Republican identification advantage among Catholics reversed itself in 2004, it was still at a level noticeably higher than it was in earlier eras. Furthermore, since the mid-1990s there has been virtually no difference between the percentage of Catholic and non-Catholic Republicans.

Figures 6.6 and 6.7 add another dimension to this examination into the perceptions of the two major political parties among Catholics and non-Catholics. The ANES regularly asks respondents how they feel toward major political figures and institutions on a scale from 0 to 100, with 0 representing the coolest response and a value

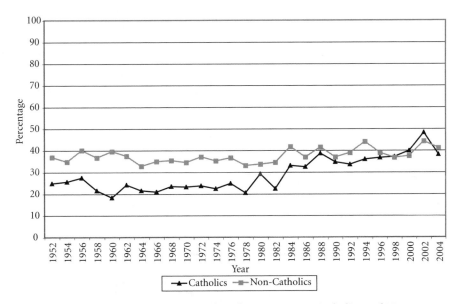

FIGURE 6.5   *ANES Republican Party Identification among Catholics and Non-Catholics, 1952–2004*

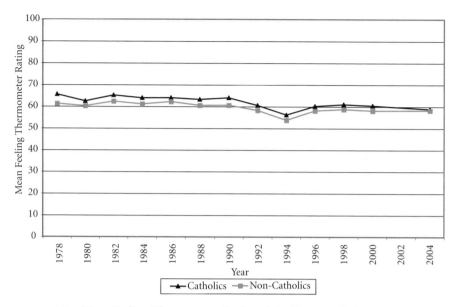

FIGURE 6.6   *Mean Feeling Thermometer Rating of the Democratic Party among Catholics and Non-Catholics, 1978–2004*

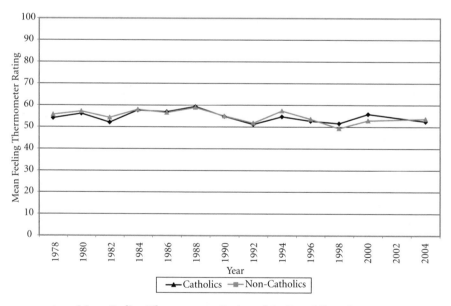

FIGURE 6.7   *Mean Feeling Thermometer Rating of the Republican Party among Catholics and Non-Catholics, 1978–2004*

of 100 the warmest. Unfortunately, it was not until 1978 that the feeling thermometer question was asked about the two major parties. Thus, we can not analyze changes
from the John F. Kennedy era until contemporary times as is the case with the data
presented earlier. Nevertheless, it is possible to glean whether there have been any systematic differences in the affective responses to the major political parties among
Catholics and non-Catholics over the past two and one-half decades. Figure 6.6 includes the mean feeling thermometer rating of the Democratic Party for Catholics and
non-Catholics from 1978 to 2004.[33] In every year the question has been asked,
Catholics feel warmer toward the Democratic Party than toward the GOP. However,
in only six of the thirteen years is the difference between the two groups statistically
significant at the .05 level. Even in the cases when statistical significance did occur,
though, it is hard to argue that the results are substantively meaningful; in no election cycle does the difference exceed three points. In 2004 the mean feeling thermometer rating toward the Democratic Party for both groups was almost identical
at around 58.

The data in figure 6.7 for the mean Republican Party feeling thermometer rating largely comport with the results just discussed. In all but two of the election years
displayed in this graph, is the mean rating for non-Catholics higher than for Catholics.
Again, the differences are minor and only statistically significant in two of the thirteen election years. In fact, in 2000, Catholics rated the Republican Party more favorably than non-Catholics by about three points (p < .020). In 2004 non-Catholics were
again slightly more favorable toward the GOP, but by less than one point. Figures 6.6
and 6.7 confirm the basic theme of this study, that Catholics are no longer a cohesive
political force markedly different from non-Catholics.

Figures 6.8–6.11 bolster this conclusion even further. They present the mean
number of things respondents liked and disliked about the two major parties cited by
Catholic and non-Catholic respondents from 1952 through 2004.[34] Figures 6.8 and 6.9
compare the mean number of likes and dislikes toward the Democratic Party for the
two groups. From 1952 through 1980, Catholics listed more things they liked about
the Democratic Party than did non-Catholics, and these differences were statistically
significant at the .05 level (figure 6.8). After 1980 the mean difference achieved statistical significance only in one election year. Figure 6.9 displays the mean number of dislikes toward the Democratic Party and, in all but three years, non-Catholics cited more
things they disliked about the Democratic Party than did Catholics. However, this difference was no longer statistically significant after 1964.

Figures 6.10 and 6.11 display the numbers for the Republican Party. Here it is
quite clear that non-Catholics cited more things they liked about the GOP than did
Catholics in the 1950s and 1960s. Conversely, Catholics listed more things they disliked
about the Republican Party than did non-Catholics over the same time frame. Yet after the 1960s, in only two elections was there a significant difference (p < .05) between
the mean number of things the two groups disliked about the Republican Party. In no
year was the mean difference in the number of likes statistically significant after the
1960s either. As with other measures of political behavior, Catholics and non-Catholics
have converged in their perceptions of both political parties. Though minor variations
appear in these data, the trend is that Catholic and non-Catholic predispositions

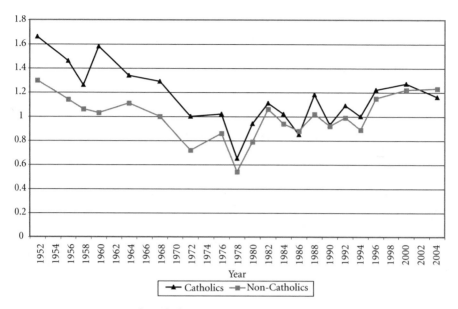

FIGURE 6.8   *Mean Number of Things Respondents Liked about the Democratic Party among Catholics and Non-Catholics, 1952–2004*

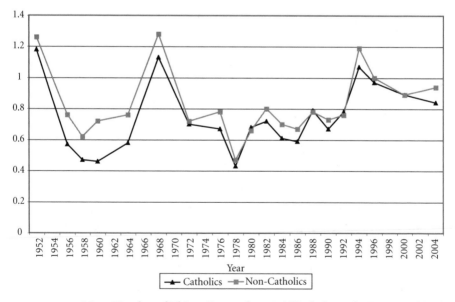

FIGURE 6.9   *Mean Number of Things Respondents Disliked about the Democratic Party among Catholics and Non-Catholics, 1952–2004*

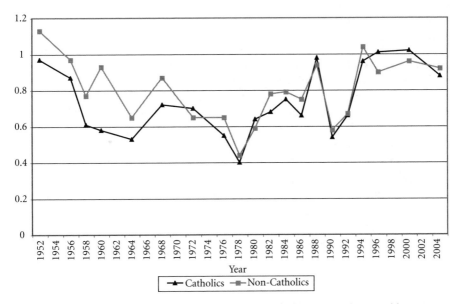

FIGURE 6.10   *Mean Number of Things Respondents Liked about the Republican Party among Catholics and Non-Catholics, 1952–2004*

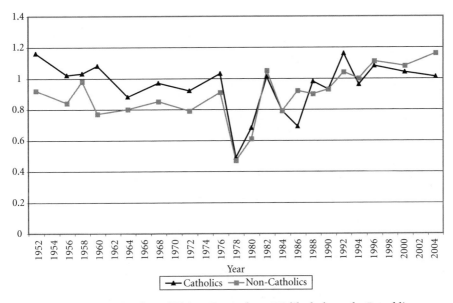

FIGURE 6.11   *Mean Number of Things Repondents Disliked about the Republican Party among Catholics and Non-Catholics, 1952–2004*

toward Democrats and Republicans largely move in tandem, depending on the prevailing political atmosphere.

The link between party identification and ideology has strengthened over the past generation. Liberals are increasingly more likely to identify as Democrats and conservatives as Republicans.[35] Considering the importance of this relationship, we look at whether there is any systematic variation in the ideological identification of Catholics and non-Catholics utilizing data from the ANES from 1972 through 2004. Unfortunately, the ANES did not begin to ask about individual ideological identification until after the height of Democratic strength among Catholics. Still, it is possible to evaluate whether there are any meaningful differences in self-reported ideological identification among the two groups. Table 6.1 presents the percentage of respondents describing themselves as liberals, moderates, and conservatives. Though there are modest differences depending on the year, the ideological profile of Catholics is congruent with non-Catholics. There are year-to-year fluctuations, but for both

TABLE 6.1　Ideological Breakdown of Catholics and Non-Catholics, 1972–2004

	Catholics			Non-Catholics		
YEAR	LIBERAL	MODERATE	CONSERVATIVE	LIBERAL	MODERATE	CONSERVATIVE
1972	18.6	32.0	25.1	18.6	25.3	26.8
1974	20.3	32.6	25.6	18.9	26.7	27.2
1976	16.1	27.0	24.8	15.8	24.7	27.1
1978	20.0	33.3	23.6	19.2	24.7	24.7
1980	17.9	20.7	25.1	15.7	19.3	29.3
1982	12.8	26.9	26.3	15.2	21.1	27.3
1984	19.0	25.6	25.3	17.4	22.5	29.7
1986	20.4	27.8	29.8	17.0	27.8	29.6
1988	17.8	23.8	28.6	15.9	21.3	32.7
1990	17.3	26.7	24.4	16.5	23.7	26.3
1992	20.1	26.1	30.0	20.4	22.1	30.2
1994	17.8	29.1	35.4	15.0	26.1	36.2
1996	21.1	27.3	34.6	19.3	22.2	34.2
1998	18.4	27.9	32.7	19.8	29.4	30.5
2000	18.6	29.9	30.7	21.4	23.0	32.8
2002	19.9	24.0	41.3	23.6	22.3	36.6
2004	23.0	26.0	26.0	19.7	22.1	28.7

Source: American National Election Studies Cumulative Data File.

Note: For ease of presentation, the percentage of those respondents answering "Don't Know" is not included.

groups there are consistently more conservatives and moderates than liberals. Slightly higher percentages of Catholics call themselves moderates over the course of this time series, but the difference is minimal. Altogether, the self reports on ideological identification support the proposition that Catholics are in line with the basic political orientation of the U.S. public as a whole. If Catholics are not ideologically distinguishable from non-Catholics, then it should come as no surprise that their voting behavior and attitudes toward the parties no longer are either.

Up to this point we have exclusively examined Catholics as a uniform group and have not looked at variation in the level of religious commitment exhibited by members of this faith. We also have not introduced any multivariate controls in the analysis. Therefore, a model has been formulated to predict Democratic Party identification, including variables representing Catholics who range from individuals who attend mass more than once a week to individuals who never attend mass. The ANES is not sufficient to get samples of these subgroups large enough to conduct a meaningful analysis. Instead, the 2004 National Annenberg Election Survey (NAES) has been utilized. The NAES includes a sample size of over 81,000 people taken over the course of the 2004 presidential campaign.[36] Hence, it permits an investigation of the impact that a number of subgroups sorely underrepresented in the ANES have on predicting party identification.

The trends in Catholics' political behavior cited earlier in this study show that Catholics as a group are not distinctive. As some researchers have noted, it may be that the degree of one's religious commitment matters more than one's status as a member of any particular faith.[37] Perhaps some groups of Catholics are more likely to identify as Democrats than are others. In order to determine whether levels of religious commitment matter in predicting identification with the Democratic Party, Catholics were disaggregated into four groups: Catholics attending mass once a week or more; Catholics attending mass once or twice a month; Catholics attending mass a few times a year; and Catholics who never attend mass. To carry out this analysis, a logit model was relied on to predict whether the respondent identified with the Democratic Party in the 2004 election. The dependent variable is coded 1 for those respondents who said they were Democrats and 0 otherwise.[38] Dummy variables for each of the four groups of Catholics just mentioned are incorporated as the key independent variables. The model includes a number of other factors likely to predict Democratic Party identification such as race, education, income, and union membership.

Table 6.2 presents the results of this model. In contrast to the other findings of this study, in this analysis Catholics at each level of religious commitment were still more likely than non-Catholics to identify as Democrats. The coefficients for all of these variables are statistically significant (p-value <.01). Just like women, African Americans, Jews, non-Cuban Hispanics, people with advanced degrees, members of union households, and liberals, Catholics were significantly more likely to align with the Democratic Party in 2004. Conversely, men, white evangelicals, gun owners, Cuban Americans, married people, Mormons, individuals who attend religious services more often, and Americans with higher incomes were all less likely to identify as Democrats. The data indicate that, even across all levels of faith commitment, Catholics still

TABLE 6.2 Logit Model Predicting Democratic Party Identification in 2004

INDEPENDENT VARIABLE	COEFFICIENT	S.E.
Female	.428*	.018
Age	.014*	.001
Education (highest degree)	−.034*	.006
Graduate Degree	.314*	.033
Income	−.059*	.005
African American	1.651*	.035
Hispanic	.293*	.035
Cuban American	−.522*	.157
Other (nonwhite)	.161*	.035
Jewish	.895*	.059
Mormon	−.558*	.092
White Evangelical	−.126*	.024
Frequency of Religious Attendance	−.047*	.009
Union Household Member	.491*	.024
Married	−.064*	.020
Gun Owner	−.125*	.027
Ideology (more liberal)	.694*	.010
Catholics by Mass Attendance		
Once a Week or More	.305*	.032
Once or Twice a Month	.268*	.042
Few Times a Year	.149*	.035
Never	.144**	.055
Constant	−3.321*	.062
Log likelihood	−38371.25	
Pseudo R^2	.140	
N	70519	

* p < .001, ** p < .01.

Source: 2004 National Annenberg Election Survey.

Note: Dependent variable is the respondent's party identification on the three-point scale coded 1 for Democratic and 0 otherwise.

display a greater allegiance to the Democratic Party than do non-Catholics. While Catholics may no longer be overwhelmingly Democratic when professing which party they affiliate with, it may be premature to declare that they are in no way distinctive in their political inclinations, after other factors are controlled for.

On the other hand, simply because there is a statistically significant difference between Catholics and non-Catholics in terms of party identification does not suggest that this difference is substantively meaningful. In order to parse out the substantive impact of Catholic identity, the predicted probabilities are calculated for each group of Catholics, holding all the other variables in the model at their appropriate means, medians, and modes. This technique allows for an estimate of the probability that members of each group of Catholics will identify as Democrats compared to non-Catholics. For the "average" non-Catholic, the predicted probability of identifying with the Democratic Party is .328. For a Catholic attending mass once or more a week it is .398, for a Catholic attending once or twice a month it is .390, for Catholics attending mass a few times a year it is .362, and for Catholics who never attend mass it is .360.[39] Contrary to expectations, all other things being equal, it is actually Catholics demonstrating the highest level of religious commitment who have the highest probability of identifying with the Democratic Party. Nevertheless, they are only about seven percentage points more likely than other respondents to do so. Therefore, one should be cautious about reading too much into these findings. Although more committed Catholics have a slightly higher likelihood of identifying as Democrats, all groups of Catholics have about the same likelihood of doing so. The gap between the groups is hardly a pronounced divide.

Moreover, this substantive impact for all types of Catholics is modest compared to members of other groups more likely to identify as Democrats. For instance, according to this model, African Americans are about 39 percent more likely than non-African Americans to identify with the Democratic Party. The corresponding estimate for Jews and non-Jews is a 21 percentage point differential. So this analysis does provide some evidence that status as a Catholic is not irrelevant on this metric of political behavior, but it hardly matters to the extent that it did in the 1960s and pales in comparison to being African American or Jewish. These demographic groups are much more loyal to the Democratic Party than Catholics.

CONCLUSION

We began this chapter noting that pundits and scholars often refer to Catholics as swing voters. The fact that Catholics regularly comprise about one-quarter of the electorate and have split their votes roughly between the Democratic and Republican Parties in recent presidential and congressional elections makes this perception understandable. However, it is not clear that Catholics are indeed swing voters. It is not essential for candidates to win the Catholic vote because there does not seem to be a "Catholic vote" to be had; Catholics vote quite similarly to non-Catholics, and their partisan affiliations and views toward the two major parties are basically the same.

Instead, we side with the views of Fiorina, Layman, and others who argue that candidates must distinguish between the religious and the secular, not between different denominations.[40]

Other factors, such as ideology and partisanship, also play a much greater role in shaping political behavior than does one's status as a Catholic. Some groups of voters in the electorate, such as African Americans, are distinctive voting blocs; Catholics are not one of them. When political observers speak of a monolithic Catholic vote, such a presumption is a myth that harkens back to the days of Kennedy and Roosevelt in a way that is incompatible with the evidence of contemporary times. The same electoral forces that drive Catholics are in line with those forces that drive non-Catholics. There may be nuanced differences around the edges, but by and large the two groups are indistinctive. Swings in the perceptions of voters toward candidates and parties will be manifested in nearly an identical fashion among both Catholics and non-Catholics. Politicians who seek to tailor their message toward a Catholic vote would do better to identify groups that still maintain a cohesive group identity. This common identity faded long ago and is not likely to return any time in the foreseeable future.

NOTES

1. Maurice Timothy Reidy, "Who Owns the 'Catholic Vote'?" *Sojourners,* June 2006, 12–17.

2. Ibid., 12.

3. E. J. Dionne Jr., "There Is No Catholic Vote—And It's Important," in *American Catholics and Civic Engagement: A Distinctive Voice,* ed. Margaret O'Brien Steinfels (Lanham, MD: Rowman and Littlefield, 2004); Henry C. Kenski and William Lockwood, "Catholic Voting Behavior in 1988: A Critical Swing Vote," in *The Bible and the Ballot Box: Religion and Politics in the 1988 Election,* ed. James L. Guth and John C. Green (Boulder, CO: Westview, 1991).

4. Morris P. Fiorina, with Samuel J. Abrams and Jeremy C. Pope, *Culture War? The Myth of a Polarized America,* 2nd ed. (New York: Pearson Longman, 2006); David C. Leege, "Divining the Electorate: Is There a Religious Vote?" *Commonweal,* October 20 2000, 16–19; David C. Leege and Paul D. Mueller, "How Catholic Is the Catholic Vote?" in *American Catholics and Civic Engagement.*

5. Leege and Mueller, "How Catholic Is the Catholic Vote?" 214.

6. Ibid.

7. See Paul Lazarsfeld, Bernard Berelson, and Hazel Gaudet, *The People's Choice* (New York: Duell, Sloan, and Pearce, 1944); Bernard R. Berelson, Paul F. Lazarsfeld, and William N. McPhee, *Voting* (Chicago: University of Chicago Press, 1954).

8. William B. Prendergast, *The Catholic Voter in American Politics: The Passing of the Democratic Monolith* (Washington, DC: Georgetown University Press, 1999), 114.

9. Kenski and Lockwood, "Catholic Voting Behavior in 1988," 175.

10. Leege and Mueller, "How Catholic Is the Catholic Vote?" 222.

11. Geoffrey Layman, *The Great Divide: Religious and Cultural Conflicts in American Politics* (New York: Columbia University Press, 2001); John Petrocik, "Realignment: New Party Coalitions and the Nationalization of the South," *Journal of Politics* 49 (1987): 347–75; Ted Jelen, "Religion and Public Opinion in the 1990s: An Empirical Overview," in *Understand-*

ing Public Opinion, ed. Barbara Norrander and Clyde Wilcox (Washington, DC: CQ Press, 1997); Mark M. Gray, Paul M. Perl, and Mary E. Bendyna, "Camelot Only Comes But Once? John F. Kerry and the Catholic Vote," *Presidential Studies Quarterly* 36 (2006): 203–22. For a counterargument, cf. Jeff Manza and Clem Brooks, "The Religious Factor in U.S. Presidential Elections, 1960–1992," *American Journal of Sociology* 103 (1997): 38–81; and Robert S. Erikson, Thomas D. Lancaster, and David W. Romero, "Group Components of the Presidential Vote, 1952–1984," *Journal of Politics* 51 (1989): 337–46. The authors of these two studies claim that Catholics became less Democratic but were still more Democratic than the country as a whole.

12. Layman, *Great Divide.*

13. Andrew M. Greeley, *The Catholic Myth: The Behavior and Beliefs of American Catholics* (New York: Scribner, 1990); Kenneth D. Wald, *Religion and Politics in the United States,* 4th ed. (Lanham, MD: Rowman and Littlefield, 2003).

14. Jelen, "Religion and Public Opinion in the 1990s."

15. Layman, *Great Divide;* Lyman A. Kellstedt, John C. Green, James L. Guth, and Corwin E. Smidt, "Religious Voting Blocs in the 1992 Election: The Year of the Evangelical?" *Sociology of Religion* 55 (1994): 307–26.

16. Layman, *Great Divide,* 198–99.

17. Ibid.

18. Wald, *Religion and Politics in the United States,* 252.

19. Ibid., 253.

20. Ibid.

21. Dionne, "There Is No Catholic Vote—And It's Important," 254.

22. Gray, Perl, and Bendyna, "Camelot Only Comes but Once?" 203–22.

23. John C. Green and James L. Guth, "The Bible and the Ballot Box: The Shape of Things to Come," in *The Bible and the Ballot Box;* Geoffrey C. Layman and Edward G. Carmines, "Cultural Conflict in American Politics: Religious Traditionalism, Postmaterialism, and U.S. Political Behavior," *Journal of Politics* 59 (1997): 751–77.

24. Fiorina, *Culture War?*

25. Ibid., 131.

26. Leege, "Divining the Electorate"; Leege and Mueller, "How Catholic Is the Catholic Vote?"

27. Leege, "Divining the Electorate," 18.

28. Leege and Mueller, "How Catholic Is the Catholic Vote?"

29. Alan I. Abramowitz and Kyle L. Saunders, "Exploring the Bases of Partisanship in the American Electorate: Social Identity vs. Ideology," *Political Research Quarterly* 59 (2006): 175–87.

30. Gray, Perl, and Bendyna, "Camelot Only Comes but Once?" 203–22.

31. Ibid., 209. See also Gray and Bendyna, chapter 5, in this volume.

32. See, for example, Gray, Perl, and Bendyna, "Camelot Only Comes but Once?" 203–22.

33. This question was not included in the 2002 survey.

34. This question was not included in the 1954, 1962, 1966, 1970, 1974, 1998, and 2002 surveys.

35. Abramowitz and Saunders, "Exploring the Bases of Partisanship in the American Electorate"; Alan I. Abramowitz and Kyle L. Saunders, "Ideological Realignment in the U.S. Electorate," *Journal of Politics* 60 (1998): 634–52.

36. For a more detailed explanation of the National Annenberg Election Survey, see Daniel Romer, Kate Kenski, Kenneth Winneg, Christopher Adasiewicz, and Kathleen Hall Jamieson, *Capturing Campaign Dynamics 2000 & 2004* (Philadelphia: University of Pennsylvania Press, 2006).

37. Fiorina, *Culture War?*; Leege and Mueller, "How Catholic Is the Catholic Vote?"

38. The three-point party identification scale is utilized in this model.

39. A separate model was run using a dummy variable indicating Catholic status without reference to religious attendance. It produced substantively similar results. In this model the predicted probability that Catholics would identify with the Democratic Party was .372 versus .320 for non-Catholics, a difference of only 5.2 percent.

40. Fiorina, *Culture War?*; Layman, *Great Divide*.

7

POLITICS *Y LA IGLESIA*

*Attitudes toward the Role of Religion in
Politics among Latino Catholics*

ADRIAN PANTOJA, MATTHEW BARRETO, AND RICHARD ANDERSON

*T*HE U.S. CONSTITUTION prohibits government from establishing or promoting a particular religion or intruding on citizens' religious beliefs or activities. Although the constitutional wall separating church and state was designed to keep religious conflicts and influences at bay, the American political and legal landscape is not free from religious strife and influences. Politicians frequently appeal to voters' religious sentiments through symbolic gestures or by supporting policies particular to religiously oriented persons. Religious leaders are increasingly active in the political arena through voter mobilization efforts and endorsements of particular candidates. Perhaps none has had the longevity or been as influential as the Christian Right. The election of a Republican majority to Congress in the mid-1990s and the presidential victories of George W. Bush, a deeply religious Christian, both with strong backing from conservative Christians and their organizations, have renewed interest among scholars in examining the role of religion in American politics.[1]

Scholars have largely considered the impact of religious orientations in structuring a wide range of political attitudes among voters and in determining electoral outcomes.[2] More specifically, the beliefs held by evangelical Protestants are regarded as a significant force driving many contemporary political cleavages, or the so-called God gap.[3] The influence of religious fundamentalist beliefs is most pronounced when it comes to policy issues with religious or moral underpinnings such as abortion, gay marriage, embryonic stem cell research, and school prayer.[4] Measures of religious fundamentalism also correlate strongly with support for the Republican Party and politically conservative candidates.[5] Polls in the 2004 presidential election showed that 22 percent of voters, many of them religious conservatives, ranked "values" as the most important motivator in casting their vote, and about 80 percent of those voters supported Bush.[6] Conservative evangelicals are a crucial constituency group for the Republican Party, and they played a crucial role in George W. Bush's margin of victory over John Kerry in 2004.

The resurgence of conservative evangelicals and other conservative Christians in politics coincides with the fourth wave of mass immigration and the growth of the Latino population. According to census estimates, at over forty million, Latinos are now the largest minority group in the nation and are the fastest-growing segment of the electorate, growing from 2.4 million voters in 1980 to 7.5 million in 2004.[7] Recent reports noting the dramatic growth of the Hispanic electorate in states with large numbers of electoral votes and statements that the Hispanic vote is "up for grabs" have raised their political capital.[8] Against the backdrop of a closely divided national electorate, it is little wonder that they have been the focus of intense campaign efforts by both political parties, which have spent record amounts in their efforts to woo Latinos to their ranks.

Exit polls placed the Latino vote for John Kerry at almost 68 percent, while President Bush garnered 31 percent. These numbers suggest that Latinos' traditional Democratic moorings have not wavered. Yet while most Latinos have long been aligned with the Democratic Party, pundits and journalists have argued that Republicans are beginning to make significant inroads by appealing to their religious values. This makes strategic sense, since Hispanics hold conservative attitudes on a number of social issues, and these attitudes are reinforced by the growth of evangelical groups and fundamentalist beliefs in Hispanic communities.[9] Despite the fact that Latinos are becoming an influential voice in American politics and are deeply religious, little research has been undertaken to examine the interplay between their religious beliefs and political behavior.[10] Hence, in order to gain a better understanding of political and religious change in America, it is essential to analyze the affiliation and religious beliefs of the Latino population.

This chapter is intended to fill a critical gap in the literature on religion and politics by examining the politicoreligious beliefs of Latinos. The study draws on a unique data source: the Hispanic Churches in American Public Life (HCAPL) 2000 public opinion survey. The HCAPL is based on a national telephone survey with 2,310 Latinos carried out between August 21 and October 31, 2000, in Los Angeles; San Antonio; Houston; Chicago; Miami; New York; rural Colorado; rural Iowa; and San Juan, Puerto Rico. (The analysis excludes the sample drawn from Puerto Rico, leaving a total of 2,060 respondents.) Presently, it is the largest national bilingual survey of Latino religious practices and beliefs in the United States.[11]

Our primary interest is to explore Latino attitudes toward the role of religious leaders and organizations in politics. Among Latinos, nearly 70 percent are practicing Catholics, and we probe whether Latino Catholics view their local church as playing an active role in politics and, further, whether they support church attention to political issues.

PUBLIC OPINION TOWARD CHURCH AND STATE

The growing involvement of religious groups in American politics and public contro-versies over the Establishment and Free Exercise Clauses in the Constitution have led public opinion scholars to examine mass attitudes toward the role of religion in poli-tics and other public spheres. Some of the earliest works focused on the issue of reli-gion in public schools, in particular school prayer and Bible reading. Despite U.S. Supreme Court decisions striking down these practices, the American public, by large margins, has favored returning prayer and Bible reading to the schoolhouse.[12] The 1980 American National Election Study found that 72.1 percent of respondents believed that schools should be allowed to start each day with a prayer. More recent studies find similar results, highlighting the stability of these beliefs despite the growth in religious diversity.[13] Within these studies, support for religion in public schools was highest among older individuals, persons with lower levels of education, and self-identified conservatives. Beyond these sociodemographic and ideological characteristics, evangel-ical Protestants and varying measures of religiosity and religious orthodoxy correlated strongly with support for religious expressions in the public schools.[14]

Other scholars have gone beyond church–state controversies in the public schools to examine attitudes toward abstract principles surrounding the Establishment and Free Exercise Clauses and concrete issues such as the display of religious symbols in public spaces and the involvement of religious groups in politics.[15] Differences be-tween elites and the mass public are noted in attitudes toward abstract principles, but smaller differences are observed when it comes to concrete issues such as the public display of Christian symbols or extending religious freedoms to religious groups that are perceived to be dangerous.[16]

Beyond issues surrounding the Establishment and Free Exercise Clauses in the Constitution, much has been written on the impact of religious views on voter pref-erences.[17] Arthur H. Miller and Martin P. Wattenberg explore the emergence of a new partisan cleavage pitting evangelicals, who closely identify with the Republican Party, against religiously moderate groups, which are supportive of the Democratic Party.[18] Their study and others note that evangelically oriented Christians and evangelically oriented Catholics vote more heavily for the Republican Party and conservative can-didates than other individuals professing a different religious identity.[19] In addition, evangelicals exhibit higher rates of voter turnout and are more involved in persuad-ing others how to vote.[20] In fact, the politicization of religious beliefs is often cred-ited for the many victories of the Republican Party since the 1980s.[21]

The most consistent finding of the studies previously reviewed is that doctri-nally conservative Christians, typically labeled evangelicals, fundamentalists, or born again Christians, tend to favor less separation between church and state on a wide range of issues, including the involvement of religion in politics.[22] These results have led Michael R. Welch and David C. Leege to argue that "the effects of religion on pol-itics are best measured when one moves beyond manifest characteristics such as af-filiation and church attendance to other religious values and behavior."[23] In other words, fundamentalist beliefs are not confined to traditionally fundamentalist churches and are increasingly adopted by mainline Protestants and Catholics.[24] How prevalent are fundamentalist beliefs among Latino Catholics and what, if any, effect do their religious beliefs and practices have on their political attitudes? Despite the sizable growth in the Latino population as well as the Latino vote, little research has examined the potentially political role played by Catholicism. In the next section, we review the findings of the HCAPL survey.

LATINO POLITICORELIGIOUS BELIEFS

Respondents were asked whether they agreed or disagreed with four statements pertaining to the involvement of religious leaders in U.S. politics and the experiences at their own churches. Table 7.1 shows the percentage of Latino Catholic respondents who "agreed somewhat" and "agreed strongly" with each of the four statements.

From the data we note that a solid majority of Latino Catholics endorse the idea of religious leaders encouraging followers to be active in their communities. Sixty percent of respondents agreed that they would like to see their church more involved in social, educational, and political issues. However, when the question turns to religious leaders attempting to exert influence in public affairs instead of the more general and less political categories of "social, educational, or political" issues, support amongst Catholics is less enthusiastic, though still noteworthy at 48 percent. The support for these activities among Latinos should not be surprising as the Catholic Church has been socially engaged in Hispanic communities since the 1960s.[25] The differences between the answers in the first two questions may also illustrate a divide on involvement in social issues as defined by the traditional culture war issues versus issues pertaining to social justice and community betterment. Where the first question implies a more benign involvement with community assistance as its main objective and receives stronger support, the second question brings to mind an individual advocating for a cause or consulting political leaders. Or, with the focus on religious leaders in general, some respondents may have envisioned non-Catholic religious leaders influencing public affairs and stated that they disagreed. With respect to activities within

TABLE 7.1 Latinos and Church Activity in Political Issues	
	AGREE (%)
Would you like your church to become more involved than it is now with social, educational, or political issues?	60
Religious leaders should try to influence public affairs.	48
How often do the leaders at your local church or place of worship talk about the pressing social or political issues of the day?	39
During the past two years, have you been asked by your church or religious organization to engage in activities on behalf of specific social, educational, or political issues?	22

the Church, 39 percent stated that priests or other leaders regularly discussed political issues of the day. However, only 22 percent of Latino Catholics report that they were asked to become involved in such issues by their church. While the church can be one important place of political socialization and a source of mobilization, Sidney Verba, Kay Lehman Schlozman, and Henry E. Brady note that the Catholic Church is not quite as adept at mobilization as Protestant and evangelical churches, citing the Church's more hierarchical structure.[26]

As a follow-up to the questions reported in table 7.1, we asked respondents what sorts of political activities their churches had engaged in over the past few years. Table 7.2 reports the results of political activity among Catholic churches. The most frequent political activity was voter registration drives, reported by 22 percent of our respondents. In contrast to the higher percentages in table 7.1, we found that only 8 percent of Latino Catholics were asked to support a specific candidate in an upcoming election, and only 9 percent stated their church had organized a political rally. However, it should be noted that six years after our survey was in the field, the Catholic Church became heavily involved in the single largest Latino political rally ever, the immigration protest rallies in March, April, and May of 2006.

In general, the initial results in table 7.1 show a strong desire on the part of Latino Catholics to have a church that is socially, and to some extent politically, active. Support for political involvement is rather high considering that the Catholic Church within the Mexican American community is noted for its political passivity in electoral politics.[27] What are the sources of support for a politically active church among Latino Catholics? Given the diversity of religious practices and beliefs among Catholics, it is clear that attitudinal differences are not only going to be driven by differences in respondents' sociodemographic or ideological characteristics, but also by differences in religious beliefs and practices and the religious context.[28] In particular, Latino Catholics have often been characterized as a highly religious group.[29] In table 7.3 we detail the degree of religiosity among Latino Catholics in our sample. Almost half of the sample stated that religion provides a great deal of guidance in their daily life, with an additional 22 percent saying religion provides quite a bit of guidance. Overall, 69 percent of Latino Catholics could be described as quite religious in the

TABLE 7.2 Political Activities of Church in Last Five Years

	AGREE (%)
Voter registration	22
Rides to polling places	14
Distributing campaign materials	10
Advocating for ballot issue, proposition, or referendum	12
Asked people to support specific candidates	8
Organized/participated in political protest or rally	9
Church has done at least one of these activities	39

TABLE 7.3   Religiosity of Latino Catholics

	AGREE (%)
Religion provides a great deal of guidance in daily life	47
Religion provides quite a bit of guidance in daily life	22
Attend mass every week	48
Attend mass once or twice a month	20
Read Bible weekly (outside of Mass)	23
Never read Bible (outside of Mass)	28
Attended religious school as child	31
Are faith and morals relevant to vote choice?	70

sense that religion is more than a weekly appointment, but rather plays a significant role in their daily lives. Furthermore, almost the same percent (68 percent) attend mass regularly, including half who go to church every week. Finally, we found that 70 percent of Latino Catholics stated that "faith and morals" are important to how they vote and whom they vote for.

To provide a more definitive picture of the connection between religion and politics, we turn to multivariate analysis to consider the differential impact of selected factors on Latino Catholic attitudes. We draw on the unique HCAPL public opinion survey of Latino adults.[30]

DATA, METHODS, AND RESULTS

The HCAPL survey of Latino adults was conducted in the fall of 2000, cosponsored by the Alianza de Ministerios Evangelicos Nacionales (AMEN), the Mexican American Cultural Center (MACC), and the Tomás Rivera Policy Institute (TRPI). The survey was implemented using random digit dial in high-density Latino areas and from directory-listed households with Spanish surnames in low-density Latino areas. The survey was carried out in Los Angeles; San Antonio; Houston; Chicago; Miami; New York City; rural Colorado; rural Iowa; and San Juan, Puerto Rico (although the San Juan sample is excluded from this chapter). The design also included an oversample of 351 Protestants. In addition to the telephone survey, the overall project also included a national leadership mailout survey of 436 Latino political, civic, and religious leaders and community profiles of 268 religious and lay leaders attending 45 congregations representing 25 religious traditions in 8 urban and rural areas across the United States.[31]

Our interest is in understanding the factors underlying Latino Catholic attitudes toward religious involvement in politics (table 7.1). The first two questions reported in table 7.1 will serve as our dependent variables as we examine the social and demographic predictors of support for a politically active church (see table 7.4). Because the responses are coded dichotomously (agree-disagree), we ran logistical regression analyses for both models and report changes in predicted probability (in addition to coefficients). From the survey, we are able to construct fourteen predictors for our multivariate analyses. These predictors can be grouped into three broad categories: religious expressions and beliefs, religious context, and sociodemographic and ideological characteristics.

Under religious expressions and beliefs, the variables selected measure religious salience and evangelicalism.[32] The first variable, labeled *Religiosity,* is based on three questions measuring the frequency of prayer, reading the Bible, and attending religious services. Responses range from 0 "never" to 5 "everyday." The three questions are combined to create a religiosity scale ranging from 0 to 15. The second variable, *Guidance,* is based on a common measure asking the individual how much guidance religion provides in their daily life. The variable is categorical and ranges from none (1) to a great deal (4). As reported in table 7.3 among the respondents, 47 percent of Latino Catholics said religion provides a great deal of guidance in their day-to-day living. Increasingly, many Catholics are embracing practices long associated with evangelically oriented Protestants, as well as with the mystical side of religion known as *espiritismo.*[33] These include having a born-again experience, forming Bible study groups, proselytizing, performing faith healing, believing in *curanderismo* and *brujeria,* and speaking in tongues. Two questions capture evangelical and *espiritismo* orientations among Catholics. The first is whether they consider themselves to be born again or to have had a conversion experience related to Jesus Christ, and the second is whether they believe in practices such as *espiritismo, curanderismo,* and *brujeria.* Twenty-eight percent of Latino Catholics identified as "born-again" and 17 percent claim to believe in *espiritismo*-oriented theology. The hypothesis is that the variables falling under religious expressions and beliefs will be positively related to supporting greater religious involvement in politics. Evangelically oriented Catholics and Catholics with a deep sense of religiosity possess beliefs and practices similar to evangelical Protestants, the latter being strong supporters of religion's participation in politics.[34] *Espiritismo*-oriented Catholics may have a more mystical sense of religiosity and perhaps are less likely to embrace the convergence of religion with politics.

Kenneth D. Wald, Lyman A. Kellstedt, and Leege write that "the ties between religion and political behavior are to some degree the product of what goes on in the churches that Americans join and support so abundantly."[35] Churches can provide the means, motive, and opportunity for members to become politically informed and mobilized. The clergy frequently use the pulpit to transmit overt and symbolic political messages.[36] While most Americans do not identify the church or clergy as influential sources of political mobilization, there is evidence noting that the clergy can mobilize members around moral and family issues.[37] Given the central role of churches in the lives of most Americans, we argue that individuals who hear political messages or are encouraged to participate in politics will display more favorable attitudes toward religion's involvement in politics. Two variables are used to measure the religious context: *Political Information* and *Encouraged to Participate.* The first is based on a question asking, "How often do religious leaders at your local church or place of worship talk about the pressing social or political issues of the day?" The second variable comes from a question asking, "During the past two years, have you ever been asked by your church or religious organization, or one of its leaders to engage in activities on behalf of specific social, educational, or political issues, such as calling or writing to public officials, coming to a meeting, or signing a petition?" Both are coded dichotomously, with 1 for "yes" responses. As we reported in table 7.1, among our respondents, 39 percent said political issues were discussed at their place of worship and 22 percent were encouraged to participate. These variables are important because they will help understand whether activities by the Catholic Church can further politicize the religious experience for Latinos.

Finally, the models include sociodemographic and ideological variables as controls. While a cross section of the American public claims evangelical orientations, the salience of religion is stronger among older individuals, women, and persons with lower incomes and less formal education.[38] The effects of sociodemographic characteristics vary depending on the particular issue surrounding the Establishment and Free Exercise Clauses in the Constitution.[39] For example, when it comes to abstract principles surrounding the separation of church and state, individuals with higher levels of education and income favored greater separation than lower socioeconomic status persons. Women were less likely than men to hold separationist attitudes. Finally, self-identified political conservatives favored a greater presence of religion in politics.[40] On concrete issues, such as the display of religious symbols in public or school prayer, the effects of sociodemographics were less consistent. Nonetheless, political conservatives were consistently more likely to favor religious displays, school prayer, and public funding of religious schools.

The models control for age, income, education, marital status, gender (female), nativity, national origin (Mexican), and political ideology (Republican). While having some expectation regarding the direction of the coefficients, we are agnostic as to the effects of these controls on Latino attitudes, as all of the previous research is based on samples with non-Hispanic whites. This agnosticism is also founded on recent scholarship showing that the traditional sociodemographic predictors of political participation and attitudes do not neatly apply to Latinos and other ethnic or racial minorities.[41] However, we have some expectations regarding the effects of political ideology, given the strong connection between conservatives, the Republican Party, and religious sentiments. Thus, it is expected that self-identified Latino Republicans will be stronger supporters of religion's participation in politics than non-Republicans.

In table 7.4, two columns of results are presented for both of our models. The first reports the logistic coefficients with the standard errors in parentheses, while the second set of results reports changes in the predicted probability that the dependent variable will take on a value of one, given a fixed change in the independent variable from its minimum to its maximum value, holding all others constant at their mean.[42]

Among the religious expression variables, only religiosity has a statistically significant effect on attitudes towards the convergence of religion and politics. Latino Catholics who attend mass and pray more frequently and read the Bible are much more likely to support their church being more involved in political issues, as well as to support religious leaders having influence in public affairs. Thus, Latino Catholics who are

TABLE 7.4 Determinants of Support for Religious Involvement in Politics among Latino Catholics

	Model 1 Church More Involved		Model 2 Influence Public Affairs	
	COEFFICIENTS	MIN-MAX	COEFFICIENTS	MIN-MAX
RELIGIOUS EXPRESSIONS				
Religiosity	0.074^t (0.023)	0.211	0.048** (0.022)	0.145
Guidance	0.060 (0.063)	0.059	0.093 (0.062)	0.091
Born Again	0.168 (0.149)	0.040	0.178 (0.142)	0.045
Espiritismo	−0.211 (0.167)	−0.051	0.106 (0.163)	0.026
RELIGIOUS CONTEXT				
Political Information	0.166*** (0.064)	0.118	0.269^t (0.062)	0.199
Encouraged to Participate	0.830^t (0.179)	0.186	0.467*** (0.160)	0.116
SOCIODEMOGRAPHICS AND IDEOLOGICAL CHARACTERISTICS				
Age	−0.009** (0.004)	−0.163	−0.013*** (0.004)	−0.218
Education	−0.082* (0.047)	−0.099	−0.016 (0.046)	−0.019
Income	−0.616*** (0.256)	−0.152	−0.612** (0.257)	−0.147
Married	−0.163 (0.130)	−0.039	−0.115 (0.127)	−0.029
Female	0.057 (0.131)	0.014	−0.002 (0.128)	−0.001
U.S. Born	−0.495^t (0.140)	−0.120	−0.020 (0.136)	−0.005
Mexican Origin	0.314** (0.135)	0.076	−0.182 (0.132)	−0.045
Republican	−0.021 (0.199)	−0.005	0.080 (0.196)	−0.020
Constant	−0.130 (0.347)		−0.779** (0.341)	
PPC	63.8%		59.9%	
PRE	0.124		0.152	
Sample Size	1,171		1,171	

Significance levels: * p <= .100, ** p <= .05, *** p <= .01, ^{t} p <= .001, one-tailed.

the most religious would like to see religion injected into the political sphere. Interestingly, there was no difference in how born-again Catholics, *espiritismo* Catholics, and traditional Catholics viewed the connection between religion and politics.

The data strongly suggest that the political context (*Political Information* and *Encouraged to Participate*) exerts a significant effect across both models. Receiving political information, or being asked to get involved in politics through the Church, leaves Latinos Catholics wanting even more. The effects for political information were robust in both models, with Latinos about 12 percent more likely to support more political involvement from their church and 20 percent more likely to support religious leaders influencing public affairs if their church talked about social and political issues of the day. When the Catholic Church encourages Latinos to get involved in political issues, they likewise support additional involvement in political affairs by the church and by religious leaders. In short, belonging to a politically active church leads followers to develop a positive outlook toward religion's involvement in politics.

The effects of the sociodemographic variables also yielded interesting patterns. Older and more educated and higher-income individuals were less supportive of the church or religious leaders taking a role in political affairs. Perhaps older individuals hold a more traditional view of the Catholic Church as an apolitical institution, given the historically passive role of the Catholic Church in politics. Because education is found to have a politically liberalizing effect, it may be the case that Latinos with higher levels of education are skeptical of a politically active church, since its involvement may largely be equated with support for conservative candidates.[43] With respect to just church involvement in politics (model I), we find that U.S.-born Latinos are less likely to be supportive than foreign born, and that Latinos of Mexican origin are more likely to be supportive.

CONCLUSION

Evangelicals and Latinos are increasingly becoming influential actors in American politics. While the nexus between these two groups has yet to be fully explored by social scientists, it is increasingly evident that the future political success of the Christian Right depends on its ability to recruit emerging minority groups such as Latinos. This sentiment is noted by John C. Green, Mark Rozell, and Clyde Wilcox, who write that "Ethnic diversity presented both a challenge and a largely untapped opportunity for the movement. . . . Hispanic Catholics shared many of the religious values of the movement's core supporters but rarely backed movement organizations . . . few [Hispanic Catholics] joined the movement in backing Republican candidates."[44]

It is well-known that Latinos are deeply religious and hold many values, beliefs, and political attitudes similar to those of evangelical Christians. For example, in the survey analyzed here, 60 percent of Latino Catholics supported the teaching of evolution and creationism side by side, while an additional 20 percent think only creationism should be taught in biology class. Furthermore, the survey found that 64 percent are strongly opposed to abortion and 62 percent are opposed to homosexuality. All three of these religious-influenced issues are topical political issues today as well. It also finds a strong desire among Latinos for a politically active Catholic Church. However, within Hispanic communities the Catholic Church has historically been reluctant to promote participation in electoral politics. In the survey only a small percentage of respondents reported being politically mobilized by their church. Only 10 percent stated that their church distributed campaign materials, and 8 percent asked parishioners to support a specific candidate. These findings then paint a pessimistic picture regarding the role of the Catholic Church in mobilizing Latino voters and may present an opportunity for recruitment by evangelicals seeking to make inroads into the Hispanic community. This, of course, presumes that Latino evangelical groups are more likely to mobilize Latinos politically. Would evangelical churches spur Latino political participation and foster beliefs favoring greater ties between religion and politics?

In their classic work on political participation, Verba, Schlozman, and Brady found Latino Catholics to be less politically engaged than Latino Protestants, while the latter were as engaged as Anglo Protestants.[45] Verba, Schlozman, and Brady concluded that the Catholic Church was a politically demobilizing institution. Jongho Lee, Harry Pachon, and Matt Barreto found that being Catholic per se did not lead to lower political involvement among Latinos.[46] Instead, the Catholic Church tended to offer Latinos less opportunities to become politically engaged within the church. However, Latino Catholics who were politicized at church were as likely as any other denomination to be politically active outside the Church.

Gastón Espinosa has sought to challenge the belief that Hispanic Catholics are more politically disengaged than other groups.[47] Drawing on the same data analyzed here, Espinosa finds evidence that the Catholic Church can be a source of political mobilization. Yet he also confirms the findings by Verba, Scholzman, and Brady by noting that "Latino Protestants are more proactive than Catholics in most forms of political and social action."[48] While Latino Protestants claimed higher levels of religious-based mobilization than Latino Catholics in the HCAPL survey, the differences were for the most part negligible, suggesting that under multivariate scrutiny, those differences might wash out when controlling for other factors beyond denominational affiliation. This is precisely what Michael Jones-Correa and David L. Leal found using data from the Latino National Political Survey. When differences were observed between Latino Catholics and Protestants, it was the former who participated at higher rates.[49] In short, the differences in Latino civic engagement and politicoreligious attitudes may not be as stark across denominational affiliations as previously believed.

Taking our results as a whole, it appears that high levels of Latino politicoreligious mobilization by Catholics has yet to occur. Nonetheless, there is a relatively strong interest on the part of Latino Catholics to have politically engaged churches. We believe Latino parishioners on the whole will be responsive to any religious group seeking their recruitment and political mobilization. Whether Latino religious politicization is undertaken by the Catholic Church or Protestant churches, evangelical or mainline, remains to be seen. What is clear is that the political influence of any religious group will be significantly enhanced by the presence of large numbers of politically engaged Latinos.

NOTES

1. Laura R. Olson and John C. Green, "The Religion Gap," *PS: Political Science and Politics* 39 (July 2006): 455–58.

2. Ted Jelen, *The Political Mobilization of Religious Beliefs* (New York: Praeger, 1991); Ted Jelen, "Political Christianity: A Contextual Analysis," *American Journal of Political Science* 36 (1992): 692–714; Ted Jelen, "The Political Consequences of Religious Group Attitudes," *Journal of Politics* 55 (1993): 178–90; Ted Jelen, "Religion and Public Opinion in the 1990s: An Empirical Overview," in *Understanding Public Opinion,* ed. Barbara Norrander and Clyde Wilcox (Washington, DC: CQ Press, 1997); Arthur H. Miller and Martin P. Wattenberg, "Politics from the Pulpit: Religiosity and the 1980 Elections," *Public Opinion Quarterly* 48 (1984): 301–17; Stuart Rothenberg and Frank Newport, *The Evangelical Voter* (Washington, DC: Free Congress Research and Education Foundation, 1984); Ted Jelen and Clyde Wilcox, *Public Attitudes toward Church and State* (Armonk, NY: M. E. Sharpe, 1995).

3. Kathleen Beatty and Oliver Walter, "Fundamentalists, Evangelicals, and Politics," *American Politics Quarterly* 16 (1988): 43–59; Andrew Kohut, John C. Green, Scott Keeter, and Robert C. Toth, *The Diminishing Divide, Religion's Changing Role in American Politics* (Washington, DC: Brookings Institution Press, 2000); Olsen and Green, "Religion Gap."

4. Ted Jelen, "Religious Beliefs and Attitude Constraint," *Journal for the Scientific Study of Religion* 29 (1990): 118–25; Ted Jelen, *Political Mobilization of Religious Beliefs;* Clyde Wilcox, "The New Christian Right and the Mobilization of Evangelicals," in *Religion and Political Behavior in the United States,* ed. Ted G. Jelen (New York: Praeger, 1989); Clyde Wilcox, "Fundamentalists and Politics: An Analysis of the Effects of Differing Operational Definitions," *Journal of Politics* 48 (1986): 1041–51.

5. Geoffrey C. Layman, "Religion and Political Behavior in the United States: The Impact of Beliefs, Affiliations, and Commitment from 1980 to 1994," *Public Opinion Quarterly* 61 (1997): 288–316; Miller and Wattenberg, "Politics from the Pulpit."

6. Peter Wallsten, "Evangelicals Want Faith Rewarded," *Los Angeles Times,* November 12, 2004.

7. Andy Hernandez, "The Latino Vote in 2000, 2002, and 2004," Report of the United States Hispanic Leadership Institute, available from www.ushli.org.

8. John Garcia, *Latino Politics in America: Community, Culture, and Interests* (New York: Rowman and Littlefield, 2003).

9. Gastón Espinosa, Virgilio Elizondo, and Jesse Miranda, *Hispanic Churches in American Public Life: Summary of Findings,* Interim Reports, no. 2 (Notre Dame, IN: Institute for Latino Studies, University of Notre Dame, 2003).

10. Michael Jones-Correa and David L. Leal, "Political Participation: Does Religion Matter?" *Political Research Quarterly* 54 (2001): 751–70. Gastón Espinosa, "Latino Clergy and Churches in Faith-Based Political and Social Action in the United States," in *Latino Religions and Civic Activism in the United States,* ed. Gastón Espinosa, Virgilio Elizondo, and Jesse Miranda (New York: Oxford University Press, 2005).

11. For a detailed description see Espinosa, Elizondo, and Miranda, *Hispanic Churches in American Public Life.*

12. Kirk W. Elifson and C. Kirk Hadaway, "Prayer in Public Schools: When Church and State Collide," *Public Opinion Quarterly* 49 (1985): 317–29.

13. Mariana Servin-Gonzalez and Oscar Torres-Reyna, "Trends: Religion and Politics," *Public Opinion Quarterly* 63 (1999): 592–621; Clyde Wilcox and Rachel Goldberg, "Public Opinion on Church-State Issues in a Changing Environment," *Journal for the Scientific Study of Religion* 41 (2002): 369–76.

14. Elifson and Hadaway, "Prayer in Public Schools."

15. Joseph Tamney and Stephen Johnson, "Church-state Relations in the Eighties: Public Opinion in Middletown," *Sociological Analysis* 48 (1987): 1–16; Clyde Wilcox, Joseph Ferrara, John O'Donnell, Mary Bendyna et al., "Public Attitudes toward Church-State Issues: Elite-Mass Differences," *Journal of Church and State* 34 (1992): 259–77; Jelen and Wilcox, *Public Attitudes toward Church and State.*

16. Wilcox, Ferrara, O'Donnell, Bendyna et al., "Public Attitudes toward Church-State Issues"; Jelen and Wilcox, *Public Attitudes toward Church and State.*

17. Corwin Smidt and Paul Kellstedt, "Evangelicals in the Post-Reagan Era: An Analysis of Evangelical Voters in the 1988 Presidential Election," *Journal for the Scientific Study of Religion* 31 (1992): 330–38.

18. Miller and Wattenberg, "Politics from the Pulpit."

19. Jelen, *Political Mobilization of Religious Beliefs;* Jelen, "Political Consequences of Religious Group Attitudes"; Michael R. Welch and David C. Leege, "Dual Reference Groups and Political Orientations: An Examination of Evangelically Oriented Catholics," *American Journal of Political Science* 35 (1991): 28–56; Smidt and Kellstedt, "Evangelicals in the Post-Reagan Era"; Layman, "Religion and Political Behavior in the United States."

20. Miller and Wattenberg, "Politics from the Pulpit."

21. Kevin Eckstrom, "U.S. Evangelicals Flexed Their Muscles in 2004," *The Times Union* (Albany, New York), December 18, 2004; Olsen and Green, "Religion Gap."

22. Lyman A. Kellstedt and John C. Green, "Knowing God's Many People: Denominational Preference and Political Behavior," in *Rediscovering the Religious Factor in American Politics,* ed. David C. Leege and Lyman A. Kellstedt (Armonk, NY: M. E. Sharpe, 1993); Tamney and Johnson, "Church-state Relations in the Eighties: Public Opinion in Middletown," *Sociological Analysis* 48 (1987): 1–16; Jelen, "Political Consequences of Religious Group Attitudes"; Jelen and Wilcox, *Public Attitudes toward Church and State.*

23. Welch and Leege, "Dual Reference Groups and Political Orientations."

24. Jelen, *Political Mobilization of Religious Beliefs.*

25. Richard Edward Martinez, *PADRES: The National Chicano Priest Movement* (Austin, TX: University of Texas Press, 2005).

26. Sidney Verba, Kay Lehman Schlozman, and Henry E. Brady, *Voice and Equality: Civic Volunteerism in American Politics* (Cambridge, MA: Harvard University Press, 1995).

27. Espinosa, Elizondo, and Miranda, *Hispanic Churches in American Public Life.*

28. David C. Leege and Michael R. Welch, "Religious Roots of Political Orientations: Variations among American Catholic Parishioners," *Journal of Politics* 51 (1989): 137–62; Welch and Leege, "Dual Reference Groups and Political Orientations."

29. Espinosa, "Latino Clergy and Churches in Faith-Based Political and Social Action in the United States."

30. Espinosa, Elizondo, and Miranda, *Hispanic Churches in American Public Life.*

31. For more on these other data and results, see ibid.

32. James L. Guth and John C. Green, "Salience: The Core Concept?" in *Rediscovering the Religious Factor in American Politics.*

33. Welch and Leege, "Dual Reference Groups and Political Orientations"; Christian Smith, *Latin American Religion in Motion* (New York: Routledge, 1999).

34. Corwin E. Smidt, "Evangelicals within Contemporary American Politics: Differentiating between Fundamentalist and Non-Fundamentalist Evangelicals," *Western Political Quarterly* 41 (1988): 602–20; Guth and Green, "Salience: The Core Concept?"

35. Kenneth D. Wald, Lyman A. Kellstedt, and David Leege, "Church Involvement and Political Behavior," in *Rediscovering the Religious Factor in American Politics,* 122.

36. Kenneth D. Wald, Dennis E. Owen, and Samuel S. Hill Jr., "Churches as Political Communities," *American Political Science Review* 82 (1988): 531–48.

37. Jelen, "Political Christianity: A Contextual Analysis"; Michael Welch, David C. Leege, Kenneth D. Wald, and Lyman A. Kellstedt, "Are the Sheep Hearing the Shepherds? Cue Perceptions, Congregational Responses, and Political Communication Processes," in *Rediscovering the Religious Factor in American Politics.*

38. Miller and Wattenberg, "Politics from the Pulpit"; Guth and Green, "Salience: The Core Concept?"

39. Jelen and Wilcox, *Public Attitudes toward Church and State.*

40. Ibid.

41. S. Karthick Ramakrishnan, *Democracy in Immigrant America: Changing Demographics and Political Participation* (Stanford, CA: Stanford University Press, 2005).

42. J. Scott Long, *Regression Models for Categorical and Limited Dependent Variables* (New York: Sage Publications, 1997).

43. John L. Sullivan, James Pierson, and George E. Marcus, *Political Tolerance and American Democracy* (Chicago: University of Chicago Press, 1982).

44. John C. Green, Mark Rozell, and Clyde Wilcox, *The Christian Right in American Politics: Marching to the Millennium* (Washington, DC: Georgetown University Press, 2003), 8–9.

45. Verba, Schlozman, and Brady, *Voice and Equality.*

46. Jongho Lee, Harry Pachon, and Matt Barreto, "Guiding the Flock? Church as a Vehicle of Latino Political Participation" (paper presented at the American Political Science Association annual conference, Boston, 2002).

47. Espinosa, "Latino Clergy and Churches in Faith-Based Political and Social Action in the United States."

48. Verba, Schlozman, and Brady, *Voice and Equality,* 280.

49. Jones-Correa and Leal, "Political Participation."

PART III
Catholics and the Federal Government

8

CATHOLICISM, ABORTION, AND THE EMERGENCE OF THE "CULTURE WARS" IN THE U.S. CONGRESS, 1971–2006

WILLIAM V. D'ANTONIO, STEVEN A. TUCH, AND JOHN KENNETH WHITE

*M*UCH SCHOLARLY ATTENTION has been devoted in recent years to the polarization resulting from the so-called culture wars that have wracked American society during the latter part of the twentieth century and into the twenty-first.[1] According to proponents of the culture wars thesis, conflict over social and moral issues such as abortion, homosexuality, affirmative action, and school prayer is so divisive and intractable that compromise is rendered difficult, if not impossible, to achieve. As groups lacking the common ground necessary for consensus stake out increasingly polar positions, the argument goes, the stability of the two-party political system is threatened.

What is the source of this conflict? James Davidson Hunter has argued that the divisions reflect opposing ideological visions of the "good society."[2] For some, the good society is grounded in an orthodox, transcendent understanding of the world, based on God-ordained, fundamental beliefs, values, and norms. With regard to abortion, those who hold this vision of the good society see life as sacred from conception; human beings are not free to undo what God has wrought. The Catholic bishops, Christian Right, other Protestants, Mormon leaders, and pro-life (anti-abortion) groups have taken an absolutist stand against abortion as intrinsically evil.

For others, a progressive view of the good society sees life as unfolding, with truth to be sought and discovered through science and reason. This view does not deny the existence of God; rather, it affirms the ability of human beings to create their moral codes and value systems based on the use of reason in their lived experience. The National Abortion and Reproductive Rights Action League (NARAL) and other pro-choice groups—including mainline Protestant denominations and leaders—see abortion as a moral choice, and they generally support the right of a woman to choose in accord with the *Roe v. Wade* decision.[3] Thus, in the progressive view of the good society, the embryo has the potential to become a human being, and its value increases during gestation as it becomes a fully sentient fetus. Once born, the orthodox see people as responsible for their own behavior within a family context in their quest for salvation; the progressives see individuals as members of communities and society as being obligated to help ensure the welfare of all.

In this chapter we focus our attention on how Roman Catholic members of the U.S. Congress have responded to abortion and the emergence of the culture wars by examining their roll-call votes from 1971 through 2006. We have selected these years first because they have been studied by a wide range of social scientists, and thus there is much systematic data available for this period, and second because they include the period just before the U.S. Supreme Court's *Roe v. Wade* decision in January 1973 that established a woman's constitutional right to an abortion. Where relevant, we will also include comparisons in voting patterns between Mainline and Conservative Protestants to help clarify our findings.

BACKGROUND

Seymour Martin Lipset addressed the issue of political polarization throughout his writings. In an essay on moralism, social movements, and violence in American politics, Lipset described polarization as "the condition whereby significant sections of the population move to the left and right of normal two-party politics. This polarization process always involves two forces which react not only to specific issues but to each other. As this occurs, politics increasingly is perceived in purely moralistic terms involving a struggle between good and evil forces rather than as a series of collective bargaining issues."[4] Paul DiMaggio, John Evans, and Bethany Bryson found polarization between self-identified Republicans and Democrats on eight of the seventeen issues they examined, with abortion attitudes being the most dramatic example.[5] Reflecting on the implications of these party divisions, they stated, "In traditional pluralist theory, social conflict emerges from struggles between groups in civil society. Political parties, seeking support from the vital center, take the rough edges off of such conflicts. Our findings—that the social attitudes of groups in civil society have converged at the same time that attitudes of party identifiers have polarized—raise troubling questions about the role of political parties in a pluralistic society."[6]

Has ideological conflict within the halls of the U.S. Congress challenged the two-party system and raised new concerns about the ability of our parties to function in the face of growing polarization and culture wars?[7] To answer this question, we examine the roll-call votes of Catholic members of the House and Senate on abortion and abortion-related legislation during the period 1971–2006. We address the following questions:

> Did roll-call voting on abortion issues become more or less polarized during this time period?
>
> How did party affiliation affect roll-call votes on abortion?
>
> Did the Catholic affiliation of members of the House and Senate impact abortion votes independent of party affiliation?
>
> What evidence is there that particular religious groups—for example, Evangelical Protestants, Catholic bishops, other Catholic groups— played a role in trying to influence the executive or legislative branches of the government on the abortion issue?

The emergence of abortion as a polarizing issue among elected Catholic leaders corresponds to the rise of Catholics in American society at large. In 1960 Democrats chose the first Catholic, John F. Kennedy, to head their presidential ticket since Al Smith in 1928. Subsequently, Democrats have chosen other Catholics for top spots on their tickets—for example, Edmund Muskie in 1968, Geraldine Ferraro in 1984, and John F. Kerry in 2004. But the Ferraro and Kerry choices highlighted a movement among Catholic prelates away from seeking inclusion in the realm of politics to one whereby Catholic politicians risked being denounced by Church leaders and priests if they opposed the Church's stance on abortion. When Geraldine Ferraro attacked Ronald Reagan on religious grounds—observing that he was "un-Christian" because his policies were so unfair—she became the target of many Catholic prelates who took her to task for her pro-choice positions.[8] Similarly, many Catholic prelates took John Kerry to task for his pro-choice views in 2004. That year, Catholic prelates in Camden, New Jersey, St. Louis, Missouri, Lincoln, Nebraska, Denver, Colorado, and Colorado Springs, Colorado, issued statements forbidding Kerry from receiving Holy Communion should he attend mass in their dioceses. The Colorado Springs bishop, Michael Sheridan, went further, noting that Catholics who supported Kerry were jeopardizing their salvation by supporting a candidate who backed abortion rights.[9] And Charles Chaput, the Denver bishop, described Catholic voters for Kerry as "co-operating in evil."[10]

In a 1984 speech at Notre Dame University, then–New York governor Mario Cuomo enunciated a position that attempted to reconcile Catholic beliefs with public responsibilities. Cuomo's speech became a kind of political doctrine for elected Democratic Catholic leaders. In it, he defended his view that Catholics can and should participate in public life and in doing so should give their highest priority to their oaths of office—not to religious dogma—when it comes to faithfully executing public laws:

> The Catholic who holds political office in a pluralistic democracy—who is elected to serve Jews and Muslims, atheists and Protestants, as well as Catholics—bears special responsibility. He or she undertakes to help create conditions under which all can live with a maximum of dignity and with a reasonable degree of freedom;

where everyone who chooses may hold beliefs different from specifically Catholic ones—sometimes contradictory to them, where the laws protect people's right to divorce, to take birth control, and even to choose abortion.

In fact, Catholic public officials take an oath to preserve the Constitution that guarantees this freedom. And they do so gladly. Not because they love what others do with their freedom, but because they realize that in guaranteeing freedom for all, they guarantee our right to be Catholics: our right to pray, to use the sacraments, to refuse birth control devices, to reject abortion, not to divorce and remarry if we believe it to be wrong.[11]

This chapter examines abortion not as a conflict of opinions within the populace at large, but as a political issue involving the votes of members of Congress. DiMaggio, Evans, and Bryson point out that increases in disagreement are important because they "militate against social and political stability by reducing the probability of group formation at the center of the opinion distribution and by increasing the likelihood of the formation of groups with distinctive, irreconcilable policy preferences."[12]

ROE V. WADE: THE TIPPING POINT

The Supreme Court decision supporting a woman's right to abortion was adopted in January 1973 by a 7 to 2 vote. In the years that followed, anti-abortion groups identified as pro-life began to lobby for restrictions on abortion, including eliminating federal funding to support abortion (for example, for people in the military and government and for the poor). Party alignments on the issue were rather unclear, especially at the presidential level, until 1980.[13] That year, a strong anti-abortion plank became part of the Republican platform, while the Democrats took a pro-choice stance.[14] During the time between *Roe v. Wade* and the 1980 election, Catholic bishops, the Christian Right, Southern Baptists, and other conservative and evangelical Protestant groups, as well as leaders of the Mormon Church, took strong stands against abortion. Pro-choice and pro-life groups became major lobbying forces in the halls of Congress, and both political parties gradually hardened their positions on abortion.[15] By 1984 the parties' stances had become political dogma, with Republicans under Ronald Reagan being ardently pro-life and Democrats vehemently pro-choice. The selection of a pro-choice Catholic, Geraldine Ferraro, to join Walter Mondale on the Democratic ticket only served to heighten the partisan divisions on this issue.

During the 1990s candidates from both major parties tried to soften the differences on the abortion issue. In 1992 Bill Clinton's refrain was that abortions should be "safe, legal, and rare," with an emphasis on the latter. Bob Dole disliked the harsh language of the 1996 GOP platform on the subject, arguing instead for a line in the platform that would read, "We recognize that members of our party have deeply held and sometimes differing views on issues of personal conscience."[16] Dole believed that his party could hardly reject the insertion of a plank Ronald Reagan himself had once approved as governor of California. He was wrong. Ralph Reed, the executive director of the Christian Coalition, threatened to withdraw his support for the Republican ticket unless its presidential and vice-presidential candidates opposed abortion. Right-to-lifers maintained that abortion could not be "tolerated."[17] GOP platform chairman and ardent pro-life activist Henry Hyde threatened to quit. Dole acknowledged defeat, and his faith that virtuous citizens would make sound decisions on abortion was rejected by Republican delegates, who handed him a stinging rebuke on the eve of his party's nomination. Fed up, Dole claimed he did not have time to read the platform and that, in any event, he did not feel honor bound by it.[18]

In 2008 presidential candidates from both parties were attempting to defuse the abortion issue. Hillary Clinton echoed her husband's "safe, legal, and rare" mantra, adding that she considers every abortion to be a "tragedy." Barack Obama told voters not to automatically peg him as a firm pro-choice vote. John McCain, meanwhile, presented himself as pro-life, even though he antagonized social conservative groups on a variety of issues. Despite these attempts by Democratic and Republican leaders to find common ground on the abortion issue, the data presented in this chapter show abortion to be a continuing source of polarization between the parties that transcends the religious preference of the congressional member.

DATA, METHODS, AND ANALYSIS

Data

Our primary source of data on abortion-related voting in Congress is the National Abortion and Reproduction Rights Action League (NARAL). NARAL provides information regarding roll-call votes on abortion separately for the House and Senate. Since NARAL's lists do not identify members of Congress by political party or religion, we used various editions of Michael Barone's *Almanac of American Politics* for information on party affiliation and, where available, religion. Information about the religious affiliation of members of Congress was also gleaned from a number of Internet sites.

Analysis

The primary focus of this chapter is the role played by Catholics elected to the U.S. House and Senate during the period encompassed by the historic Supreme Court decision in *Roe v. Wade*. It begins with a brief overview of the changing numbers of Catholics in the House and Senate by party affiliation, starting with the 92nd Congress (1971–72), just before *Roe v. Wade*, and ending with the 110th Congress (2007–08), which reflects the 2006 national elections. Figure 8.1 shows that, in the House

1. Throughout this thirty-seven-year period, Catholic Democrats have outnumbered Republicans, but with a gradual and somewhat uneven closing of the gap over time.
2. The gap between Democratic and Republican Catholics was four to one in 1971–72, but only two to one after the 2006 election.

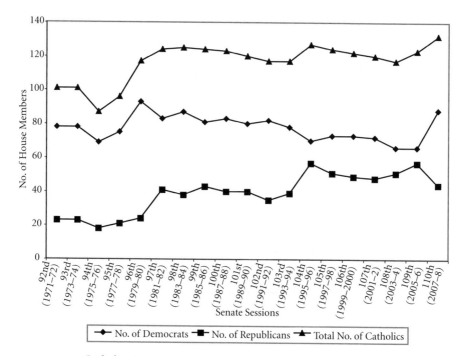

FIGURE 8.1   *Catholics in U.S. House, 92nd to 110th Session*

3. The range for Democrats has been between a high of 93 and a low of 66; for the Republicans it has been between 18 and 57.
4. The gap was widest just prior to the 1980 presidential election, narrowed during the Reagan years, then closed most dramatically with the Gingrich-led victory of 1994 and again with George W. Bush's victory in 2004. Following the 2006 elections, the gap widened noticeably.
5. The closing of the gap has been accompanied by an increasing presence of Catholics as a percent of the total. In 1971 they comprised about 20 percent of the House membership; today, they are 30 percent—somewhat larger than their numbers in the general society.
6. Within parties, Catholics have grown from 29 percent of all House Democrats to 38 percent. On the Republican side, they have grown from 13 percent to about 25 percent.

Figure 8.2 shows that, in the Senate

1. Never have the Democrats had fewer Catholics than the Republicans, though twice during the Reagan years their numbers were tied, and they were again in the last years of the Clinton administration.
2. The gap between the parties was five to one in 1971, completely closed three times, and for the 110th Congress is five to three.

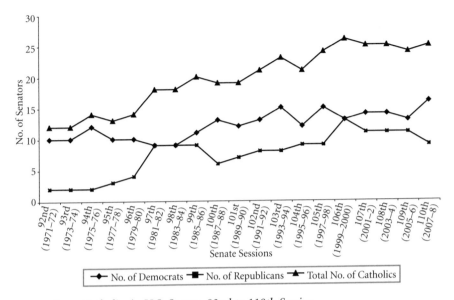

FIGURE 8.2   *Catholics in U.S. Senate, 92nd to 110th Session*

3. There have never been fewer that nine Catholic Democratic senators during this thirty-seven-year period, with a high of sixteen in 2007. Republicans have increased their numbers from two to a high of eleven, and nine
as of 2007.

4. Catholics have increased their numbers in the Senate during these years.
In 1971 they comprised only 12 percent of all senators; as of 2007 they
were 25 percent of the Senate. Within parties, Catholics are currently 31
percent of Democrats, while they were less than 20 percent in 1971. The
Catholic presence within the Republican Party is more impressive, growing from less than 5 percent in 1971 to 20 percent in 2007.

We begin our analysis of abortion roll-call votes with the Congress of 1977–78.
Included in the period examined is the so-called Gingrich Congress (the 104th),
which followed the 1994 elections. The analysis concludes with the 2003–4 Congress
(the 108th). Our examination of roll-call votes reveals a pattern that emerged after
1980, with little or no change—except in whether Democrats or Republicans controlled the House or Senate. The larger picture is that party affiliation eventually
trumped religion, except for a significant minority of Catholic House Democrats, who
consistently cast anti-abortion votes.

Table 8.1 reports the number of votes on abortion legislation in the House and
Senate during each of the Congresses under study. It shows that the sweeping Republican victory in 1994 brought with it the largest number of abortion-related roll-call
votes in a single Congress (the 104th): thirty in the House and twenty-three in the
Senate.[19] On average, there were fifteen abortion-related votes in the House and twelve
in the Senate per Congress over this time frame.[20]

TABLE 8.1 Number of Votes Cast in the House and Senate on Abortion-Related Issues

						Session						
	95TH 1977–78	96TH 1979–80	98TH 1983–84	100TH 1987–88	101ST 1989–90	102ND 1991–92	103RD 1993–94	104TH 1995–96	105TH 1997–98	106TH 1999–2000	107TH 2001–02	108TH 2003–04
No. of Votes												
House	18	9	6	7	13	13	14	30	35	22	11	6
Senate	12	11	9	16	13	12	10	23	12	9	2	16

TABLE 8.2 U.S. House Votes on Abortion, 1977–2004[a]

	95TH 1977–78	96TH 1979–80	98TH 1983–84	100TH 1987–88	101ST 1989–90	102ND 1991–92	103RD 1993–94	104TH 1995–96	105TH 1997–98	106TH 1999–2000	107TH 2001–02	108TH 2003–04
Pro-choice	39	44	45	48	42	54	48	44	45	45	44	44
Pro-life	61	56	55	52	58	46	52	56	55	55	56	56

[a] Percentages supporting either the pro-choice or the pro-life position.

TABLE 8.3 U.S. Senate Votes on Abortion, 1977–2004[a]

	95TH 1977–78	96TH 1979–80	98TH 1983–84	100TH 1987–88	101ST 1989–90	102ND 1991–92	103RD 1993–94	104TH 1995–96	105TH 1997–98	106TH 1999–2000	107TH 2001–02	108TH 2003–04
Pro-choice	61	55	49	57	49	57	56	49	50	53	48	47
Pro-life	39	45	51	43	51	43	44	51	50	47	52	53

[a] Percentages supporting either the pro-choice or the pro-life position.

ABORTION VOTES WITHOUT REGARD TO PARTY OR RELIGION

Tables 8.2 and 8.3 display pro-choice and pro-life votes in the House and Senate, respectively, on all abortion-related legislation from the 95th through the 108th Congresses, without controlling for political party or religious affiliation. In the House (table 8.2), pro-choice votes varied within a range of fifteen percentage points over the course of the twelve sessions, from a high of 54 percent in the 102nd to a low of 39 percent in the 95th; in the Senate (table 8.3), the proportion of pro-choice votes fluctuated within a range of fourteen percentage points, from a high of 61 percent in the 95th to a low of 47 percent in the 108th. During this time the House was more pro-life than pro-choice and the Senate was slightly more pro-choice than pro-life. However, examining roll-call votes without taking party and religion into account tells an incomplete story. The struggle within both parties to find a position on abortion that would mollify Catholic and conservative Protestant leaders was a focus of the presidential candidates in the 1976 and 1980 elections, but it was not without consequences for members of Congress, as further analysis will attest.

THE ROLES OF PARTY AND RELIGION

What happens to the pattern of abortion voting when we take into account the political party affiliations of House and Senate members? Figures 8.3 and 8.4 display these patterns for the House and Senate, respectively. In the House (figure 8.3), Democrats (without regard to religion) became increasingly pro-choice, from a low of 57 percent pro-choice votes in the 95th Congress (1977–78) to a high of 80 percent in the 104th, leveling off above 70 percent in the 106th and 108th Congresses. House Republicans since the 95th Congress have been overwhelmingly pro-life, at no time exceeding 22 percent in pro-choice voting. Since the Gingrich revolution, that figure has hovered around 10 percent or lower. Thus, in the House, Democrats

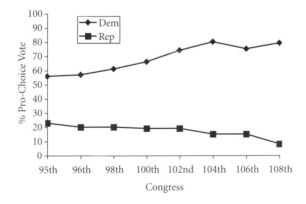

FIGURE 8.3   *U.S. House votes on Abortion, 1979–2004, by Party Affiliation*

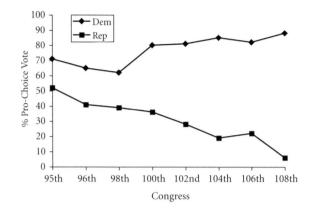

FIGURE 8.4   *U.S. Senate Votes on Abortion, 1979–2004, by Party Affiliation*

became more pro-choice over time while Republicans remained overwhelmingly pro-life.

Figure 8.4 reveals that, in the Senate, both parties experienced change: Democrats became overwhelmingly pro-choice, from 71 percent in the 95th Congress to 88 percent in the 108th. Republicans, meanwhile, moved from being slightly pro-choice in the 95th Congress (52 percent) to overwhelmingly pro-life. Thus, in the Senate as in the House, polarization shifted away from a struggle within each of the two parties to a clear-cut cleavage between the parties.

What role does religion play in the roll-call voting of House and Senate members? To understand the influence of religion when controlling for party affiliation, figures 8.5 and 8.6 compare Catholic votes with Mainline and Conservative Protestant votes in both the House and Senate. The religious affiliation of members of Congress provides no information on the degree to which that identification was a salient factor in their thinking or basic value orientations—in other words, we measure religious affiliation only, not religiosity. However, in an earlier study, Peter L. Benson and Dorothy L. Williams found religion in the U.S. Congress to be very much alive and influential in voting behavior. According to their study, a majority of members acknowledged that their votes were influenced by their religious beliefs and values.[21] So, for at least the 95th and 96th Congresses they studied, religion was salient to a majority of the members. Most members were reelected to the 98th Congress, and some still remained into the 108th.

Figures 8.5 and 8.6 present the trends in abortion votes by religion and party. The religious typology used here is taken from Wade Clark Roof and William Mc-Kinney, who divided Protestant denominations into three major groupings: (1) Liberal Protestants-Episcopalians, Presbyterians, and Congregationalists (United Church of Christ); (2) Moderate Protestants–Methodists, Lutherans, Northern Baptists, Christians (Disciples of Christ), and Reformed; and (3) Conservative Protestants–Southern Baptists, Church of Christ, Evangelicals/Fundamentalists, Nazarenes, Pentecostals/

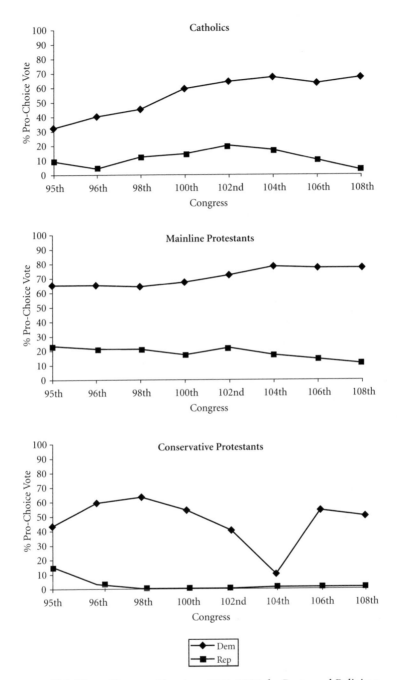

FIGURE 8.5 *U.S. House Votes on Abortion, 1979–2004, by Party and Religious Affiliation*

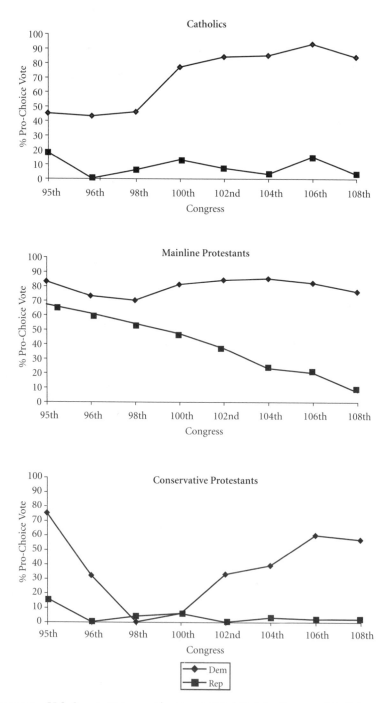

FIGURE 8.6   *U.S. Senate Votes on Abortion, 1979–2004, by Party and Religious Affiliation*

Holiness, Assemblies of God, Church of God, and Adventists.[22] Mormons, who consider themselves to be Christian but not Protestant, are included in the Conservative Protestant category. Given the similarity in their voting patterns, we have combined the Liberal and Moderate Protestant denominations into one category called Mainline Protestants, following Roof and McKinney and Guth and colleagues.

In the House (figure 8.5), both Catholic and Mainline Protestant Democrats became increasingly pro-choice from the 95th to the 108th Congresses, from 32 percent to 67 percent among Catholics, and from 65 percent to 78 percent among Mainline Protestants. A majority of Conservative Protestant (CP) Democrats voted pro-choice through the 100th session, but by the 104th, those remaining in the Democratic Party were overwhelmingly pro-life. Still, the trend reveals a mix of pro-choice and pro-life votes.

Among House Republicans, Catholics remained overwhelmingly pro-life: their pro-choice votes decreased from 9 percent in the 95th Congress to a low of 3 percent in the 108th. Four out of five Mainline Protestant Republicans voted pro-life throughout, with the most recent pro-life votes near 80 percent; Conservative Protestants were the most consistently pro-life throughout the period, being close to 100 percent pro-life in most sessions.

Across-party polarization by religion increased for Catholics and Mainline Protestants. Regardless of party, Conservative Protestants were strongly pro-life by the 104th session. Figure 8.5 makes it clear that the increasing polarization in the House was not the result of changes across all major religious groups. Catholic and Protestant Republicans were overwhelmingly pro-life throughout the time period. The largest change occurred among Catholic Democrats, as pro-choice voting grew from 32 percent to 67 percent. Polarization also decreased among Mainline Protestant Democrats as their pro-choice votes increased by 12 percentage points. Conservative Protestants became much less polarized as they moved toward a consensus pro-life position in the 108th session. However, a new gap appears to be emerging.

Figure 8.6 shows that the pattern in the Senate was similar to that of the House. Catholic Democrats became increasingly pro-choice, while Republicans remained overwhelmingly pro-life, leading to near-total polarization across parties. Mainline Protestant Democrats maintained their pro-choice strength, thus reducing intraparty tendencies toward polarization. Mainline Protestant Republicans changed; from being moderately polarized with a pro-choice majority, they became dramatically pro-life and much less internally divided. Conservative Protestant Democrats changed dramatically from pro-choice before 1980 to almost 100 percent pro-life in the mid- to late 1980s, then to a current position that is moderately pro-choice. Conservative Protestant Republicans have remained overwhelmingly pro-life.

ABORTION AS A UNIQUE VOTING ISSUE

Is abortion an exemplar of a long-standing trend toward ideological polarization that has characterized Congress at least since the late 1970s, or is it a uniquely polarizing issue? DiMaggio, Evans, and Bryson warned that "to generalize from the abortion controversy to other issues, or to view it as evidence of more deep-seated polarization, is profoundly misleading."[23] To address this possibility, we examined a number of key social justice votes—that is, votes on bills that U.S. Catholic bishops supported or opposed. These votes illustrate a legislator's stance on important votes where he or she must vote for or against a national issue. If DiMaggio, Evans, and Bryson are correct that abortion is a uniquely polarizing issue, the polarization that we documented above should substantially decline when votes on other, nonabortion-related issues are examined.

Our analysis of key votes for the 98th through the 108th Congresses indicates that across-party polarization increased from 1983–84 to 2003–04 in both the Senate and the House. The U.S. Catholic Bishops Council, through its Office of Government Liaison, lobbies extensively not only on abortion-related issues, but also on a broad range of social justice issues—including raising the minimum wage, opposing more funding for nuclear weapons research, and lifting the embargo against Cuba for humanitarian reasons. They are joined in these efforts by other religious lobbying groups and interest groups that range from the extreme right to the extreme left. Many key votes reflect social justice concerns; cited here are a few that reflect the whole range.

Despite some fluctuations, the trend for within-party polarization is one of decline among congressional Democrats and Republicans. Thus, on social justice votes—as in the case of abortion—across-party polarization increased and within-party polarization decreased. An analysis of these votes supports our hypothesis that the culture wars are about more issues than abortion. The vision of the good society propounded by those who see the world through orthodox religious eyes is not only antiabortion, but also antitax and antigovernment-supported social welfare. It extends across major areas of life and is increasingly coherent. The progressive view of the good society is less coherent and consistent.[24]

To further understand the degree to which tendencies toward polarization have increased and to which, at the same time, party has come to dominate religion, we rearranged these votes into nine categories (see table 8.4).

The consensus-building expected on the basis of pluralist theory is not evident in these votes. In areas like taxes, welfare, and the military, a majority of votes revealed high levels of cleavage or polarization between Democrats and Republicans in both the House and Senate. Voting totals in the 80 percent to 95 percent ranges make it clear that Catholic Democrats and Republicans were hardly ever distinguishable from their party colleagues. Republicans were consistently closer to the bishops' positions on abortion and related issues, while Democrats were consistently closer on taxes, welfare, military spending, social services, and the environment.

We take for granted that the bishops support raising the minimum wage; providing decent housing for the poor and aged; and opposing abortion, stem cell research, and the like. It is not well-known that the bishops have long supported lifting the Cuban embargo for humanitarian reasons. In the 107th House vote on this issue, sixty-two of the seventy-four Catholic Democrats (84 percent) voted to lift the ban, while only three of the forty-nine Catholic Republicans (6 percent) did so.

DISCUSSION

Our findings indicate the following:

1. A consistently high level of polarization in the roll-call votes on abortion in both the House and Senate from 1977 through 2006. In the earlier period the polarization was brought about by a mix of across- and within-party voting. That is, a significant minority of Republicans in the Senate voted pro-choice, just as a significant number of Democrats voted pro-life.
2. When we controlled for political party, we found that a majority of congressional Democrats supported the pro-choice position. At the same time, a majority of congressional Republicans voted pro-life. Over time, voting patterns within the parties converged, while they diverged more and more across parties. Thus, even as polarization within the House and Senate remained high, it became more closely identified with political party identification. Republicans became predominantly pro-life; Democrats became predominantly pro-choice.
3. The significant changes in voting behavior were found among Catholics and white Protestants. Congressional Catholic Democrats became strongly-to-overwhelmingly pro-choice, while Catholic Republicans became as strongly pro-life.[25] Jennifer Strickler and Nicholas L. Danigelis found Catholics becoming slightly more pro-choice over time. Evans found similar patterns of divergence and convergence within and between these major religious groups.[26]
4. The high level of polarization during the period 1977–2006 is consistent with what DiMaggio, Evans, and Bryson reported for the opinions of the party identifiers during this same time period. Evans was even more emphatic, as was Mark J. Hetherington, along with Geoffrey C. Layman and Thomas M. Carsey.[27]

Over time, the Republican Party has assumed the mantle of pro-life, thanks to a variety of influential advocates that have gained power within the GOP.[28] At the same time, Democrats have moved from being fairly polarized within their own ranks on the abortion issue to being a pro-choice party. This is seen in the dramatic decrease in the level of polarization within the party; instead, today's Democrats have a high level of consensus on abortion issues—especially when it comes to reducing abortions via legislation that provides more health care and other options for single and poor women and couples. That consensus is further evident in the changing voting patterns of Catholic members of Congress. Catholic Democrats are strongly pro-choice; Catholic Republicans are even more strongly pro-life.[29] The phrases appear to have different meanings within the two parties. Thus, over time, while polarization in the Congress has remained high, it has become much more a function of party alignment than of individual decision making. According to the findings by Strickler and Danigelis, the conservative movements of the 1980s and 1990s (family values, sanctity of life) were very effective in countering the liberal movements of the 1970s (feminism

TABLE 8.4 Barone's Key Issues 1983–2004, Percentages Supporting and Opposing Legislation in Nine Areas, by House and Senate, and by Political Party

		House		Senate	
		DEM	REP	DEM	REP
1. Taxes	Cap Tax Cuts	89–11	0–100	91–9	6–94
	Stop Tuition Credit	—	—	80–20	45–55
	Impose Tarifs on Imports	78–22	10–90	—	—
	Deficit Reduction	83–17	1–99	—	—
	Capital Gains Debate	—	—	0–100	91–9
	Override China Veto	—	—	91–9	19–81
	Tax Rich, Cut Middle				
	Class Taxes	80–20	1–99		
2. Welfare	Extend Social Security	51–49	1–99	68–32	0–100
	Minimum Wage Increase	—	—	94–6	20–80
	Increase Minimum Wage	97–3	33–67	100–0	53–47
	Housing for Aged	—	—	66–34	18–82
	Restrict $ for Homeless	19–81	94–6	—	—
	$ for GHW Bush Homes	16–84	97–3	9–91	80–20
	Remove Budget Walls	—	—	85–15	7–93
	Reduce Medicare Growth	2–98	98–2	0–100	99–1
	Welfare Reform	15–85	98–2	50–50	98–2
3. Immigration	Extend Amnesty	30–70	70–30	44–56	6–94
	Immigration Reform	47–53	56–44	85–15	77–23
4. Abortion	Limit (Need 2/3 vote)	40–60	79–21	33–67	64–36
	Deny Abortions	36–64	81–19	38–62	84–16
	Ban DC Abortions	39–61	80–20	—	—
	Abortion Gag Rule	—	—	14–86	63–37
	Provide Overseas Military				
	Abortions	70–30	22–78	—	—
	Override Partial Birth				
	Abortion Veto	35–65	93–7	34–66	88–12
5. Military	Missiles	73–27	11–89	12–88	81–19
	No Aid to Contras	78–22	11–89	77–23	15–85
	Aid Contras	19–81	93–7	23–77	85–15
	El Salvador Aid	22–78	95–5	24–76	91–9
	Block Nuclear Freeze	—	—	21–79	85–15
	Bar Nuclear Testing	84–16	11–89	—	—
	Support Nuclear freeze	84–16	36–64	—	—
	Strategic Defense	20–80	90–10	24–76	80–20
	Chemical Weapons	—	—	37–63	74–26
	Ban Chemical Weapons	63–37	17–83	—	—
	More $ for Defense	—	—	0–100	80–20
	Use Force in Gulf, 1991	33–67	97–3	18–82	95–5

TABLE 8.4 *(continued)*

		House		Senate	
		DEM	REP	DEM	REP
5. Military (continued)	Table Amend to Ban				
	Keep Salvador Aid	—	—	9–91	88–12
	Cut 1B$ from SDI	68–32	17–83	75–25	12–88
	FY 1993: 15B$Defense Cut	85–15	3–97	—	—
	Cut U.S. Military Aid Abroad	73–27	25–75	—	—
	Cuba Trade Embargo	56–44	85–15	51–49	96–4
	Table Anti-Missile Defense	—	—	9–91	89–11
	Ban Bosnia Troop Funds	10–90	82–18	2–98	40–60
	Cut Vietnam Aid	—	—	22–78	62–38
	Cuban Embargo	35–65	98–2	—	—
	Cut Anti-Missile Defense	94–6	1–99	—	—
	Bar UN Uniforms	35–65	95–5	—	—
6. Judicial	Robert Bork Nomination	—	—	4–96	87–13
	Death Penalty for Drug Felony	57–43	95–5	—	—
	Clarence Thomas Nomination	—	—	19–81	95–5
	Limit Death Row Appeals	—	—	29–71	100–0
	Death Penalty by Jury	24–76	93–7	—	—
7. Social Values Issues	School Prayer OK	48–52	90–10	42–58	67–33
	MLK Jr Holiday	—	—	90–10	67–33
	ERA Approve	85–15	33–67	—	—
	Ban Plastic Guns	—	—	26–74	81–19
	Japanese Reparations	—	—	86–14	55–45
	Delete Provision to Ban Drug Tests	11–89	74–26	—	—
	Handgun Sales	42–58	78–22	—	—
	Handgun Waiting Period	68–32	37–63	84–16	44–56
	Ban $ for Obscene Art to NEA	54–46	91–9	—	—
	Flag Desecration Amendment	46–54	95–5	30–70	92–8
	Gay Employment Rights	—	—	89–11	15–85
	Repeal Assault Weapons Ban	30–70	81–19	—	—
8. Social Services	Auto Protection	74–26	20–80	—	—
	Override Highway Veto	—	—	100–0	28–72
	Kill Plant Closing Notice	11–89	83–17	7–93	78–22
	Ban Striker Replacements	87–13	12–88	91–9	12–88
	Limit Product Liability Damages	17–83	98–2	26–74	89–11
9. Environment	Endangered Species Moratorium	—	—	89–11	13–87
	Drop Proposed EPA Limits	85–15	28–72	—	—

and equal rights) and thus served to stabilize abortion attitudes, rather than seeing them evolve more into a pro-choice direction.[30] Thus, they concluded that in framing public attitudes toward abortion since the 1980s, the pro-life movement led by evangelicals and Catholic Church leaders has been more successful than the pro-choice movement in setting the terms of the public debate.

According to DiMaggio, Evans, and Bryson, "Whereas, in the 1970s, Republicans were less opposed to abortion than Democrats, the groups moved in opposite directions, crossing in the mid-1980s and diverging thereafter. At the same time, Republicans divided more sharply over abortion."[31]

Our findings present a different picture; while it is true that Democrats and Republicans in Congress have been moving in opposite directions on the abortion issue, it is also true that a majority of Democrats (but not Catholics) have been pro-choice since 1979. Moreover, the DiMaggio, Evans, and Bryson finding that Republicans in the general population were more pro-choice than the Democrats before 1980 is not consistent with our findings of actual votes in the Congress. Pro-choice support among Republicans in the House never exceeded 20 percent, and it decreased steadily toward the current level of just above 10 percent. In the Senate, pro-choice Republicans declined from above 60 percent to less than 10 percent during this time. This provides further evidence of a gap between the public and its representatives in Congress.

Evans used General Social Survey (GSS) and American National Election Study (NES) data through the year 2000 and stated that the evidence was even more inescapable that increasing polarization within the public may be a result of polarization in our political system.[32] This finding was supported by Gregg D. Adams, who found that the abortion issue transformed the two parties over a twenty-five-year period following *Roe v. Wade*.[33] Furthermore, he found strong evidence that this gradual shift in Congress caused a similar shift among the voting public. Hetherington makes the further point that "greater partisan polarization in Congress has clarified the parties' ideological positions for ordinary Americans, which in turn has increased party importance and salience on the mass level."[34] Using NES data for the same period as did DiMaggio, Evans, and Bryson, Layman and Carsey, and Evans suggest that the evolving polarization in Congress primarily impacted strong party identifiers rather than the voting masses as a whole.[35]

This study's findings on the changing religious composition of the House and Senate, along with their changing pro-choice and pro-life votes, raise questions about the relationship between the public and the members of Congress regarding the direction of the influence flow. For example, Mainline Protestant (MP) churches have formal positions acknowledging the right to abortion under certain conditions. Thus, it is not surprising that MP Democrats have been pro-choice over the entire time period, as have a minority of Republican MPs. On the other side, the Catholic bishops have consistently condemned abortion under any and all conditions, but their impact on Catholics in the House and Senate has been mixed. There has been a growing gap between the bishops and the Catholic public. Over time, congressional Catholic Democrats have become more pro-choice, also mirroring the Catholic public. Catholic Republicans have been strongly pro-life, mirroring the bishops' positions. But when it comes to issues like taxes, minimum wages, health care, removing sanctions against Cuba, nuclear weapons, and the like, Catholic Democrats provide strong support for positions taken by the bishops, whereas Catholic Republicans do not.[36]

The conflict and division caused by the controversy over abortion and related issues differ in one important way from earlier moralistic movements: they have led to a tightening of party ties rather than a loosening of them. Part of the explanation for this is suggested by Richard Fleisher, who developed and tested a set of constituency variables to understand and explain the impact of the Voting Rights Act of 1965 on the South.[37] In brief, Fleisher found that

1. Southern Democrats now take into account the size of their black constituency as they consider running for office. In districts with sizeable black populations, Democratic candidates move toward the center or become more liberal, or both.
2. Conservative Democrats either move to the middle or, if deeply committed to conservative ideology, become Republicans. One consequence has been the rise of the Republican Party in the South.
3. The other consequence has been the rise of a more liberal Democratic Party in the South.
4. There has also been a steady increase in the number of blacks in public office, especially in the U.S. House.
5. House rules have been changed to create more intraparty discipline in the years after 1980; members have become more party conscious. Southerners who want to have input into party politics now must adhere more closely to party discipline. But the party is also more sensitive to the needs and concerns of its members, as in, for example, the case of former senator John Breaux, a Catholic conservative Democrat from Louisiana until 2005. His generally pro-life stance did not cost him positions in his party leadership.
6. The South has a more competitive two-party system, one which is more ideologically divided than before.[38]

A further tightening of party ties occurred with the Gingrich revolution of 1994. It increased tensions between parties, making friendships across party lines suspect and leading a number of moderates to retire from Congress.

CONCLUSION

At the height of the Vietnam War in 1968, Representative John Brademas explained that Congress's job was to seek consensus through rational debate and compromise.[39] Today, consensus building has been marginalized. As this chapter's findings show, issues are defined and decided on party lines, with each side claiming the moral high ground. Can the center hold? Part of the answer may lie in the reality that there are two publics being polled nationally: one has little or no commitment to the political system; the other has a discernible degree of commitment, manifested in poll data by its self-identification with a political party. Evans, Hetherington, Layman and Carsey, and Adams all provide further support for this position.[40]

DiMaggio, Evans, and Bryson's expressed concern about political mobilization becoming a problem when groups "(a) hold very different opinions and (b) are internally unified" may more aptly be directed to events taking place in Congress than in public opinion polling.[41] The latter seems to provide much more support for the culture wars hypothesis than do GSS findings. However, more recent studies by Evans, Adams, Hetherington, and Layman and Carsey support our findings that abortion is and has been the source of a high level of polarization within Congress at least since 1980. Evans raises the question whether the polarization between religious groups in the United States may presage the kind of culture war that has plagued Ireland for so many years.[42] This concern may be unwarranted, as polarization is occurring primarily within religious groups (especially Catholics and Mainline Protestants), while smaller groups like evangelicals, Jews, and black Protestants have a high level of internal cohesion on the abortion issue.

Hunter may be correct that there are two opposing world views of the good society, and that abortion and other issues make those two positions clear. In Tom Robbins's 1976 novel, *Even Cowgirls Get the Blues*, one of the characters rhetorically asks, "You really don't believe in political solutions, do you?" The startling response is, "I believe in political solutions to political problems. But man's primary problems aren't political; they're philosophical. Until humans can solve their philosophical problems, they're condemned to solve their political problems over and over again. It's a cruel, repetitious bore."[43]

Robbins effectively summarizes the problems both parties currently face on the abortion issue. Even though the Democrats took control of Congress in 2006, the party positions show little movement and the polarization continues. Unless and until the parties solve their philosophical problems on this issue—that is, develop a position that is not either-or but some form of *both* that captures what Arthur Schlesinger Jr. once called the Vital Center—the political polarization so apparent in today's culture wars will continue to be a dominant feature of American life. Until that happens, Catholic members of Congress will reflect the views of their constituents. Breaking this cycle will require real leadership, which is not yet in sight.

NOTES

The authors are indebted to Karla Yoder and Todd Schribner for assistance with data compilation and to Rosemary Chien for preparing the figures. The authors also express their appreciation to members of the Life Cycle Institute and the Dean of Arts and Sciences office, both at Catholic University of America, and the American Sociological Association Fund for the Advancement of the Discipline. Each of these entities provided much-needed support.

1. Greg D. Adams, "Evidence of an Issue Evolution," *American Journal of Political Science* 41, no. 3 (1997): 718–37; Paul DiMaggio, John Evans, and Bethany Bryson, "Have Americans' Social Attitudes Become More Polarized?" *American Journal of Sociology* 102 (1996): 690–755; John H. Evans, Bethany Bryson, and Paul DiMaggio, "Opinion Polarization: Important Contributions, Necessary Limitations," *American Journal of Sociology* 106, no. 4

(2001): 944–59; John H. Evans, "Polarization in Abortion Attitudes in U.S. Religious Traditions, 1972–1998," *Sociological Forum* 17 (2002): 397–422; John H. Evans, "Have Americans' Attitudes Become More Polarized?—an Update," Working Paper 24, Working Papers Series of the Center for Arts and Cultural Policy Studies at Princeton University, spring 2002; Todd Gitlin, *The Twilight of Common Dreams: Why America Is Wracked by Culture Wars* (New York: Henry Holt, Metropolitan Books, 1995); John A. Hall and Charles Lindholm, *Is America Breaking Apart?* (Princeton, NJ: Princeton University Press, 1999); Marc J. Hetherington, "Resurgent Mass Partisanship: The Role of Elite Polarization," *American Political Science Review* 95, no. 3 (2001): 619–31; James Davison Hunter, *Culture Wars: The Struggle to Define America* (New York: Basic Books, 1991); James Davison Hunter, *Before the Shooting Begins: Searching for Democracy in America's Culture Wars* (New York: The Free Press, 1994); Geoffrey C. Layman and Thomas M. Carsey, "Party Polarization and 'Conflict Extension' in the American Electorate," *American Journal of Political Science* 46, no. 4 (2002): 786–802; Kristin Luker, *Abortion and the Politics of Motherhood* (Berkeley: University of California Press, 1984); Thomas E. Mann and Norman J. Ornstein, *The Broken Branch: How Congress Is Failing America, and How to Get It Back on Track* (New York: Oxford University Press, 2006); Ted Mouw and Michael E. Sobel, "Culture Wars and Opinion Polarization: The Case of Abortion," *American Journal of Sociology* 106, no. 4 (2001): 913–43; Pietro S. Nivola and David W. Brady, *Red and Blue Nation: Characteristics and Causes of America's Polarized Politics* (Washington, DC: The Brookings Institution, 2006); Neil J. Smelser and Jeffrey C. Alexander, eds., *Diversity and Its Discontents: Cultural Conflict and Common Ground in Contemporary American Society* (Princeton, NJ: Princeton University Press, 1999); John Kenneth White, *The Values Divide: American Politics and Culture in Transition* (Washington, DC: Congressional Quarterly Press, 2003); Rhys Williams, ed., *Cultural Wars in American Politics* (New York: Aldine de Gruyter, 1997); Robert Wuthnow, *The Restructuring of American Religion: Society and Faith since World War II* (Princeton, NJ: Princeton University Press, 1988).

2. Hunter, *Culture Wars;* Hunter, *Before the Shooting Begins.*

3. *Roe v. Wade* permits abortions without restrictions during the first trimester of pregnancy and with increasing restrictions during the second and third trimesters. States have the right to impose restrictions in the second and third trimesters. In recent years, the states have become more and more active in adopting legislation regarding abortion, e.g., laws requiring parental consent for underage women, restricting late-term abortions, and banning abortion except to save the life of the mother.

4. Seymour Martin Lipset, *Consensus and Conflict: Essays in Political Sociology* (New Brunswick, NJ: Transaction, 1985), 316.

5. DiMaggio, Evans, and Bryson, "Have Americans' Social Attitudes Become More Polarized?" 735–36.

6. Ibid., 738. Even at the height of the Vietnam conflict, U.S. representative John Brademas (D-IN) described the role of members of Congress as explaining, justifying, interpreting, and interceding with the public and with each other slowly to build consensus making it possible to pass controversial legislation. (Brademas, "The Emerging Role of the American Congress," *Proceedings of the Indiana Academy of Social Sciences* (1968). See also Ralph Goldman, *Behavioral Perspectives on American Politics* (Homewood, IL: Dorsey Press, 1973), chapters 6, 8.

7. Hall and Lindholm, in *Is America Breaking Apart?* argue that our loosely structured two-party system, with the broad separation of powers at all levels, the perception of a rather

blurred class system, the Constitution with its guarantees, and our devotion to freedom of speech, press, religion, and assembly, have been crucial to understanding how we have been able to fashion sufficient consensus out of conflicts that often seem irreconcilable.

8. John Kenneth White, *The New Politics of Old Values* (Hanover, NH: University Press of New England, 1988), 20.

9. Daniel J. Wakin, "A Divisive Issue for Catholics: Bishops, Politicians, and Communion," *New York Times,* May 31, 2004.

10. Maureen Dowd, "Vote and Be Damned," *New York Times,* October 17, 2004.

11. Mario Cuomo, "Religious Belief and Public Morality: A Catholic Governor's Perspective" (speech, Notre Dame University, Notre Dame, IN, September 13, 1984).

12. DiMaggio, Evans, and Bryson, "Have Americans' Social Attitudes Become More Polarized?" 693. In March 1974 representatives of the United States Catholic Conference gave testimony on a "Constitutional Amendment Protecting Unborn Human Life" before the Subcommittee on Constitutional Amendments of the Senate Committee on the Judiciary. The representatives declared that their testimony, as well as prior statements made by the National Council of Catholic Bishops, have "two central themes: 1. The right to life is a basic human right which should be protected by law. 2. Abortion, the deliberate destruction of an unborn human being, is contrary to the law of God and is a morally evil act." The testimony also made the major point that abortion was not just a violation of a Church teaching, but a violation of morality that should be apparent to all people who value the use of reason.

In November 1974 the Vatican Congregation for the Doctrine of Faith, with the formal approval of Pope Paul VI, published *Declaration on Procured Abortion.* This declaration was, in effect, a validation of the earlier testimony by the U.S. Catholic Bishops. The twelve-page document reviews the traditional teaching, quoting sources from the Didache to the present that "you shall not kill by abortion the fruit of the womb" and "Life must be safeguarded with extreme care from conception" (3). The document further states that "from a moral point of view this is certain: even if doubt existed concerning whether the fruit of conception is already a human person, it is objectively a grave sin to dare to risk murder" (ibid., 5). And further, "One can never approve of abortion; but it is above all necessary to combat its causes. This includes political action [on behalf of social justice]" (ibid., 8). A major focus of the argument is that the Church's teaching is not just a religious teaching, but is a moral teaching that all right-minded people should be able to come to. Still, it is clear that "in showing the unity of the Church, it will confirm by the authority proper to the Holy See what the bishops have opportunely undertaken." (ibid., 2).

Ten years later Kristin Luker, in *Abortion and the Politics of Motherhood,* observed that the activism of pro-life adherents was "premised on the deeply held belief that every embryo is a baby. [Thus], they cannot be expected to compromise on their belief that every abortion takes a baby's life. Yet in order to capture the middle ground, this is exactly what they will have to do. All the available poll data suggest that American support for certain categories of abortion is deeply ingrained and that any unswerving application of pro-life principles that ignores that support will create massive obstacles to capturing the middle ground" (228–29). The battle for the middle ground continued through the 1990s and into the twenty-first century, and the support for the middle ground is no less provided by Catholics as others. Which may raise the question of exactly how one is to interpret the phrase cited above in the Vatican document, namely that it shows "the unity of the Church." Is the Church primarily and principally the hierarchy, or does the word *Church* also include the laity?

13. In the 1976 campaign, Jimmy Carter was personally opposed to abortion but did not support an anti-abortion constitutional amendment. Gerald Ford held a moderate pro-choice position but allowed a plank supporting a constitutional amendment to affirm life. A compelling and provocative account of this period is provided by George McKenna, political science professor at the City College of New York, in his 2006 article, "Democrats, Republicans, and Abortion," in *Human Life Review* (Summer-Fall 2006): 57–79. He argued that the Democratic Party, with its commitment to social justice programs that were at the heart of Catholic teachings, was more appropriately the pro-life party, while the Republican Party seemed more committed to the values that supported population control. He recounted the efforts by U.S. cardinals and then-Archbishop Bernadin to convince candidate Carter in 1976 to support a constitutional amendment to outlaw abortion. While Carter was sympathetic, he rejected that strategy and ultimately broke with the bishops. By this time labor unions, civil liberties groups, and feminist organizations such as NOW had become active advocates within the Democratic Party supporting *Roe v. Wade*. Abortion as a potential party divider was actualized in 1980 when Ronald Reagan, a pro-choice supporter as governor of California, embraced the pro-life stand of the Republican Party platform while President Carter maintained his ambivalent position. Interesting accounts of how the evangelical Christians became crucial to the adoption of the anti-abortion plank and in the process became active players in the Republican Party are provided by Charles Moore, first national field director of the Moral Majority, at Moorereport.com, and by Adams, who asserted that "More than anyone, Ronald Reagan helped establish his party's signals on abortion" ("Evidence of an Issue Evolution," 735).

14. The Republican Party's anti-abortion platform plank stated, "We believe the unborn child has a fundamental individual right to life that cannot be infringed. We therefore reaffirm our support for a human life amendment to the Constitution, and we endorse legislation to make it clear that the Fourteenth Amendment's protections apply to unborn children." The Democratic Party platform in 1980 stated that "a woman has a right to choose whether and when to have a child" and affirmed its support for *Roe v. Wade*, going well beyond the 1976 platform's statement that it would be undesirable to overturn that decision. The 1980 platform also called abortion a "fundamental human right," and with that statement the divide between the two parties became clear, and the first signs of the culture wars began (George McKenna, "Democrats, Republicans, and Abortion," 71).

15. Using GSS data, Michael Hout, in "Abortion Politics in the United States, 1972–1994," *Gender Issues* (spring 1999): 3–34, examined the process by which liberals and conservatives coalesced around pro-choice and pro-life issues respectively, and how these growing ideological divides finally manifested themselves in the presidential election of 1988.

16. White, *Values Divide*, 87.

17. Ibid, 88.

18. Ibid.

19. We included in our analysis all abortion-related roll-call votes regardless of whether they were ultimately dropped or modified in the final write-up of particular bills. Nonvoters and abstentions were deleted.

20. Typical of the bills and amendments regularly voted on in the House and Senate were those to allow Medicaid funding of abortions where the mother's life was in danger or the pregnancy was the result of rape or incest; prohibit funding of abortions in such cases; stop the District of Columbia from using any federal funds to pay for abortions; outlaw courts from ordering states to fund abortions with state money; stop federal employees' health

insurance from covering abortions; ban military personnel and their dependents from obtaining privately funded abortions at overseas military hospitals except in cases of rape or incest; withhold funds from international family planning programs that might include abortion counseling; and forbid certain late-term abortion procedures.

21. Peter L. Benson and Dorothy L. Williams, *Religion on Capitol Hill* (San Francisco: Harper and Row, 1982). Benson and Williams also found that it was not possible to predict how members of Congress voted based only on their religious affiliation, but that religiosity also mattered.

22. Wade Clark Roof and William McKinney, *American Mainline Religion* (New Brunswick, NJ: Rutgers University Press, 1987), 82ff; also cited in Kevin J. Christiano, William H. Swatos Jr., and Peter Kivisto, eds. (Lanham, MD: Alta Mira Press, 2002), 114–16.

23. DiMaggio, Evans, and Bryson, "Have Americans' Social Attitudes Become More Socialized?" 739.

24. This finding is supported by Layman and Carsey, who found that the Democratic and Republican Parties have become increasingly polarized on all three of the major domestic policy agendas: social welfare, racial, and cultural issues ("Party Polarization and 'Conflict Extension' in the American Electorate," 786).

25. The steady increase in the Catholic pro-choice vote in Congress leading to polarization across parties seems to reflect the support for choice among Catholics generally. Michele Dillon, "Institutional Legitimation and Abortion: Monitoring the Catholic Church's Discourse," *Journal for the Scientific Study of Religion* 34, no. 2 (1995): 141–51, suggests that the Catholic Church's adoption of a variety of action strategies similar to those used by other political actors has delegitimated its voice as a source of moral authority on the issue of abortion in Congress and threatens its position as a public, socially engaged church. Research on American Catholics reveals strong trends across gender and generations, with growing majorities looking to their own conscience rather than to church leaders for moral guidance on such issues as abortion (William V. D'Antonio, James D. Davidson, Dean R. Hoge, and Mary L. Gautier, (Lanham, MD: Alta Mira, 2001, chapter 5). For a detailed analysis of the Catholic bishops' lobbying efforts on abortion and other social issues, see also Gene Burns, *The Frontiers of Catholicism* (Berkeley: University of California Press, 1992). For an overview of the Catholic bishops' position on abortion and other issues, see Office of Government Liaison, U.S. Catholic Conference, *Final Legislative Report*, 102nd, 104th, 105th Congresses.

26. Evans, "Polarization in Abortion"; Jennifer Strickler and Nicholas L. Danigelis, "Changing Frameworks in Attitudes toward Abortion," *Sociological Forum* 17 (2002): 187–201.

27. Evans, *Have Americans' Attitudes Become More Polarized? An Update;* Hetherington, "Resurgent Mass Partisanship"; Layman and Carsey, "Party Polarization and 'Conflict Extension' in the American Electorate."

28. Jeffrey Berry, *The New Liberalism: The Rising Power of Citizen Groups* (Washington, DC: Brookings Institution Press, 1999) delineates the process by which liberal interest groups have gained ascendancy in American politics and civic life. While he points out that the conservative "family values" groups have failed to overturn *Roe v. Wade*, our findings support the argument that they have significant influence within the public at large and in the Republican Party, especially within the House (74). See also Jennifer Strickler and Nicholas L. Danigelis, "Changing Frameworks in Attitudes toward Abortion," *Sociological Forum* 17 (2002):187–201, and also Adams, "Evidence of an Issue Evolution."

29. Four Catholic Democrats were in the Senate during the congressional sessions of this study. Two were 100 percent pro-choice throughout the time period, one was predominantly pro-

choice, and the fourth was 100 percent pro-life in the 96th Congress and still predominantly pro-life in the 104th Congress. Despite the increasing criticism by the Catholic bishops of pro-choice Catholics in the House and Senate, their numbers have increased.

30. Strickler and Danigelis, "Changing Frameworks in Attitudes toward Abortion," *Sociological Forum* 17 (2002): 187–201.

31. DiMaggio, Evans, and Bryson, "Have Americans' Social Attitudes Become More Polarized?" 737.

32. Evans, *Have Americans' Attitudes Become More Polarized?*

33. Adams, "Evidence of an Issue Evolution."

34. Hetherington, "Resurgent Mass Partisanship," 619.

35. Layman and Carsey, "Party Polarization and 'Conflict Extension' in the American Electorate"; Evans, "Polarization in Abortion Atitudes in U.S. Reigious Traditions, 1972–1998."

36. For example, in the Senate all the fourteen Catholic Democrats supported the Prescription Drug Bill; by contrast, only one in ten Catholic Republicans supported the bill. In the House, seventy-one of seventy-four Catholic Democrats supported the bill, while only one of forty-nine Catholic Republicans did so. On lifting the Cuban Embargo sanctions, sixty-two of seventy-four House Catholic Democrats supported the bill, while only three of forty-nine Catholic Republicans did.

37. Richard Fleisher, "Explaining the Change in Roll-Call Voting Behavior of Southern Democrats," *Journal of Politics* 55, no 2 (1993): 327–41.

38. Ibid.

39. John A. Brademas, "The Emerging Role of the American Congress," *Proceedings of the Indiana Academy of Social Sciences,* 1968.

40. Evans, "Polarization in Abortion Attitudes"; Hetherington, "Resurgent Mass Partisanship"; Layman and Carsay, "Party Polarization and 'Conflict Extension' in the American Electorate"; Adams, "Evidence of an Issue Evolution."

41. DiMaggio, Evans, and Bryson, "Have Americans' Social Attitudes Become More Socialized?" 745.

42. Evans, "Polarization in Abortion Attitudes."

43. Tom Robbins, *Even Cowgirls Get the Blues* (Boston: Houghton Mifflin, 1976), preface.

9

CATHOLICS AND
THE SUPREME COURT
From the "Catholic Seat" to the New Majority

Barbara A. Perry

*I*N JUNE 1963 President John F. Kennedy made a sentimental pilgrimage to Ireland, the land from which his family was only three generations removed. JFK, not noted for the public emoting that is seen with annoying frequency from our politicians in the twenty-first century, told a gathering in Limerick, "So I carry with me as I go the warmest sentiments of appreciation toward all of you. This is a great country, with a great people, and I know when I am back in Washington I . . . will not see you, but I will see you in my mind and feel all of your good wishes, as we all will in our hearts."[1] Bidding farewell to the crowds that turned out to say good-bye to the youthful Irish American president at Shannon Airport, he again waxed nostalgic: "What gives me the greatest satisfaction and pride, being of Irish descent, is the realization that even today this very small island sends thousands . . . of its sons and daughters to the ends of the globe to carry on an historic task, which Ireland assumed 1,400 or 1,500 years ago."[2]

The president then took out a slip of paper on which he had scrawled a verse, quoted to him the previous evening by the wife of Irish president and national hero Eamon De Valera, because JFK thought the words were "so beautiful":

'Tis it is the Shannon's brightly glancing stream,
Brightly gleaming, silent in the morning beam,
Oh, the sight entrancing,
Thus returns from travels long,
Years of exile, years of pain,
To see old Shannon's face again,
O'er the waters dancing.[3]

Turning to the throngs one last time, he promised, "Well, I am going to come back and see old Shannon's face again, and I am taking, as I go back to America, all of you with me."[4] Earlier in his trip through the Emerald Isle, he had paraphrased an old Irish ballad, vowing "I shall come back in the springtime."[5] He never returned, falling victim to an assassin's bullets just five months later.

Two days after the president's murder, the Irish writer Frank O'Connor wrote of JFK's importance to his compatriots: "John Fitzgerald Kennedy was a miracle. In three different ways he broke through age-old American prejudices against Catholics, against Irishmen and against intellectuals, and you have to have lived in America to realize how strong these prejudices are. Eleven years ago [1952], in the bar of an exclusive Boston club, an old Bostonian said to me: 'Do you know, you're the first educated Irishman I've ever met?'"[6]

The Irish author, playwright, and poet had been so proud to hear the night before Kennedy died that the president had quoted him in a San Antonio speech describing America's goal to put a man on the moon within the decade. The novelist, JFK noted, had written of the Irish parable about embracing the challenge of climbing a high wall by tossing one's cap over it. O'Connor observed in his elegiac tribute that President Kennedy "was not the man to be afraid of quoting some Irish writer, whom most of his audience had never heard of. He was leading the Irish out of a ghetto of humiliation and pretense and telling them that they were a people with a history and literature as good as the best." From triumph to tragedy, O'Connor heard on one night that the president of the United States was quoting him and the next evening that he was dead. "I wept," the novelist reported, "partly for ourselves, who have lost a man that represented not only his own country but ours."[7]

In addition to the emerald thread that ties the Kennedy clan together and links it to the Irish wherever they may have settled, the remarkable story of JFK's ascent to the presidency is inextricably bound to the role of immigration, religion, and ethnicity in American politics. This fascinating mixture also played an identifiable role in appointments to the U.S. Supreme Court from the latter part of the nineteenth century until President Kennedy's election, which signaled that Catholics had made their way into the mainstream of American politics. Until that time, presidents had felt the political need to reach out to religious minorities, as waves of Catholic and Jewish immigrants entered the country, to give them "representation" on the nation's highest tribunal. Such presidential recognition was meant to instill constituency loyalty and garner votes in campaigns for the White House.[8]

Furthermore, the only way that an Irish Catholic could be elected president in 1960 was to emphasize his belief in the absolute separation of church and state, along with keeping his own religious faith carefully restricted within the realm of his private life. Not coincidentally, in the midst of Kennedy's presidency, one that he predicated on his secular approach to public life, the Supreme Court issued its landmark 1962 ruling, *Engel v. Vitale,* in which it invalidated compulsory recitation of state-written prayers in public schools.[9]

As Frank O'Connor observed, Kennedy also reflected a cool intellectualism that made it stylish to cite literary allusions in speeches, invite New England Yankee Robert Frost to recite his poetry at the inauguration, and fete the nation's literati at White

House state dinners.[10] The triumph of reason and intellect during the Enlightenment had led America's Founders (particularly Thomas Jefferson, James Madison, and George Mason) to protect religious freedom and insulate religion and government from the excesses of each other, eventually via the First Amendment to the U.S. Constitution.[11] Although Doris Kearns Goodwin argues that JFK liked the pomp and circumstance of Roman Catholic ritual and transformed that pageantry into a civic symbolism for the political world, President Kennedy also moved easily among WASPs, who had constituted the nation's governing elite since the nation's founding. Joseph P. Kennedy Sr. had demanded that his sons receive a secular education, while their sisters, whose schooling his wife Rose Kennedy engineered, attended convent schools and Catholic colleges.[12]

As American electoral politics evolved, religious affiliation began to wane as a criterion for Supreme Court nominees, to be replaced first by race (in the 1960s) and then gender (in the 1980s) as characteristics more germane to attracting votes in presidential campaigns.[13] The fading of religious affiliation as a consideration carrying symbolic weight meant that presidents were free to appoint members of the Catholic and Jewish faith in numbers that filled more than one seat—one seat having been the custom for over a century. Currently, the U.S. Supreme Court has five Catholic and two Jewish justices.[14] For the first time in its history, the high tribunal has a majority of minority religion adherents and a majority of Roman Catholics, as shown in table 9.1.

TABLE 9.1   Catholic Supreme Court Justices

JUSTICE	APPOINTING PRESIDENT	COURT TENURE
Roger B. Taney	Jackson	1836–64
Edward D. White Jr.	Cleveland	1894–1910
Joseph McKenna	McKinley	1898–1925
Edward D. White Jr.[a]	Taft	1910–21
Pierce Butler	Harding	1922–39
Frank Murphy	F. Roosevelt	1940–49
William J. Brennan Jr.	Eisenhower	1956–90
Antonin Scalia	Reagan	1986–
Anthony M. Kennedy	Reagan	1988–
Clarence Thomas[b]	G. H. W. Bush	1991–
John G. Roberts Jr.[c]	G. W. Bush	2005–
Samuel A. Alito Jr.	G. W. Bush	2006–

[a] Promoted to chief justice from associate justice.
[b] Reconverted to Catholicism in 1996.
[c] Chief justice.
Source: Author.

Yet while Catholicism is no longer a factor in helping presidents to attract voters through symbolic representation on the high court, it may have shifted to serving as a signal to conservative presidents that the potential Supreme Court nominee is a traditional Catholic whose beliefs may coincide with Christian fundamentalists. Presidents may now want Catholics actively, not passively or symbolically, to represent conservative political values once they are ensconced on the nation's highest court. Indeed, over the last decade a majority of justices have supported government accommodation of religion, rather than separation therefrom. Notably, the separationist approach to government and religion now remains intact only through judicial bans on state-organized prayer in public schools, and that precedent may not survive a more conservative Supreme Court, which ABC News legal affairs correspondent Jan Crawford Greenburg argues in her 2007 book, *Supreme Conflict,* may well be President George W. Bush's major victory in America's contemporary battle between red and blue states.[15]

THE CATHOLIC SEAT'S HISTORY

Understanding this transformation of presidential motives in appointing members of religious, racial, or ethnic groups to the U.S. Supreme Court entails grasping distinctions in the concept of representation. The juxtaposition of "representative" and "Supreme Court" may initially seem oxymoronic. Aren't judges supposed to be above politics and the constituencies it engenders? As Chief Justice John Roberts explained at his Senate confirmation hearings in 2005, judges should be like umpires at a baseball game—scrupulously neutral, with no bias toward either team. This conceptualization of the judicial process is certainly the ideal. In reality, presidents and the American people have wanted the Supreme Court, at the very least, to mirror various characteristics of the body politic. Theorists have labeled this view "descriptive representation," which concerns "who the representative is or what he or she is like, rather than what he or she does." This perspective has been defined as follows: "The representative does not act for others; he 'stands for' them, by virtue of a correspondence or connection between them, a resemblance or reflection."[16] A similar label is "passive representation," or the mirroring of societal characteristics, in contrast to "active representation," with its vigorous pursuit of the constituents' interests, as in legislatures.[17]

In a memorable segment of his eloquent, passionate dissent from the Supreme Court's 1943 decision invalidating mandatory flag salutes for public school children (successfully challenged by Jehovah's Witnesses as a violation of their religious beliefs), Justice Felix Frankfurter declared: "As judges we are neither Jew nor Gentile, neither Catholic nor agnostic."[18] In replacing Catholic justice Frank Murphy with Protestant Tom Clark, President Harry Truman exclaimed with characteristic pugnacity, "I do not believe religions have anything to do with the Supreme Bench. If an individual has the qualifications, I do not care if he is a Protestant, Catholic, or Jew."[19]

Preceding presidents had not followed Truman's approach. A "Catholic seat" eventually evolved on the Supreme Court, as did a "Jewish seat" some decades later.

While "representing" (in the passive or symbolic sense) members of these two minority religions on the Court, presidents also were cognizant of the electoral ramifications of their appointments. When Catholics and Jews emerged as potentially significant voting blocs, occupants of the White House attempted to woo their votes through Supreme Court appointments. Thus, presidential electoral and "representative" motivations may be indistinguishable. What better way to attract or "pay off" Catholic and Jewish ballots than by offering "representation" on the Court to minority religious groups?

Although Catholics gradually gained political parity with the Protestant majority, anti-Romanist suspicions lurked just beneath the surface in American politics and society. During the first century and a half of U.S. history, there emerged a cyclical pattern in which anti-foreign nativism bubbled to the surface in episodes of virulent, and sometimes violent, displays of anti-Catholicism. Between incidents, the nativist outbreaks would subside and anti-Romanism would fester under the surface of politics, only to erupt when next provoked. In the nineteenth century, provocations came often as relentless waves of immigrants carved out enclaves and remade the American political landscape.[20]

Between 1790 and 1850, 1,071,000 Catholic immigrants arrived on the shores of the United States, outstripping the native Catholic population by quantum leaps and giving the Church a decidedly foreign flavor, which provided grist for the nativist mill. Traditional anti-Catholicism combined with new and worrisome economic conditions, including increased competition for jobs, to produce a fresh campaign of nativism in 1830, marked by the establishment by non-Catholic clergy of an explicitly anti-Catholic weekly newspaper, *The Protestant*. Over the next several decades, numerous local nativist societies spread the case against the foreign born, particularly Catholics, as did a national political party, labeled the Know-Nothings.[21]

The indictment against Catholics charged that they could never be proper Americans because they owed their allegiance to a foreign prelate—the pope, or the Prince of Rome. Moreover, nativists argued that the hierarchical church structure produced an anti-democratic ethos among Romanists that was incompatible with the American political system. Further, in these "huddled masses," xenophobic Americans saw a threat to the nation's social and economic well-being as the "dregs" of European societies flooded the labor market and turned sections of U.S. cities into teeming, vice-ridden ghettoes. At the most extreme were nativists who foresaw the introduction of the Inquisition to American soil.[22]

Overcoming Anti-Catholicism: Roger Taney (1836–64)

The first Catholic nominated to serve on the nation's highest tribunal was Roger Brooke Taney, whom President Andrew Jackson nominated to be chief justice in 1836, amid the rise of nativism. No evidence exists to indicate that Taney's religion played any role in Jackson's decision. Indeed, given such a hostile and extreme anti-Catholic climate, Taney's rise to the highest judicial position in the land proves the strength of other factors, namely, his demonstrable merit, native state (Maryland, with its large Catholic population), politics (emphatically Jacksonian), and friendship with Old Hickory.[23] Yet Taney was known to be a devout Catholic and, the *New York Herald* commented, "on that ground may offend a certain sect of religionists. But the selection of such a man for chief justice, is a signal example of practical religious liberty in the actions of the government of the United States."[24] Serving until his death in 1864, Taney paved the way for what would become the "Catholic seat" on the high court.

Edward D. White Jr. (1894–1910)

Nominated by President Grover Cleveland in 1894, Edward D. White Jr. was the next Roman Catholic appointed to the bench. A Protestant minister had accused Democrat Cleveland in his first run for the White House in 1884 as representing the party of "rum, Romanism, and rebellion."[25] In the midst of a revival of anti-Catholicism spearheaded by the American Protective Association (APA), founded in 1887, President Cleveland, in his second term, appointed White, a U.S. senator from Louisiana. Machinations of legislative and executive politics during the late nineteenth century probably outweighed religion among the factors leading to Cleveland's choice. Yet White's piety and morality had impressed the president when, as they once departed a Saturday evening party, White asked his host where he might attend an early mass the next morning. As one historian has explained, "Either from gratitude for Catholic principles [Taft had called Catholicism 'one of the bulwarks against socialism and anarchy in this country'] or from fear of the increasing Catholic voting power, politicians began to extend governmental aid to the Church. . . . Both major political parties gave Catholics greater recognition than ever before."[26]

Attracting Catholic Voters: Joseph McKenna (1898–1925)

Although Taney and White had roots and educational experience in old Catholic traditions based in Maryland and Louisiana, the third Catholic to be nominated to the Supreme Court—Joseph McKenna, by President William McKinley in 1898—was rooted in immigrant Catholicism. McKenna's parents had emigrated from England and Ireland to Philadelphia, where the future justice was born in 1843—just one year before nativist-Catholic riots scarred the City of Brotherly Love. Twelve years later, in order to escape continuing nativist bigotry, the McKenna family escaped to California.[27]

Religious affiliation was a mere coincidence in Taney's appointment and peripheral to White's, but in the case of McKenna's nomination, Catholicism was a more significant factor (perhaps even a tipping point) in his nomination to the Supreme Court. His geographic roots (in California, the home state of the justice he replaced), along with political compatibility and personal friendship with McKinley, probably trumped religion. But McKinley had been fighting the American Protective Society for most of his political career, and he was well aware that McKenna's appointment to the high court could attract Catholic votes in his 1900 reelection bid.[28]

Catholicism as the tipping factor was at work again in 1910, when President William Howard Taft promoted Associate Justice White to chief justice. White's judicial experience, meritorious legal skills, strong moral character, and age were foremost in Taft's consideration of White. (Taft wanted the chief justice position himself, and White was old enough not to have a lengthy tenure. When White died in 1921, President Warren Harding nominated former President Taft to his much-coveted chief justiceship.)[29]

Anti-Catholicism had hardly disappeared from politics in the early twentieth century, despite the demise of the Know-Nothings and the American Protective Association. Indeed, some suggested that Taft, a Freemason, should not have appointed a Roman Catholic to such a high position, but the president argued that to reject an appointee based on religious affiliation would violate his oath of office.[30] Moreover, Taft was convinced that his past and future electoral success depended on the support of Catholics, whose numbers had increased to over sixteen million by 1910.[31] His aide wrote that Taft was "very strong with the Catholics, and in nearly every city we visit he manages to show some special mark of respect for them and to have a few minutes conference with some of their leaders." The aide worried that Taft "might pay very dearly" among Protestants who resented what they considered pandering to Catholics. Later, Taft's assistant even accused the president of encouraging Catholics to separate themselves from others to attract his attention.[32]

Developing the Catholic Seat: Pierce Butler (1922–39)
Like Joseph McKenna, the next Catholic to be selected for the Supreme Court, Minnesotan Pierce Butler, was a first-generation Irish American. Appointed in 1922 by Harding, Butler had garnered the support of now–Chief Justice Taft, who trusted his conservative ideology and legal acumen, which he had demonstrated as a corporate lawyer for railroad interests. In addition, a close friend of Taft advocated placing a Catholic on the high bench because, in the aftermath of White's death in 1921 and the anticipated demise of the ailing McKenna, there would be a "demand" for another Roman Catholic on the Court. Indeed, with Butler's appointment, religion moved beyond its status as a factor that could put a nominee over the top to an element that had now become one of the primary considerations in choosing a Supreme Court justice. Religion was still an insurmountable obstacle to the presidency, however, as evinced by Catholic Al Smith's lopsided defeat at the hands of Herbert Hoover in 1928.[33]

Franklin Roosevelt, who would appoint the next Catholic to the Court, had recognized the importance of Catholic electoral influence early in his New York political career. By 1932 he was well aware of the significance of Catholic support, especially if he hoped to carry the eastern states in a national election. A substantial portion of FDR's twelve-million-plus victory margin over President Herbert Hoover that year undoubtedly came from Roosevelt's strong showing in the country's twelve largest urban areas, which contained sizable Catholic populations.[34]

As one historian has noted, "It was FDR who maintained the allegiance of American Catholics toward the [Democratic] party by the recognition he extended them and the finesse with which he treated them."[35] Roosevelt nurtured Catholic support, in part, by appointing Roman Catholics to office in unprecedented numbers. Up to his presidency, which began in 1933, only four Catholics had ever served in presidential cabinets. FDR appointed two in his first term alone. Roosevelt averaged one Catholic for every four judicial appointments during his twelve-year tenure in the White House.[36] No wonder a Gallup poll in October 1936 revealed that 78 percent of Catholics surveyed intended to vote for FDR in his first attempt at reelection.[37] As in 1932, he racked up overwhelming majorities in urban areas, where most of the Catholic votes were concentrated.[38]

Frank Murphy (1940–49)

Another victor in the 1936 elections was one of Roosevelt's earliest and staunchest supporters, Frank Murphy, who became the first Roman Catholic governor of Michigan in 1936. Two years later the president named him attorney general and then promoted him to the Supreme Court in 1940. Like the four Catholics who preceded him on the high bench, Murphy was of Irish ancestry. Arthur Krock, the eminent journalist, once attended mass with Murphy and Joseph Kennedy Sr., father of the future president and FDR's stunning choice to serve as ambassador to the Court of St. James, the first Irishman to represent the United States to the United Kingdom. Krock later joked with Kennedy that he found Murphy the better model to follow in order to keep up with the service's rituals that called for kneeling, standing, or sitting at the proper times. Kennedy, referring to Murphy's prowess in the formalities of the Catholic mass, replied: "That character . . . ought to have been a priest."[39] Instead, Murphy would join the "priestly tribe," as justices are sometimes labeled.

Murphy had served as attorney general for less than a year when Justice Butler died in November 1939. President Roosevelt wasted no time in making his decision on Butler's replacement, telling Murphy after a Cabinet meeting on the day of Butler's death that he would take the seat. In addition to having the right religious affiliation, Murphy possessed partisan and ideological compatibility with FDR, along with a close friendship. Thus, the historical record indicates that Catholicism had risen to the top two or three considerations in Roosevelt's continuance of the Court's "Catholic seat." As if to emphasize the role of Murphy's Catholicism in the new justice's life, as well as his appointment, an FDR confidante pointedly remarked that with Murphy on the Court, FDR would achieve his goal of increasing the number of seats on the high bench, because the new justice would "bring with him as colleagues Father, Son and Holy Ghost!"[40]

Indeed, Murphy's selection to fill the "Catholic seat" that had evolved on the Court over the first half of the twentieth century was the pinnacle of Catholic "representation" on the high bench. Upon Justice Murphy's death in 1949, President Truman—as has been noted—nominated a Protestant, Tom C. Clark, stating defiantly that religious affiliation should have nothing to do with Supreme Court selection criteria. For him, personal and political friendship was the primary factor.

Nevertheless, a 1953 article in the Catholic magazine *Commonweal* noted the absence of Catholics on the U.S. Supreme Court: "The president is under no obligation to appoint a Catholic to any position, but in recognition of the fact that Catholics constitute about one-fifth of the total population, it had been deemed equitable, and perhaps politically expedient, to allocate a certain number of top appointive positions to members of the Roman Catholic Church."[41]

Catholic "representation" had become a prominent issue in American politics. The continued concentration of America's single largest religious denomination (20 percent of the total population) in urban areas gave Catholics an important role in the presidential Electoral College system. Historian Lawrence Fuchs has noted that "more than 80 percent of the Catholic voters lived in fewer than a dozen key industrial states including those with the largest Electoral College vote."[42] In recognition of this demographic fact, Democratic politicians, as they approached the presidential nominating convention in the summer of 1956, debated the strategy of putting a Catholic vice-presidential candidate on the ticket.[43] Senator John F. Kennedy of Massachusetts nearly captured the honor but lost a hard-fought convention struggle with Tennessee senator Estes Kefauver, the eventual nominee for vice president on the unsuccessful Democratic ticket headed by Adlai Stevenson Jr. Kennedy's father was uncharacteristically delighted at his son's defeat. Old Joe predicted that the Stevenson ticket would lose again to incumbent president Dwight Eisenhower, and JFK's Catholicism might be blamed for the loss, thus ending his chance to lead a future presidential ticket.

William J. Brennan Jr. (1956–90)

Just two months before Eisenhower overwhelmed the Stevenson-Kefauver ticket with his landslide reelection victory in November 1956, he was faced with a vacancy on the Supreme Court. He found the perfect nominee—William J. Brennan Jr., an associate justice of the New Jersey Supreme Court. A Harvard Law School graduate, he had been an outstanding trial lawyer before becoming a judge lauded by the bar. Only fifty years old, a youngster to the elderly president, the Irish Catholic Brennan fit the bill. Eisenhower may have promised Francis Cardinal Spellman, whom he knew from the latter's days as "Military Vicar" during World War II, that he would restore the "Catholic seat," which had been vacant since Murphy's death in 1949. In a 1985 interview about his appointment, Justice Brennan voluntarily launched into a story of Spellman's possible influence on Eisenhower. He also recalled that, after his appointment, his pastor at the New Jersey church where he had long worshiped informed him that a priest who was the brother of Ike's appointments secretary had made inquiries "to see if Brennan was a good Catholic." When Eisenhower's press secretary heard that the virtually unknown Brennan was the president's choice for the Court, the only descriptive credentials that came to mind were that Brennan was "a judge on the New Jersey Supreme Court and a good member of the Holy Name Society."[44]

In that same 1985 interview, Justice Brennan offered another possible motivation for Eisenhower's selection of an Irish Catholic for the Supreme Court in the months preceding the 1956 election. Senator Kennedy's near victory at that summer's Democratic Convention in the race for his party's vice-presidential nomination may have prompted the president to recognize the Irish Catholic constituency.[45] Some three million of the Catholics who voted in the 1952 presidential election had cast their votes for General Eisenhower.[46] At a minimum, Ike must have been anxious to maintain that Catholic support in the upcoming 1956 election, especially in the traditionally Democratic Northeast, with its abundance of electoral votes. As Arthur Krock, the veteran New York Times editorialist, explained, "The appointment to the Supreme Court of a Catholic to succeed the retiring Justice Minton was not only service to a fine American tradition: it was obviously good politics as well."[47]

The impact of John F. Kennedy's landmark victory in 1960 on the Supreme Court's "Catholic seat" may have been indirect, but it was nevertheless profound. Less than a century removed from "No Irish Need Apply" signs, Kennedy's success symbolized the removal of a stigma that had prevented Roman Catholics from reaching the highest elected office in the land and punctuated their long assimilation process into American society and politics. As Fuchs has argued, JFK's electoral success invigorated the forces of modernization within the American Catholic Church because Kennedy represented "the antithesis of the stereotyped, separat[ed], parochial, anti-intellectual, superstitious, tribalistic, and fatalistic Catholic of Protestant literature and conversation."[48] University of Chicago religion professor Martin Marty agreed that Kennedy's 1960 victory was symbolic of the complete transition for Catholics but believed that their "mainstreaming" into the general population actually began with their use of the G.I. Bill after World War II. The resulting increase in their levels of education and migration to the suburbs made them full participants in American society and politics.[49]

Ironically, the movement of Catholics to center stage of American politics and society may have eliminated the raison d'être of the Court's "Catholic seat." That is, the assimilation of Catholics into American politics to the point of capturing the Oval Office in 1960 arguably removed the "equitability" justification, and perhaps even the electoral motivation, for offering "representation" on the Court to Catholics as a group. James Hennesey has stated that "JFK's election lessened the psychological defensiveness that had historically marked the Catholic American."[50] Presidents would no longer have to compensate for Catholic feelings of inferiority or inequity by reserving one seat on the Supreme Court for Roman Catholics.

SEPARATION OF CHURCH AND STATE: FROM KENNEDY TO THE MODERN COURT

Kennedy presented himself to the American electorate as a young member of a new generation, a survivor of World War II for whom religion was purely a personal trait. His secular public persona came easily to him, as he had heeded his father's lessons in attending non-Catholic schools. Ever the political tactician, Joe Kennedy reasoned that his sons would have to succeed in a non-Catholic world of politics. JFK's political success would be based on mastering the WASP power structure. Much to his mother's delight, however, Jack attended Mass at his neighborhood parish church in Georgetown the morning of his snowy inauguration on January 20, 1961, but he would not have dared held a public religious service to mark the commencement of his presidency.[51] (JFK did invite Kennedy family friend Richard Cardinal Cushing of Boston to deliver the invocation at his inauguration.) Kennedy had eloquently and definitively explained to the Greater Houston Ministerial Association, a gathering of Southern Baptist clerics, during the 1960 campaign that "what kind of church I believe in . . . should be important only to me."[52] He then described the nation he believed in: "I believe in an America where the separation of church and state is absolute—where no Catholic prelate would tell the president (should he be a Catholic) how to act and no Protestant minister would tell his parishioners for whom to vote—where no church or school is granted any public funds or political preference." With a repetitive syntax and cadence that JFK had perfected on the campaign trail, he told the ministers,

> I believe in an America that is officially neither Catholic, Protestant nor Jewish— where no public official either requests or accepts instructions on public policy from the Pope, the National Council of Churches or any other ecclesiastical

source. . . . For, while this year it may be a Catholic against whom the finger of suspicion is pointed, in other years it has been, and may someday be again, a Jew—or a Quaker—or a Unitarian—or a Baptist. It was Virginia's harassment of Baptist preachers, for example, that led to Jefferson's Statute for Religious Freedom. Today, I may be the victim—but tomorrow it may be you—until the whole fabric of our harmonious society is ripped apart at a time of great national peril.

"Finally," he continued, "I believe in an America where religious intolerance will someday end . . . where there is no Catholic vote, no anti-Catholic vote, no bloc voting of any kind."

Senator Kennedy then expanded the theme to include the office of the president, "whose views on religion," he said, "are his own private affair, neither imposed upon him by the nation nor imposed by the nation upon him as a condition to holding that office." As a member of "the greatest generation," he made a powerful statement to an audience that must have included many World War II veterans: "This is the kind of America I believe in—and this is the kind of America I fought for in the South Pacific and the kind my brother died for in Europe. No one suggested then that we might have a 'divided loyalty.'" For emphasis, he declared, "I do not speak for my church on public matters—and the church does not speak for me." Kennedy came to a stark conclusion: "If this election is decided on the basis that 40 million Americans lost their chance of being president on the day they were baptized, then it is the whole nation that will be the loser in the eyes of Catholics and non-Catholics around the world, in the eyes of history, and in the eyes of our own people."

Just a year and a half after Kennedy took office, the U.S. Supreme Court firmly separated organized, state-sanctioned religious observances from the nation's public schools. *Engel v. Vitale,* which the justices decided in 1962, invalidated a brief nondenominational prayer drafted by the New York State Board of Regents for mandated use in the Empire State's public schools. With Justice Hugo Black writing for an 8 to 1 majority, the Court declared that such a devotional violated the First Amendment's Establishment Clause, which Black argued, in Jeffersonian terms, created a wall of separation between church and state.[53]

When asked about his views on the Court's school prayer ruling, President Kennedy urged support of the Supreme Court's decisions "even when we may not agree with them." Then, following the views of Jefferson and Madison, Kennedy added, "We have in this case a very easy remedy and that is to pray ourselves. And I would think that it would be a welcome reminder to every American family that we can pray a good deal more at home, we can attend our churches with a good deal more fidelity, and we can make the true meaning of prayer much more important in the lives of all of our children. That power is very much open to us."[54]

Justice Brennan voted with the majority in *Engel* and was a separationist in religion cases for his entire thirty-four-year tenure on the high bench. Like John Kennedy, he attended mass faithfully each weekend but found little room for accommodating state-sponsored religion in the public square. As a staunch liberal, Brennan did not even follow his church's anti-abortion policy, voting with the Court's majority in *Roe v. Wade.*[55] While Brennan fulfilled his weekly mass obligation, pro-life protestors stationed themselves outside St. Matthew's Cathedral in Washington so he would have to see them while entering the church. When he passed away in 1997, the protestors were back one more time; as his coffin was brought up the aisle at St. Matthew's, mourners could hear the pro-lifers shouting their anti-Brennan slogans outside the basilica.

The Catholic Seat in Decline: Antonin Scalia (1986–)

Justice Brennan had been the Court's only Catholic from his appointment in 1956 until he was joined on the high bench by Antonin Scalia three decades later. Although Brennan's and Scalia's presence on the nine-person Court reflected the approximate percentage of Catholics in the American population in 1986 (25 percent, or 52,000,000), it is unlikely that President Reagan or his advisers were guided by such a consideration or that they were concerned about the inevitable departure of the eighty-year-old Brennan and the implications for the "Catholic seat."[56] When asked in 1988 if he would be willing to discuss the Court's "Catholic seat," Justice Scalia replied in typically pithy fashion, "if that's what you think I sit in."[57] Though the Reagan administration was not particularly interested in Scalia's religious affiliation (his conservatism was much more determinative), they were aware that he would be the first Italian American on the nation's highest tribunal. Once he took his seat on the high tribunal, Italians wrote to him frequently, expressing their pride that he was on the Supreme Court—an obvious counter to the lawless Mafia stereotype.[58]

True to his conservative jurisprudence, Scalia embraces accommodation, not separation, between church and state. His posture on the Establishment Clause is another indication that Catholics no longer have to dichotomize their public and private lives. Scalia is a devout Catholic with nine children, one of whom is a priest. The first Italian American on the Court swears that his judicial views on religion and abortion do not derive from his Catholicism, but rather the text of the Constitution. That may be, but he does not have to worry, as his Catholic predecessors in public life had to do, that they would be an easy target for critics if it appeared that they were basing their public decisions on their church's teachings.

Anthony M. Kennedy (1988–)

No one could have predicted that a little over a year after Scalia's appointment, President Reagan would nominate another Catholic to the Supreme Court, but in the fall of 1987, America's Catholic press reported that, if confirmed, Reagan's nominee, Anthony M. Kennedy (no relation to JFK), would become the third Catholic to sit on the Rehnquist Court.[59] There is no evidence that Justice Kennedy's religious affiliation played any part in Reagan's decision to nominate him as the replacement for retiring Justice Lewis F. Powell, then the Court's swing vote. Kennedy's primary attraction for Reagan was that the moderately conservative, mild-mannered California federal judge epitomized the antithesis of the contentious Robert Bork, Reagan's first choice, whom the Democratic Senate had failed to confirm because of his staunch conservatism. Kennedy's appointment brought Catholic religious affiliation full circle to its previous status as a purely coincidental factor in nominations to the Supreme Court.[60]

The trio of Catholics on the Court represented three different segments on the political spectrum, from liberal (Brennan) to moderate (Kennedy) to conservative

(Scalia). Nowhere was this fact more striking than in abortion cases. In addition to voting with the majority in *Roe v. Wade*, Brennan continued to support the right to abortion throughout his next nearly two decades on the Court. Conversely, Scalia has repeatedly called for the Court to overturn its *Roe v. Wade* precedent. Justice Kennedy, however, has often been the swing voter in abortion cases, most obviously in the 1992 case of *Planned Parenthood of Southeastern Pennsylvania v. Casey*, when he helped fashion a compromise opinion (with Justices Sandra Day O'Connor and David Souter) to scrap *Roe's* trimester system of determining the levels of abortion rights based on the three stages of pregnancy, but to uphold the basic right of women to seek the procedure without "undue burden" from state limitations.[61]

Maintaining the swing-vote tradition of his predecessor, Justice Powell, in church–state cases, Justice Kennedy has cast the deciding vote, and written the majority opinion, in several Establishment Clause decisions. Depending on the facts before the Court, Kennedy's opinions have supported separation, as well as accommodation, of religion and government. In the midst of the Court's internal discussions in *Lee v. Weisman* (1992) over whether clergy could present nonsectarian prayers at public high school graduations, Kennedy switched his initial vote and struck down the practice as an Establishment Clause violation, prompting a stinging dissent from his fellow Catholic, Justice Scalia.[62] In *Rosenberger v. University of Virginia* (1995), however, he wrote for another closely divided Court that the institution founded by separationist Thomas Jefferson had to allow a student-run Christian magazine to receive monetary support from the student activities fee.[63]

THE NEW CATHOLIC MAJORITY

With the addition of Justice Samuel A. Alito Jr. in 2006, an unprecedented quintet of Catholics occupy a majority of the Court's positions. They include, along with Alito, Justices Antonin Scalia, Anthony Kennedy, and Clarence Thomas, as well as Chief Justice John Roberts.

Clarence Thomas (1991–)
In 2008 Catholic justices occupy five seats on the high tribunal. One of the three, in addition to Scalia and Kennedy, is Justice Clarence Thomas (appointed by President George H. W. Bush in 1991), who reconverted to Catholicism in 1996. He was born into a Southern Baptist household, raised as a Catholic by his grandparents, briefly studied for the priesthood in a seminary, received his undergraduate degree from the College of the Holy Cross, married his second wife in and joined the Episcopal church, and then returned to the Catholic fold. He proudly announced his reconversion to Catholicism during a speech at a Holy Cross reunion in 1996. The justice attends daily mass on Capitol Hill with his Catholic clerks.[64]

As with fellow conservative Justice Scalia, Thomas votes for accommodation, not separation, between religion and government. The reconverted Catholic has written victorious opinions upholding the expenditure of government funds to purchase computers and other instructional materials for religious schools, as in *Mitchell v. Helms*

(2000), and requiring public schools to make their facilities available for after-hour use by an evangelical religious club for elementary students, in *Good News Club v. Milford Central School* (2001).[65] He is also a reliable vote against abortion.

John G. Roberts Jr. (2005–) and Samuel A. Alito Jr. (2006–)

The two George W. Bush appointees, Chief Justice John Roberts and Associate Justice Samuel Alito, are lifelong Catholics. Their religious affiliation, however, had nothing to do with their appointments, in contrast to the days of the "Catholic seat." They are not "representing" Catholics in the old passive or symbolic sense, nor was the president attempting to show Roman Catholics that they were receiving equitable treatment in appointments. Nevertheless, Roberts's and Alioto's traditional Catholic beliefs assured Bush that he was selecting ideological soul mates whose beliefs squared with his own self-proclaimed Christian worldview. In a recent informal discussion between President Bush and a group of students from the University of Louisville, he began his opening remarks on political leadership by describing the importance of religious faith in his life, particularly how it saved him from alcoholism.[66] His theology also forms the core for his faith-based initiatives, where government and religious groups join forces to mitigate social ills. The Christian fundamentalist constituency, which has supported the president, was delighted with Bush's two Supreme Court picks. They believe that this President Bush has avoided the sins of his father, who placed WASPy David Souter on the Court, only to discover that he was a closet liberal.

John Roberts, a graduate of Harvard College and Harvard Law School, had served as a law clerk for Justice William Rehnquist, worked in the Reagan Justice Department and White House Counsel's Office, and was a deputy solicitor general in the George H. W. Bush administration. In private practice, Roberts had been a successful appellate advocate before the Supreme Court, arguing thirty-nine cases there. President George W. Bush's appointment of him to the U.S. Court of Appeals for the District of Columbia in 2003 provided a stepping-stone to the nation's highest tribunal. Bush initially nominated him in July 2005 for the seat vacated by Justice Sandra Day O'Connor's announced retirement.[67] In an article about Catholics on the Supreme Court, the *New York Times* reported, "Friends and political allies have described Judge Roberts's active and conservative brand of Catholicism, which he shares with his wife . . . as an important part of their lives. Many social conservatives clearly took his religious background as a positive sign about his judicial and political philosophy."[68] Such conservatives felt particularly triumphant over Roberts's replacement of swing voter O'Connor, whose position in favor of maintaining a fundamental right to abortion was anathema to them.

Before Roberts could appear before the Senate Judiciary Committee for confirmation hearings on his nomination to be an associate justice, Chief Justice Rehnquist, his mentor, died of cancer over the Labor Day weekend of 2005. President Bush wasted no time in naming Roberts to the Court's center chair. After a tour de force performance at his hearings, and confirmation by the full Senate on a vote of 78–22 (representing more affirmative votes than any chief justice had previously received), Roberts became the seventeenth chief justice of the United States on September 29, 2005.

President Bush then had to find another replacement for O'Connor, who had delayed retirement until her successor could be invested. For this second chance to name a justice to the seat that O'Connor had claimed in 1981 as the first woman on the high court, Bush began searching for a female candidate. A host of reasons led him to Harriet Miers, his friend from Texas and the White House counsel. Miers initially did not want the position and urged the president to nominate Third Circuit U.S. Court of Appeals judge Samuel Alito, who had been second on the short list to Roberts that past summer. Bush was insistent, however, and nominated Miers in October 2005. From the outset, her nomination was a disaster. Bush assured social conservatives that Miers, a former Catholic who had embraced evangelical Protestantism as a born-again Christian, shared their views, particularly on abortion. They were not convinced, citing her lack of a clear position in the pro-life debate. In addition, her unfamiliarity with constitutional law made Miers's courtesy meetings with senators on Capitol Hill torturous for both sides in the conversations. Eventually, the president's advisers had to convince Miers that withdrawing her name was the only course of action to save the White House and herself from an even more humiliating public defeat.[69]

Ironically, shortly after Miers announced her withdrawal, President Bush selected her initial choice for the O'Connor seat, Judge Alito. A fifteen-year veteran of the Third Circuit, the conservative judge, sometimes called "Scalito" for his perceived kinship with Justice Scalia's ideology, had impeccable credentials. A graduate of Princeton University and Yale Law School, Alito had served in the Reagan Justice Department and as the U.S. attorney in his native New Jersey. A 1990 appointee to the Third Circuit by the first President Bush, Alito was the sole dissenter in a 1991 Pennsylvania abortion case which had struck down a state requirement that married women tell their husbands they were seeking an abortion.[70] (The Supreme Court subsequently upheld that portion of the Third Circuit's majority ruling, with Justice O'-Connor expressing the opinion that the Pennsylvania requirement would pose an "undue burden" on married women.[71])

In a 1997 Third Circuit church–state ruling, Alito held that a Jersey City, New Jersey, holiday display of a crèche and menorah did not violate the First Amendment's Establishment Clause because the city had included secular figures such as Frosty the Snowman.[72] Alito's accommodationist ruling followed the Supreme Court's precedent, *Lynch v. Donnelly* (1984), in which the majority had upheld a similar display in Pawtucket, Rhode Island, because "total separation [of church and state] is not possible."[73]

Once more the *New York Times* noted the Catholic affiliation of another Bush appointee to the Supreme Court. "Alito Could Be 5th Catholic on Current Supreme Court," the *Times*'s headline declared. The article reported that experts on judicial appointments suggested that "religious affiliation means less now than does a discernable track record on social issues."[74]

Because Alito had such a clear track record and would take the seat of swing voter Sandra Day O'Connor, his confirmation hearings before the Senate Judiciary Committee were more contentious than those of John Roberts just four months previously. The politics of swing-seat appointments are always more acrimonious; they highlight the battle over a potential shift in the high court's rulings. Senator Richard

Durbin (D-IL) pressured Alito to respond to Roberts's view that *Roe v. Wade* was "settled law." The judge, resorting to a standard answer of judicial nominees, replied that he could not comment on a subject that might come before the high court. By a straight party-line vote (10 Republicans to 8 Democrats), the Judiciary Committee sent Alito's nomination to the full Senate. Massachusetts Democratic senators John Kerry and Edward Kennedy, both Catholics who support abortion rights, attempted to mount a filibuster against Alito's confirmation, but it fell short. The Senate voted 58–42 to make Alito the 110th justice of the U.S. Supreme Court, which he joined on January 31, 2006.[75]

Protestant evangelical and Catholic social conservatives had their prayers answered in the first abortion case, *Gonzales v. Carhart* (2007), to come before the Court with its new Catholic majority.[76] With Justice Kennedy swinging to the conservative side, providing the fifth vote to secure a majority and writing the Court's opinion, in which the four other Catholic justices joined, he upheld the federal ban on so-called partial-birth abortions. The ruling marked the first time the high tribunal had approved a government ban on a particular type of abortion.[77] Alito's appointment had made the difference. With O'Connor in that seat seven years previously, she had provided the crucial fifth vote to invalidate a similar *state* prohibition in *Stenberg v. Carhart*.[78]

The symbolic "Catholic seat" had truly given way to a substantive Catholic majority. Yet the Supreme Court's "Catholic seat" tradition (along with that of the "Jewish seat") may offer precedents for addressing our nation's more recent immigrant groups. For example, President Bush had hoped to appoint the first Hispanic member of the high court and groomed Alberto Gonzales for the position by bringing him to Washington, initially as White House counsel and then as attorney general. A close friend of the president and former member of the Texas Supreme Court, Gonzales, who holds a Harvard Law degree and is the son of poor Mexican immigrants, seemed perfectly cast to play that historic role. But the Republican Party base did not trust him on affirmative action and abortion (despite his Catholic affiliation), particularly to take the "swing seat" vacated by Justice Sandra Day O'Connor. The joke among conservatives was that the word *Gonzales* was Spanish for *Souter*.[79] They did not want symbolic representation of Hispanics; rather, conservatives wanted active representation of their ideology on the Supreme Court. In light of subsequent scandals surrounding Gonzales's tenure as White House counsel and attorney general, Bush is fortunate not to have nominated him to the high court.

CONCLUSION

In presidential politics, the move from a "Catholic *seat*" to a "Catholic *Court*" exemplifies a shift from electoral considerations (attracting Catholic votes through mere symbolism) to ideological ones (establishing a conservative Court majority). This shift's impact on church–state decisions is clear in the Court's trend away from separationism and toward accommodationism. Prior to the 1980s, liberal Catholics in public life inevitably turned to the Jeffersonian wall between church and state as a bulwark against anti-Catholicism. In the wake of the Reagan Revolution, however, conservative Catholics joined forces with Christian fundamentalists to implement their common social agenda that is explicitly based on religious dogma.

An intriguing question for future Supreme Court appointment politics is how presidents will respond to Islam in public life. President Bush reached out to American Muslims immediately after September 11, 2001. If there is a recognizable end to the war on Islamic terror, will presidents offer Muslims "representation" on the U.S. Supreme Court? Will Virginia Republican congressman Virgil Goode's diatribe against Keith Ellison (D-MN), the first Muslim congressman, and attacks on the Muslim lineage of Senator Barack Obama (D-IL) one day seem as antiquated as nineteenth-century anti-Catholicism? Apparently, some Americans also have reservations about a Mormon president, with over one-quarter responding that they would not vote for a qualified Mormon candidate to occupy the Oval Office. In contrast, the same poll showed that 95 percent of respondents would vote for a Catholic and 92 percent for a Jewish presidential candidate.[80] Those figures provide additional evidence that Catholics and Jews have joined the mainstream of American politics, making the single Catholic and single Jewish seat on the nation's highest court anachronistic.

NOTES

1. John F. Kennedy Library, "A Journey Home: John F. Kennedy in Ireland," available from www.jkflibrary.org.html.

2. Ibid.

3. As quoted by Thomas Maier, *The Kennedys: America's Emerald Kings* (New York: Basic Books, 2003), 441.

4. John F. Kennedy Library, "A Journey Home."

5. Maier, *The Kennedys*, 441.

6. Maurice N. Hennessy, *I'll Come Back in the Springtime: John F. Kennedy and the Irish* (New York: Ives Washburn, 1966), 107.

7. Ibid., 108.

8. See Barbara A. Perry, *A "Representative" Supreme Court? The Impact of Race, Religion, and Gender on Appointments* (New York: Greenwood Press, 1991).

9. 370 U.S. 421.

10. See Barbara A. Perry, *Jacqueline Kennedy: First Lady of the New Frontier* (Lawrence: University Press of Kansas, 2004).

11. See Barbara A. Perry, "Jefferson's Legacy to the Supreme Court: Freedom of Religion," *Journal of Supreme Court History* 31, no. 2 (2006): 181–98.

12. See Doris Kearns Goodwin, *The Kennedys and the Fitzgeralds* (New York: St. Martin's Press, 1987).

13. See Perry, *A "Representative" Supreme Court?* chapters 4 and 5.

14. The Catholics are Chief Justice John Roberts and Justices Antonin Scalia, Anthony Kennedy, Clarence Thomas, and Samuel Alito. The Jewish justices are Ruth Bader Ginsburg and Stephen Breyer.

15. Jan Crawford Greenburg, *Supreme Conflict: The Inside Story of the Struggle for Control of the United States Supreme Court* (New York: Penguin Press, 2007), 315.

16. Hanna Pitkin, *The Concept of Representation* (Berkeley: University of California Press, 1967), 61.

17. Frederick C. Mosher, *Democracy and the Public Service,* 2nd ed. (New York: Oxford University Press, 1982), 12–17.

18. *West Virginia State Board of Education v. Barnette,* 319 U.S. 624.

19. As quoted by Barbara A. Perry and Henry J. Abraham, "A 'Representative' Supreme Court? The Thomas, Ginsburg, and Breyer Appointments," *Judicature* 81, no. 4 (1998): 158.

20. See Ray Allen Billington, *The Protestant Crusade, 1800–1860: A Study of the Origins of American Nativism* (New York: Rinehart, 1938).

21. John Tracy Ellis, *American Catholicism,* 2nd ed. (Chicago: University of Chicago Press, 1969), 63.

22. Theodore Maynard, *The Story of American Catholicism* (New York: Macmillan, 1942), 282.

23. Perry, *A "Representative" Supreme Court?* 22–23.

24. Editorial, *New York Herald,* March 18, 1836.

25. Lawrence Fuchs, *John F. Kennedy and American Catholicism* (New York: Meredith Press, 1967), 58–59.

26. Robert D. Cross, *The Emergence of Liberal Catholicism in America* (Cambridge, MA: Harvard University Press, 1958), 35.

27. Matthew McDevitt, *Joseph McKenna: Associate Justice of the United States* (Washington, DC: Catholic University of America Press), 1–13, 20–21.

28. Perry, *A "Representative" Supreme Court?* 28–29.

29. Alpheus T. Mason, *William Howard Taft: Chief Justice* (New York: Simon and Schuster, 1965), 40.

30. Karen Icke Anderson, *William Howard Taft: An Intimate History* (New York: W.W. Norton, 1981), 192.

31. Gerald Shaughnessy, *Has the Immigrant Kept the Faith?* (New York: Macmillan, 1925), 166, 172.

32. Archie Butt, *Taft and Roosevelt: The Intimate Letters of Archie Butt, Military Aide,* vol. 2 (Garden City, NY: Doubleday, Doran, 1930), 757.

33. Perry, *A "Representative" Supreme Court?* 31–33.

34. George Q. Flynn, *American Catholics and the Roosevelt Presidency, 1932–1936* (Lexington: University of Kentucky Press, 1968), chapter 1.

35. Ibid., ix.

36. Ibid., 50–51.

37. Leo V. Kanawada Jr., *Franklin D. Roosevelt's Diplomacy and American Catholics, Italians, and Jews* (Ann Arbor: UMI Research Press, 1982), 47.

38. Flynn, *American Catholics and the Roosevelt Presidency,* 233.

39. Sydney Fine, *Frank Murphy: The Detroit Years,* vol. 1 (Ann Arbor: University of Michigan Press, 1974), 4–12; quotation in Fine, *Frank Murphy: The New Deal Years,* vol. 2 (Chicago: University of Chicago Press, 1979), 286.

40. Sydney Fine, *Frank Murphy: The Washington Years,* vol. 3 (Ann Arbor: University of Michigan Press, 1984), 130.

41. As quoted by Daniel F. Cleary, "Catholics and Politics," in *Catholicism in America* (New York: Harcourt, Brace, 1953), 138.

42. Fuchs, *John F. Kennedy and American Catholicism,* 151.

43. Ibid.

44. William J. Brennan Jr. (associate justice, Supreme Court of the United States), interview with author, April 1985.

45. Ibid.

46. Cleary, "Catholics and Politics," 97.

47. Editorial, *New York Times,* October 2, 1956.

48. Fuchs, *John F. Kennedy and American Catholicism,* 229.

49. Martin Marty (lecture at Rollins College, Winter Park, FL, September 22, 1988).

50. James Hennesey, *American Catholics: A History of the Roman Catholic Community in the United States* (New York: Oxford University Press, 1981), 237.

51. Rose Fitzgerald Kennedy, *Times to Remember* (Garden City, NY: Doubleday, 1974), 329.

52. All quotations taken from full text of speech posted on the U.S. State Department's International Information Programs website under "Address to Southern Baptist Leaders (1960) John F. Kennedy," available from usinfo.state.gov/usa/infousa/facts/democrac/66.html.

53. Perry, "Jefferson's Legacy to the Supreme Court," 196.

54. Nicholas A. Schneider, ed., *Religious Views of John F. Kennedy: In His Own Words* (St. Louis: B. Herder, 1965), 82–83.

55. 410 U.S. 113 (1973).

56. Perry, *A "Representative" Supreme Court?* 42.

57. A 1987 correspondence with Justice Scalia, on file with author.

58. *New York Times,* June 18, 1986.

59. *Louisville Record,* November 19, 1987.

60. Barbara A. Perry, "The Life and Death of the 'Catholic Seat' on the United States Supreme Court," *Journal of Law and Politics* 6, no.1 (Fall 1989): 91.

61. 505 U.S. 833.

62. 505 U.S. 577.

63. 515 U.S. 819.

64. Barbara A. Perry, "Clarence Thomas," in *"The Supremes": Essays on the Current Justices of the Supreme Court of the United States,* ed. Barbara A. Perry (New York: Peter Lang, 1999), 111.

65. 530 U.S. 793; 533 U.S. 188.

66. George W. Bush (in discussion with University of Louisville McConnell Scholars, Louisville, KY, March 2007).

67. "John G. Roberts Dossier," *Washington Post,* available from www.washingtonpost .com.html.

68. Robin Toner, "Catholics and the Court," *New York Times,* August 7, 2005.

69. For an excellent behind-the-scenes look at the Miers nomination, see Greenburg's *Supreme Conflict,* chapters 10 and 11.

70. "Samuel A. Alito, Jr. Profile," *Washington Post,* available from www.washingtonpost .com.html.

71. See note 61, above.

72. "Samuel A. Alito, Jr. Profile," *Washington Post.*

73. 465 U.S. 668.

74. Lynette Clemetson, "Alito Could Be 5th Catholic on Current Supreme Court," *New York Times,* November 1, 2005.

75. "Samuel Alito Supreme Court Nomination: Encyclopedia," available from http://en.allex perts.com.html.

76. 550 U.S. 833.

77. Joan Biskupic, "Court Backs Abortion Ban," *USA Today,* April 18, 2007.

78. 530 U.S. 914; Associated Press, "Supreme Court Upholds Ban on Abortion Procedure," *New York Times,* April 18, 2007.

79. Greenburg, *Supreme Conflict,* 246.

80. Jeffrey M. Jones, "Some Americans Reluctant to Vote for Mormon: Strong Support for Black, Women, Catholic Candidates," Gallup News Service, February 20, 2007, available from *www.galluppoll.com.* When Gallup first proposed the Catholic question in 1937, only 60 percent of those polled responded that they would vote for a Catholic for president. Just six months prior to the 1960 presidential election, that figure had risen to 71 percent. Eight months after Kennedy's inauguration, 82 percent of respondents affirmed that they would vote for a Catholic presidential candidate.

10

WHITE HOUSE OUTREACH
TO CATHOLICS

Thomas J. Carty

*I*N APRIL 2005 the Republican president, George W. Bush, knelt in front of the deceased Pope John Paul II, and by doing so, Bush became the first U.S. president to attend a papal funeral.[1] By November 2006 this precedent-setting sign of respect for Catholicism seemed a distant memory for American Catholics. As the Iraq war dominated headlines and required more money and lives, a majority of Catholic voters repudiated the Republicans in the 2006 midterm elections.[2] Was Bush's appeal to Catholics worth the effort? This chapter examines the methods, motives, and electoral impact of White House outreach to Catholics in order to understand better the role of religion in U.S. politics.

Presidents have increasingly appealed to Catholics as this group's demographic size and political power have grown. Representing 25 percent of the U.S. population, Catholics are the nation's largest religious denomination. Political observers have labeled the Catholic vote as a "barometer" for national, especially presidential, elections for several reasons.[3] Positioned in big cities within states that possess large numbers of Electoral College voters, Catholics have the potential to determine election results—especially in close contests. Furthermore, American Catholics demonstrate no consistent loyalty to either the Democrats or Republicans. In recent years, evangelical Protestants have solidified an alliance with the Grand Old Party (GOP), and secular atheists have gravitated toward the Democrats. Yet Catholics in the aggregate have acted independently by selecting candidates based on personalities or issues unique to a particular election year more than party platforms. Based on this group's geographic position and ideological diversity, as noted by Matthew J. Streb and Brian Frederick in chapter 6, many political scientists refer to American Catholics as a "swing vote."[4]

While one might identify many constituencies that display diverse and inconsistent voting patterns, the existence of specifically Catholic, nationally recognized institutions allows presidents to target this group directly. For example, the White House has utilized the nation's most recognized Catholic institution of higher education, Notre Dame University, as a platform to announce or discuss moral—or even specifically Catholic—issues. Presidents have also exercised the opportunity to negotiate directly with America's Catholic bishops in major U.S. cities (such as George Cardinal Mundelein and Joseph Cardinal Bernardin of Chicago, Francis Cardinal Spellman and John Cardinal O'Connor of New York, John Cardinal Krol of Philadelphia, and Theodore Cardinal McCarrick of Washington, D.C.), bishops holding positions of regional authority throughout the United States, or the U.S. Catholic Conference of Bishops, a centralized organization of the national church's leadership.

In the twentieth century, presidents increasingly sought more direct access to the Catholic Church's ultimate source of authority, the Holy See.[5] Beyond their religious authority, popes also reign politically over the Vatican, a sovereign state within Italy's geographic borders. Presidents have sent personal representatives to the Vatican, engaged in direct diplomacy with popes, and—since 1984—appointed official ambassadors to the Holy See. Presidential meetings with popes have provided public relations opportunities to appear statesmanlike and exercise "soft power" by exchanging good wishes and expressing the desire for interfaith harmony and world peace.[6] Behind the scenes, however, White House negotiators work to ensure that these events cultivate common cause rather than highlight the profound public policy differences that often arise between the chief executive of the world's most technologically powerful secular state and a religious patriarch steeped in theological tradition and protected by the Italian government and the Pontifical Swiss Guard.[7]

This discussion of presidential appeals to Catholics develops in four sections. The first examines how Democratic president Franklin D. Roosevelt aligned economic reforms with Catholic teaching, appointed unprecedented numbers of Catholics to executive offices, and utilized a personal envoy to improve dialogue with the Vatican. The second section reveals how Democratic and Republican presidents cultivated the Catholic Church as an ally against communism from 1945 to 1969, despite non-Catholic protests about the rise of Catholic power. Harry S. Truman, Dwight D. Eisenhower, John F. Kennedy, and Lyndon B. Johnson treated the Vatican as a valuable partner in the Judeo-Christian consensus against atheistic communism—especially in Vietnam—yet each president felt pressure to avoid any outreach that non-Catholics would interpret as violating the principal of church–state separation. The third section focuses on how Presidents Richard M. Nixon and Ronald Reagan appealed to Catholic voters by emphasizing abortion and federal aid to Catholic schools as issues of national significance and by opening more regular ties with the Vatican between 1969 and 1989. The last section compares and contrasts the presidency of George H. W. Bush, who offered little outreach to Catholics, with Presidents Bill Clinton and George W. Bush, who actively pursued common cause with the Catholic clergy and laity. While Clinton appealed to Catholic sympathy for immigrants and the poor, George W. Bush engaged Catholics on cultural issues—such as abortion, embryonic stem cell research, and federal partnership with religious charities. In conclusion, this chapter will consider how White House approaches to Catholic Americans have contributed to this community's sense of self-identity.

FRANKLIN D. ROOSEVELT, 1933–45

President Franklin D. Roosevelt mounted the first systematic White House appeal to Catholics in the United States. In the nineteenth century, Irish immigrants found common cause with the Democratic Party because agrarian white farmers of the U.S. South offered political leverage against the financial elites, anti-immigrant nativists, and evangelical Protestants who dominated the opposition Whig, Native American (or Know-Nothing), and Republican parties. Prior to Roosevelt, however, Democrats offered few rewards for this group's loyalty. Woodrow Wilson visited the pope in 1919, a precedent that no president repeated until 1959. Yet this symbolic gesture provided small compensation for the fact that two years before, Wilson had betrayed American Catholics, especially Irish and Germans, to whom he had pledged to avoid entry into World War I. Once the United States joined the war, Wilson sought total victory over illiberal European monarchs and ignored papal pursuit of a cessation of hostilities that would restore prewar borders.[8]

Franklin Roosevelt showed a remarkably greater respect for the role of Catholics. While campaigning for the presidency in 1932, Roosevelt quoted a papal encyclical to support his criticism of economic oligarchy and to defend his progressive economic program of expanded federal assistance to the underprivileged.[9] Using the power of presidential appointments, Roosevelt advanced the political careers of many Catholics. New York's James Farley received the position of postmaster general after serving as Roosevelt's campaign manager in the 1932 presidential race. Catholic businessman Joseph P. Kennedy raised $125,000 for Roosevelt, who rewarded him with positions as the first Securities and Exchange commissioner and later as ambassador to the Court of St. James.[10] When Roosevelt's choice for attorney general, Senator Thomas Walsh, died prior to taking the oath of office, the president appointed another Catholic, future Supreme Court justice Frank Murphy, as the nation's highest law enforcement official. Catholics represented 25 percent of FDR's judicial appointments compared with previous presidents, who had appointed Catholics at a rate of one in twenty-five.[11]

The Roosevelt administration carefully managed policy and public relations as a means of maintaining Catholic loyalty to the Democratic administration. When some conservative Catholics characterized his New Deal programs as communist threats to private property, Farley asked Chicago's George Cardinal Mundelein to affirm publicly that the administration had "no communistic tendencies."[12] Roosevelt further courted Catholics by adopting a neutral position regarding the Spanish Civil War when many liberal Democrats wanted the United States to support the anti-clerical resistance to fascist general Francisco Franco.[13] Roosevelt's attention to Catholic voters facilitated his 1936 landslide, which substantially exceeded his 1932 margin of victory. When the White House solicited letters from clergymen, the responses of Catholic priests overwhelmingly favored the New Deal (73 percent supported, 12 percent opposed, and 15 percent expressed neutrality).[14] As Roosevelt prepared to pursue a third term in 1940,

Catholics Joseph Kennedy and James Farley received consideration for the presidency. According to Farley's memoirs, Roosevelt lobbied Mundelein to make the case that a Catholic candidate would revive anti-Catholic sentiments.[15]

When the United States entered World War II, most Catholics rallied around the commander in chief. One notable exception, nationally broadcast radio priest Reverend James Gillis, believed that Roosevelt pressured the National Broadcast Corporation to cancel his radio program in 1942. Nonetheless, his antiwar voice as editor of *Catholic World* prompted no echoes in the mainstream Catholic publications *Commonweal*, *America*, and *Ave Maria*, which supported the war effort.[16] Indeed, Roosevelt worked with the Catholic Church during the war by supporting the appointment of battlefield chaplains and by sending a non-Catholic envoy, Myron Taylor, as his personal representative to the Vatican.[17]

In reaching out to the Catholic Church, Roosevelt offended some Democratic Party constituents who faulted Catholicism for refusing to respect America's constitutional barriers between church and state. While wartime pressure for unity stifled this interfaith conflict, peace left Roosevelt's successors to struggle with this continued suspicion of Catholicism. Postwar presidents nonetheless cultivated good relations with Catholics, especially by emphasizing the common cause of anticommunism.

INTERFAITH CONFLICT AND CONSENSUS IN THE EARLY COLD WAR, 1945–69

According to author Charles Morris, "A team of alien anthropologists would have reported that 1950s America was a Catholic country."[18] The prominence of Catholics in postwar public life complicated White House outreach to Catholics. Presidents Truman, Eisenhower, Kennedy, and Johnson appealed to Catholics during this period with some trepidation. Some non-Catholics warned that rising Catholic power threatened American freedom, especially the principle of church–state separation.[19] Fearful of the Catholic Church's superior experience in organization, these individuals and groups formed lobbying agencies, such as Protestants and Other Americans United for Separation of Church and State (POAU).[20] Due to this pressure, presidents proved unable to fulfill the Catholic Church's two primary objectives: the Vatican's pursuit of formal diplomatic ties with the United States, and U.S. Catholic bishops' request that the federal government aid public and Catholic schools in equal proportion. Yet these presidents viewed Catholics as an important element of America's anticommunist consensus and the Catholic Church as a critical ally in the U.S. struggle to stop communism and bring peace to Vietnam.

Harry Truman's inability to cultivate goodwill in the Catholic hierarchy contributed to the Democratic president's declining popularity after 1951. While continuing to send Myron Taylor, Roosevelt's personal envoy, to the Vatican, Truman publicly denied that he would appoint a permanent representative to the Holy See. After listening to a 1946 delegation of Protestant ministers who argued that the mission violated church–state separation by showing favoritism to a particular religious institution, Truman reiterated his intention to terminate Taylor's mission after resolving all war-related issues. The Catholic archbishop of New York, Francis Spellman, directed his disappointment at the ministers—"unhooded Klansmen sowing seeds of disunion within our treasured Nation"—rather than Truman.[21] The president continued to send Taylor to the Vatican until January 1950, when he resigned for personal health reasons.[22]

Although Truman appeared to fulfill Catholic wishes in January 1952 by nominating General Mark Clark as a permanent ambassador to the Vatican, the president quickly retreated when the Senate refused to vote on his nominee. Clark's removal of his name from consideration ended the effort so abruptly that Jesuit priest and historian Gerald Fogarty has suggested that Truman merely offered the nomination as an empty gesture to mollify Catholics. The Vatican had alerted the White House that it would not accept another temporary, personal representative, which would merely conceal America's refusal to grant full diplomatic legitimacy to the papal state. Having worked with the U.S. Department of State and the Central Intelligence Agency (CIA) to block the election of communists in Italy, the Vatican felt justified in calling for open recognition of the two states' working relationship.[23] The Senate deadlock, however, revealed election-year fears of an anti-Catholic backlash at the polls. Truman's proposal, serious or superficial, ultimately succumbed to the lobbying success of the POAU.[24]

While Truman's successor, Dwight Eisenhower, avoided the issue of an ambassador to the Vatican, he cultivated Catholics as important components of America's interfaith consensus against atheistic communism. Even prior to receiving the Republican Party's presidential nomination, Eisenhower took an opportunity to ingratiate himself with Catholics. Addressing a three-day Spiritual Life Conference in The Netherlands in May 1952, Eisenhower praised the Catholic Church's opposition to "that evil thing—communism" (although he made sure to precede his remark by pointedly emphasizing his outsider status as a "convinced, nearly fanatic Protestant"). Upon becoming president, Eisenhower made further small but meaningful gestures to the Catholic Church. He seemed to reserve the secretary of labor position for a Catholic.[25] When a Catholic men's lay organization, the Knights of Columbus, lobbied Congress to add "under God" to the Pledge of Allegiance, Eisenhower signed a bill that fulfilled this ambition.[26] Upon the celebration of Pope Pius XII's eightieth birthday in 1956, Eisenhower sent a personal envoy to represent the United States. While the Vatican had previously requested a formal ambassador or none at all, the pope graciously accepted the first representative from the United States in nearly six years. Eisenhower's reelection only months later proved that the public in the United States perceived no serious danger from informal diplomatic contact with the Vatican. Many Catholics appreciated Eisenhower's effort enough to give him nearly 50 percent of their votes in 1956.

The Catholic Church figured significantly in Eisenhower's goal of creating a South Vietnamese government that would serve as an anticommunist bulwark. Eisenhower's secretary of state, John Foster Dulles, whose son converted to Catholicism and became a Catholic priest (and has since become an important Catholic theologian and a cardinal), encouraged the rise of a Catholic leader of that predominantly Buddhist region.[27] Dulles and Ambassador Claire Booth Luce, a Catholic convert, attended Pius XII's 1958 funeral, and Eisenhower himself visited the Vatican in 1959. At the Notre

Dame University graduation in that same year, the president expressed a great desire to meet the Catholic medical doctor Tom Dooley, who authored articles and books publicizing (and exaggerating, as historians have recently discovered), the plight of Vietnamese Catholics in the communist North.[28] Eisenhower's outreach to Catholics may seem modest today, but it was significant in an age when Dr. Fred Schwarz, founder of the Christian Anti-Communism Crusade, categorically rejected a formal alliance with Catholic anticommunist Phyllis Schlafly because her church "might be suspect" among his predominantly evangelical Protestant membership.[29]

While the Democratic Party's nomination and election of the nation's first Catholic president temporarily reversed the swing of Catholics toward the Republican Party, Kennedy missed an opportunity to solidify his party's alliance with his church. Having encountered anxious and outspoken resistance during the campaign from many Americans who feared Catholic power, Kennedy pledged repeatedly to avoid any favoritism toward his church. In particular, he promised to oppose both federal aid to Catholic schools and the appointment of an ambassador to the Vatican. Pressure groups, such as the POAU, anxiously monitored Kennedy's actions to ensure that he fulfilled these commitments.[30]

As president, Kennedy did not advance any new initiatives in White House outreach to Catholics. When his brother-in-law, Sargent Shriver, an active Catholic, suggested the Irish-sounding name Robert S. McNamara for secretary of defense, the president-elect required assurance that he was not Catholic prior to approving his nomination.[31] When Congress considered a bill to aid education in early 1961, the POAU opposed federal grants to Catholic and other religious schools. In response, the National Catholic Welfare Conference (NCWC) requested an alternative: the inclusion of low-interest loans for parochial schools. Without this provision, New York archbishop Francis Cardinal Spellman argued, the legislation would discriminate against families who chose a "God-centered education" for their children.[32] When Kennedy refused to advocate this compromise in public, however, other Catholic politicians endorsed a bill that would aid public schools and exclude Catholic educational institutions. Only Catholic representative James Delaney (D-NY), one of eight Democrats on the fifteen-member House Rules Committee, agreed with Spellman's view. Since seven Republicans on the committee opposed permanent federal aid to teachers' salaries as an inappropriate expansion of the national government's authority, Delaney's refusal to vote for the bill in committee doomed the measure to defeat by a margin of eight to seven.[33]

Despite his fear of confirming suspicions of Catholic power, Kennedy continued Eisenhower's precedent of direct diplomacy between presidents and popes. Kennedy's decision to visit the Vatican became easier after the enthusiastic media response to Pope John XXIII's papal encyclical *Pacem in terris* (April 11, 1963), which opposed the stockpiling of weapons and advocated a greater United Nations role in the cold war. According to the *New York Times,* this encyclical persuaded even anticlerical Catholics, Protestants, and Jews to perceive the Catholic Church as breaking with "stagnant or reactionary forces with which it often has found itself in alliance in underdeveloped societies."[34] The *Washington Post* praised this pope as "one of the enlightened philosophers and moral leaders of his time" and counseled Kennedy to see the pontiff during his previously scheduled visit to Europe.[35] After the pope's sudden illness and death, Kennedy met with the newly installed Pope Paul VI on July 2, 1963. Rather than follow traditional Catholic practice and kneel to kiss the pope's ring (which "would get me a lot of votes in South Carolina," mused Kennedy sarcastically to aide Kenneth P. O'Donnell), the nation's first Catholic president shook hands with the Vatican state's leader.[36] Although Kennedy's policies had offended Catholic leaders such as Spellman, the president's longtime ally, Boston's Richard Cardinal Cushing, embraced him with a big hug "followed by a friendly left jab and right hook to the ribs."[37] While Kennedy's death made him a martyr for many Catholics, he never established a common cause between the Democratic Party and the Catholic Church that might have promulgated a long-term political alliance.

While Lyndon Johnson pursued cooperation with the Catholic Church, the destructiveness of U.S. actions in the Vietnam War alienated the Vatican and many Catholics. Despite Catholicism's consistent anticommunism, popes voiced grave fears of U.S. military power, and especially of nuclear weapons, following World War II.[38] In his first month as president, Johnson sent a letter to Pope Paul VI with John Kennedy's brother-in-law, Sargent Shriver, in which he expressed a desire to meet the pontiff.[39] Before the pope arrived in the United States as a guest of the United Nations secretary-general U Thant, Johnson made elaborate plans to avoid appearing to favor one religious leader over others. Because the U.S. government did not officially recognize the Vatican's status as a sovereign state, the president would show deference by going around normal diplomatic protocol through pursuit of a special meeting with the Catholic Church's institutional and spiritual leader. Johnson therefore agreed to be in New York's Waldorf-Astoria Hotel during the pope's trip through Manhattan. In this way, it would appear that Pope Paul VI had initiated the unofficial summit by visiting Johnson's suite.[40] These strainings of international norms demonstrated both Johnson's exceptional outreach as well as the continued suspicion of Catholic power in the United States.

Despite Johnson's appeals to the pope, Paul VI held little sway over the president's Vietnam policy. On October 4, 1965, the pope passionately denounced war before the United Nations, saying, "No more war; never again war."[41] Less than four months later, on January 31, 1966, Johnson revived the strategy of bombing North Vietnam while claiming to be in "full sympathy" with the pontiff, who had recently repeated his appeal for peace.[42] When Johnson visited the Vatican on December 23, 1967 to ask the pope to pressure South Vietnamese leader Nguyen Van Thieu (a Catholic who followed a long line of failed presidents after Ngo Dinh Diem's death in 1963) to negotiate with North Vietnam, contemporary news reports portrayed this meeting as tense. *Time* magazine reporter Wilton Wynn alleged that Johnson irritated the pope by his hastily arranged helicopter landing in the Vatican gardens (to avoid Rome's automobile traffic). Already angered by Johnson's heavy bombing of Hanoi on December 13 and 14, the pope supposedly "slammed his hand on to his desk and shouted at Johnson."[43]

Prominent American Catholic critics of Johnson's Vietnam policy further undermined his appeal to Catholics. Eugene McCarthy, a U.S. senator from Minnesota who challenged Johnson for the 1968 Democratic presidential nomination, denounced Johnson's militaristic response to communism in a late 1967 interview with the

Jesuit magazine, *America:* "Everything the Church seems to have given up at Vatican II has now been picked up by the Pentagon and the Administration. The Church has more or less said holy wars are out."[44]

White House outreach to Catholics remained very controversial in the early cold war period, but presidents established the precedent of appealing to Catholic anticommunism. Opposition to Truman's appointment of an official ambassador to the Vatican demonstrated the restraints that the president faced in coordinating U.S. policy with Catholicism. Yet Eisenhower clarified the Catholic Church's importance within America's Judeo-Christian coalition against communism. His decision to meet with the pope set a precedent that each subsequent president has imitated. While Kennedy and Johnson recognized how the Vatican's global network, especially in Vietnam, made courting Catholicism critical to U.S. foreign policy, these Democratic presidents largely ignored the Catholic hierarchy's appeals for an end to the war in Vietnam and for executive support of federal assistance to Catholic schools. In the 1970s and 1980s, Republican presidents would exploit this opportunity for creating connections between the GOP and Catholics.

CATHOLICS AND THE LATE COLD WAR, 1969–89

Republican presidents Richard Nixon and Ronald Reagan orchestrated appeals to Catholics that resulted in a temporary political realignment among their Church's membership. While Nixon's foreign policy mirrored Johnson's, he sought common cause with Catholics on federal aid to Catholic schools and opposition to abortion. Republican Gerald Ford and Democrat Jimmy Carter both engaged the Catholic Church through meetings with the pope but not with specific issues. Reagan completed Nixon's efforts to cultivate Catholics by appointing several of the Church's members to high-level offices and by sending an official ambassador to the Vatican. Despite some Catholic discomfort with Reagan's reliance on military strength in dealing with communism, his lobbying on behalf of aid to Catholic schools and against abortion greatly pleased the Catholic hierarchy.

In 1969 Richard Nixon pointedly sought to improve relations with the Vatican and the Catholic Church. Nixon's political history demonstrated his great willingness to work with Catholics. The Reverend John F. Cronin, a Catholic priest and a National Catholic Welfare Conference expert on communism, wrote Nixon's speeches for twenty years.[45] As president, Nixon appointed a Jesuit priest, the Reverend John McLaughlin, as a speechwriter and special assistant. Mere months into his administration, Nixon met with Pope Paul VI. While tensions about the U.S. war in Vietnam remained high, Nixon showed a strong desire to ingratiate himself with the pope. Altering his schedule to coincide with the end of a papal retreat, Nixon made two trips to Rome in order to see Pope Paul VI on his second stop. The pope's official remarks admonished Nixon to bring about "total cessation of those conflicts now unfortunately in progress."[46] Nixon's earnest attempts to lighten the mood with ironic humor obliquely referred to the civil strife in the United States generated by the war. Nixon quipped that he would visit the Vatican's North American college, a seminary for

Catholic priests, because it was "one of the few college campuses I could go without a demonstration against me."[47] Even when Nixon spoke seriously about how economic growth had provided educational and employment opportunities for youth, a young seminarian whispered that many of these young people would travel as soldiers to Vietnam, according to the *New York Times* report on the meeting.[48]

Vietnam persuaded the Republican president to revisit the notion of sending a personal envoy to the Vatican. Less than a year after publicly denying that he would send a full-time ambassador to the Vatican, Nixon appointed Henry Cabot Lodge to this position on an informal basis in 1970. Both sides appeared to see benefit from this decision, which made Lodge the first regular ambassador to the Vatican since Roosevelt sent Myron Taylor in 1939. The Vatican acceded to this informal relationship (despite its previous opposition to any further unofficial appointments) because it gave the pope the opportunity to call American attention to the need for peace and the plight of poor nations. Nixon hoped that Lodge, who had served as Kennedy's ambassador to Vietnam, could obtain diplomatic victories, such as the release of prisoners of war, through dealing with the Vatican, which retained loose relations with the government in North Vietnam.[49] The mission seemed to dissipate the controversy around the appointment of an ambassador to the Vatican as evidenced by a 1971 *New York Times* headline favorably describing Lodge's privileged access to the pope as "enviable."[50] While seeking détente with the Soviet Union, Nixon also engineered the thawing of a long-standing diplomatic "cold war" with the Holy See.

The Republican president also successfully appealed to Catholics on domestic issues that had achieved national prominence in recent years. In the 1960 campaign against Kennedy, Nixon endorsed government aid to Catholic schools. This position failed to secure him Catholic votes largely because the issue remained in the hands of state and local governments.[51] With the expansion of federal aid to education in the 1960s, Catholic schools found themselves in competition with public institutions that benefited from the vast largesse of the U.S. Treasury. In late 1971 and early 1972, Nixon pledged to prevent Catholic school closings and advocated federal assistance for these institutions. Nixon campaigned on this issue in heavily Catholic New York City and Philadelphia.[52]

Even before the Supreme Court's *Roe vs. Wade* decision made abortion a national issue in 1973, Nixon aligned himself with Catholics opposed to the legalization of this procedure. When the president's Commission on Population Growth and the American Future included the practice among other methods of family planning, Nixon explicitly and publicly declared abortion "an unacceptable form of population control." After New York's Catholic archbishop, Terence Cardinal Cooke, protested the state's decision to decriminalize abortion, Nixon wrote the cardinal to express solidarity with his position. The majority of Nixon's campaign team discouraged the president from entering this controversial debate about a local issue. Yet Nixon followed the counsel of two aides, Protestant Charles Colson and Catholic Patrick J. Buchanan, who would become generals of conservatism's culture wars into the next century. Cooke's decision to publish Nixon's letter helped distinguish the Republican candidate from Democratic nominee George McGovern in the eyes of American Catholics.[53]

Democratic politicians expressed frustration with Nixon's ability to court Catholics without political penalty. One Democrat noted the double standard that had prevented John Kennedy from appealing to Catholics in the same manner: "Can you imagine the uproar if Kennedy had come out for parochial school aid or put a Jesuit on his staff or sent that abortion letter to the Cardinal?"[54] Yet Nixon fearlessly appealed to Catholic leaders while Democratic presidents tread softly around church–state issues. "Nixon's done everything except say mass," joked New York's Queens County Democratic chairman.[55] In 1972 the Democratic presidential nominee, George McGovern, selected Kennedy's Catholic brother-in-law, Sargent Shriver, for vice-president. Despite this inclusion of a Catholic on the Democrats' ticket, and despite the fact that Catholics were registered 60 percent Democratic, Nixon became the first Republican to win a majority of the Catholic vote, with 53 percent. Only 26 percent of Catholics voted for McGovern.[56]

Watergate and the continued war in Vietnam prevented the Republican president from expanding upon these alliances with Catholics in his second term. Even prior to the scandal that prompted his resignation, Nixon engendered outspoken Catholic opposition for the continued bombing of North Vietnam. Only weeks after Nixon's landslide reelection, Pope Paul VI decried U.S. military violence. While the Vatican carefully avoided a direct confrontation with the president, the pope seized the opportunity of a cessation in hostilities to speak on December 31, 1972 of "his profound bitterness" and "the shocked reaction of human—not to say, Christian—conscience" upon learning of "the horror" of the most recent U.S. assault on North Vietnam.[57] Philadelphia's John Cardinal Krol, president of the National Conference of Catholic Bishops, expressed "grief and dismay" about the "recourse to violent force and massive bombing in Vietnam."[58] The exposure of Nixon's efforts to suppress illegality among his campaign staff further eroded his stature among Catholics.

Although Gerald Ford and Jimmy Carter both met with popes, neither extended Nixon's aggressive outreach to Catholics. Ford maintained Lodge as a personal envoy to the Vatican, yet Carter returned the Catholic vote to the Democratic Party in 1976—with a 57 percent Catholic majority. Carter became the first president to choose a Catholic to serve as his personal representative to the Vatican. In 1978, however, Carter betrayed a campaign pledge to support aid to Catholic schools by opposing a bill that would have provided federal tuition tax credits to parents whose children attended nonpublic schools.[59] Furthermore, Carter's 1979 meeting with Pope John Paul II served merely to expose the vast difference in political savoir faire that separated the two men. Perhaps referring to Carter's tendency to pontificate, the president's Polish-born national security adviser, Zbigniew Brzezinski, recalled, "My impression was that the Pope would have made a wonderful politician and Jimmy Carter would have made a wonderful Pope."[60] John Kennedy's brother, Edward, challenged the president in the 1980 Democratic presidential primaries and won the Catholic vote in Massachusetts, New York, and Pennsylvania. Carter secured his party's presidential nomination with more Catholic voters than Kennedy in New Hampshire, Florida, Illinois, and Wisconsin.[61] Yet Republican nominee Ronald Reagan won 51 percent of Catholics in the general election, and Carter's Catholic percentage dropped nearly 20 points from his 1976 result.[62]

Ronald Reagan built upon Nixon's precedents in soliciting Catholic support for his presidency. Once a Democrat, this Republican politician entered the Oval Office as the president with the closest personal connection to Catholicism since John Kennedy. Reagan was the son of a Catholic father, and his oldest brother was baptized Catholic. After divorcing his first wife Jane Wyman, she converted to Catholicism and raised their two children as Catholics.[63] The new administration included Catholics as national security adviser (Richard V. Allen and later William Clark), CIA director (William J. Casey), ambassadors (such as Vernon Walters and Faith Whittlesey), and speechwriters (including Tony Dolan and Peggy Noonan). Reagan targeted Catholic audiences in presenting his political vision. At the University of Notre Dame in 1981, Reagan revived Eisenhower's emphasis on Catholicism's critical role in the Judeo-Christian consensus against communism, which he predicted would fall if Western nations united behind "our civilized ideas, our traditions, our values" against the "ideology and war machine of totalitarian societies."[64] After surviving an assassination attempt, Reagan interpreted his presidential responsibility as God's will. "Look how the evil forces were put in our way and how Providence intervened," Reagan told Pope John Paul II.[65] Several Catholics, such as Mother Theresa and Cardinal Cooke, reaffirmed this view during meetings with the president.[66]

Despite these appeals to Catholics, Reagan encountered outspoken opposition from U.S. Catholic bishops toward his core principles of military strength, uncompromising anticommunism, and economic neoliberalism. In 1982 Archbishop Joseph L. Bernardin of Chicago led a committee of five bishops in preparing a pastoral letter for the National Conference of Catholic Bishops (NCCB) that sharply challenged Reagan's foreign policy. The media actively publicized this anticipated document because the bishops' powerful moral commentary would raise national security policy to the forefront of the American Catholic Church's teaching. Many Catholic Democrats, such as Edward Kennedy, enthusiastically endorsed the NCCB's two principal messages: (1) calling the U.S. government to halt testing and production of nuclear weapons, popularly known as a nuclear "freeze," and (2) imploring the administration to make a "no first use" pledge never to initiate the use of nuclear weapons. "No Christian can rightfully carry out orders or policies deliberately aimed at killing noncombatants," read a copy of the proposed letter in 1982.[67] This statement represented Bernardin's mission to refashion the U.S. Catholic Church as, in his words, a "peace church."[68] Only months later, NCCB president Archbishop John R. Roach of St. Paul and Minneapolis complained to Reagan about members of his administration who criticized Catholic aid to communists in Central America. Just prior to a visit to this region by the pope, Vice-President George H. W. Bush and Secretary of State George P. Shultz suggested that Catholic priests were supporting Marxist revolution in El Salvador and neighboring nations. According to Roach, Catholic priests in Latin America confronted "human, moral issues" and a theology of a "conscious 'option for the poor'" rather than promoting a political or military ideology.[69] Reagan's aggressive plans to confront, and even roll back, communism in favor of capitalism seemed destined to clash with the NCCB's support of détente, peaceful coexistence, and a theology of liberation, which tolerated socialist restraint of free markets.

Yet Reagan engaged the bishops in dialogue and sought common cause with the NCCB's cultural agenda. In an August 1982 speech to the Knights of Columbus and U.S. bishops in Hartford, Connecticut, Reagan rejected the freeze and no first use doctrines, explained his justification for maintaining a nuclear deterrent, and then outlined issues where the administration and the bishops might work together. Reagan's list expanded upon the mutual agreements that Nixon had earlier established with the Catholic hierarchy on opposition to abortion and support for federal tax credits for families who send their children to Catholic schools. Reagan also expressed support for a constitutional amendment to end the Supreme Court's ban on prayer in public schools and for stronger regulations on obscenity in the media.[70]

When the U.S. Catholic bishops continued to resist Reagan's foreign policy, however, the president changed tactics and pursued formal diplomacy with the supreme leader of global Catholicism—Pope John Paul II. By appointing an official, full-time ambassador to the Vatican in 1984, Reagan gained political leverage with U.S. Catholic bishops and granted the Vatican a wish that popes had harbored for decades. Direct presidential access to the pope now allowed Reagan to circumvent the American hierarchy. Reagan increasingly justified policies by citing Pope John Paul II, whose European and specifically Polish origins and residency contributed to a less compromising attitude toward communism than that of the U.S. bishops. The pope shared Reagan's characterization of the Soviet Union as an "evil empire," having endured life with sharply curtailed freedoms in Nazi- and Soviet-occupied Poland during his formative years. While American bishops viewed nuclear weapons as a direct threat to American cities, European bishops—particularly the French and Germans—tended to welcome the threat of U.S. nuclear weapons as a deterrent to a Soviet invasion of Western Europe with conventional forces.[71] The pope's hard-line anticommunism, especially regarding Central America, allowed Reagan to disregard the American bishops' criticism of his weapons buildup.[72]

Reagan reaped the political rewards of this skillful maneuvering in the Catholic community during the 1984 campaign. While the American bishops might oppose the U.S. mission at the Holy See, "rank-and-file Roman Catholics are pleased," observed the assistant to the president for public liaison Faith Ryan Whittlesey, a Catholic.[73] In May, Reagan enjoyed a meeting and photo opportunities sure to impress Catholics by waiting an extra night to confer with Pope John Paul II as both men stopped in Alaska for refueling during trips to Asia.[74] While the NCCB remained neutral, individual bishops who favored Reagan openly campaigned for the president. In states pivotal for the Electoral College vote, Reagan stood beside Bishop Edward Head of Buffalo, New York; John Cardinal Krol of Philadelphia; and Archbishop Peter L. Gerety of Newark, New Jersey. Even legendary Catholic entertainer Frank Sinatra (who sang John Kennedy's theme song, "High Hopes," in the 1960 campaign) appeared in support of Reagan. Making no references to the NCCB's call for a nuclear freeze, Reagan defended his militant anticommunism with a reference to Pope John Paul II, saying "in Central America, we are rather more inclined to listen to the testimony of his holiness the Pope than the claims of the Communist Sandinistas."[75]

These Catholic clergy emphasized cultural issues by directly and indirectly endorsing Reagan. Cardinal Krol delivered the invocation at the Republican National Convention and introduced Reagan at a campaign rally before a Roman Catholic shrine by praising the president's support for federal tax credits to religious schools. Even though politicians such as Catholic Democrat Daniel Patrick Moynihan, a supporter of tax credit legislation, blamed Reagan for introducing it too late in his first term, Krol echoed Cardinal Spellman's strong lobbying for aid to parochial schools by arguing that Reagan's "sustained effort [served to] reduce and eliminate the ugly blemish of injustice and discrimination" against parents who sent children to Catholic schools.[76] Archbishop Bernard Law of Boston characterized the 1.5 million abortions performed annually as America's "key [political] issue."[77] Bishop James Timlin of Scranton, Pennsylvania, and New York Archbishop John O'Connor both publicly rebuked the Democratic Party's vice-presidential nominee, Geraldine Ferraro, a Catholic, for ignoring her church's teaching by advocating the legalization of abortion. At one Reagan rally in heavily Catholic Scranton, a sign read, "FERRARO—A CATHOLIC JUDAS."[78]

A majority of Catholics and non-Catholics accepted the president's justification of his outreach to those who sympathized with his religious views. When Catholic Democrats warned against the dangers of mixing personal faith and public policy, Reagan defended his moralism by referring to the first saint of American civil religion, George Washington, who claimed that the nation could not maintain morality and decency without religion. Reagan believed that politicians possessed the right to approach religious groups as they would any organization, saying, "when I'm addressing an audience who share my own religious beliefs . . . I see nothing wrong with talking of our mutual interests."[79] While Reagan actively cultivated Catholics, Democratic presidential nominee Walter Mondale canceled a speaking engagement at the New York Archdiocese's annual Alfred E. Smith dinner only days prior to the election. On Election Day 1984, 55 percent of Catholics supported Reagan, a two-percentage-point improvement upon Nixon's record Republican success among this constituency in 1972.[80]

Presidents Nixon and Reagan successfully found common cause with Catholics on several issues. Although Nixon's refusal to curtail bombing in Vietnam alienated many Catholics, especially in the Church's hierarchy, he appealed to Catholics by focusing national attention on two of the bishops' domestic goals—opposition to abortion and federal aid to Catholic schools. Both presidents improved diplomatic ties with the Vatican, culminating in Reagan's establishment of an official ambassador to the Holy See. This cooperation neutralized American Catholic opposition to Reagan's militant anticommunism and allowed Reagan to renew Nixon's engagement with the Catholic bishops' domestic agenda of limiting abortions and obtaining financial support for Church institutions. George H. W. Bush failed to expand upon these efforts, and Bill Clinton mounted active outreach to restore Catholic confidence in a Democratic president. Although George W. Bush paid much more attention to Catholics, the events of September 11, 2001, served to divide the White House and the Holy See on the issue of international security.

CATHOLICS AND THE POST–COLD WAR WORLD, 1989–2007

Of the three post–cold war presidents, two actively pursued dialogue and compromise with Catholics. From 1989 to 1993, George H. W. Bush mostly undermined the bonds that Reagan had established with Catholic leaders. Democrat Bill Clinton demonstrated a great desire to align his policies with the Catholic Church from 1993 to 2001, even though he would not compromise his fundamental disagreement with the Catholic hierarchy regarding abortion. George W. Bush's alignment with the Catholic hierarchy's positions on abortion and education most resembled Reagan's, yet the president and the pope disagreed distinctly on issues of war and peace.

Regarding outreach to Catholics, President George H. W. Bush clearly lacked, as he once said about his presidency in general, "the vision thing." Bush's words and actions betrayed little genuine support for the issues on which Reagan cultivated members of the Catholic laity and hierarchy alike. While Bush met Pope John Paul II in the first months of his presidency, the two men shared none of the camaraderie that animated this pope's political bond with Reagan.[81]

In foreign policy Bush made little effort to avoid open clashes with the Catholic hierarchy about his active deployment of U.S. military force. When the Panamanian leader, General Manuel Antonio Noriega, fled an invading U.S. Army and sought asylum in the Vatican embassy, the American military blockaded and bombarded the building with loud, thematic rock music (such as "Smugglers Blues," "Nowhere to Run," and "Voodoo Chile"). While the White House characterized this technological and psychological warfare as "fairly standard practice," the Vatican portrayed the actions as "ludicrous" and "childish" violations of international law and diplomatic norms. Describing the United States as "an occupying power," the Vatican demanded to negotiate with a legitimate Panamanian government. According to a Vatican official speaking on condition of anonymity, "The Americans have said they want to restore constitutional and democratic rule in Panama, but on the first major issue faced by the new Government there, they are stepping in and saying in effect, 'Give Noriega to us because we are in charge here.' I am afraid it is a bit contradictory."[82] Also, the pope spoke against Bush's use of military force in the Persian Gulf in 1990. Bush made no effort to dissuade the pope from this position, as evidenced by Secretary of State James Baker's failure to visit with Pope John Paul II despite frequent visits to the Persian Gulf and the Middle East in the months prior to the 1991 Gulf War.[83]

On the issues of abortion and federal aid to children in Catholic schools, Bush showed little ability, nor even intention, to maintain the political coalition with American Catholics that Nixon and Reagan had created. While these previous Republican presidents had pleased many Catholics by raising these topics to national consciousness, Bush demonstrated uncertain commitment to these causes. On the subject of federal tax credits for families with children in nonpublic schools, Bush dashed Catholic hopes. Although Bush endorsed this idea of parental "choice" in the 1988 campaign, he shockingly reversed this position in one of his first statements as president in March 1989: "Everybody should support the public school system and then, if on top of that your parents think that they want to shell out, in addition to the tax money, tuition money, that's their right. But I don't think they should get a break for that."[84] After Democratic gains in the 1990 midterm elections, Bush halfheartedly returned to lobbying for federal aid to nonpublic schools. Seventy percent of the public now favored this position, yet Bush never appealed for popular pressure against the National Education Association, the powerful public school teachers' union that sought to protect its monopoly on federal funding. In one presidential debate, Bush even retreated from the issue in deference to budgetary constraints, saying "tax credits is a good idea, but . . . there isn't enough money around when we're operating at these enormous deficits to do that."[85]

Bush appeared largely tone deaf to the themes with which Reagan animated many Catholic clerics and laypersons. When addressing Notre Dame's graduating class in May 1992, a presidential election year, Bush avoided explicitly religious themes and delivered a secular, political defense of "family values" as an alternative to big government.[86] His speech failed to resonate with those Catholics who supported Patrick Buchanan's challenge to the president in the Republican primaries. After making peace with Bush and rallying behind him at the GOP National Convention, Buchanan called on Americans to reaffirm traditional religious values in "a culture war as critical to the kind of nation we shall be as the cold war itself." Although Buchanan claimed "George Bush is on our side," the president refused to fight that war.[87] In a television interview, Bush claimed that he would support a granddaughter's decision to have an abortion. Bush's wife Barbara publicly called abortion a "personal thing," which she would have removed from the Republican platform.[88] Offering no support to those Catholics who sought compatibility between religious principle and political action, Bush (who had received 54 percent of the Catholic vote in 1988) secured only 36 percent of Catholics in his 1992 defeat.[89]

Bush's opponent in the 1992 campaign, Bill Clinton, pursued areas of agreement with Catholics despite the incompatibility of his agenda with some traditional Catholic positions, such as opposition to abortion and support for federal aid to Catholic institutions. Educated at Georgetown University, a Jesuit institution, Clinton felt confident about how to appeal for Catholic support. In an address to Notre Dame students only months after Bush's commencement speech, Clinton pointedly utilized the language of religious morality to offer Catholics a political alternative to the cultural appeal of Reagan and Buchanan. New York Times reporter Gwen Ifill described Clinton's speech as "confessional" and "like a homily to the converted."[90] Clinton appealed to Catholic sympathy for the disadvantaged by articulating the need for government aid to the poor: "If we truly believe that children are God's most precious creation, then surely we owe every child born in the U.S.A. the chance to make the most of his or her God-given potential."[91] Clinton carefully touched upon his disagreement with church teaching on abortion by quoting a woman who had adopted an AIDS-infected baby: "I respect this debate we are having in this country about life, but how I wish we would reach out and help the living."[92] Clinton's rhetorical flourish helped him win the Catholic vote in 1992.[93]

While the recurring issue of abortion threatened Clinton's goal of reaching out to Catholics, the new president engaged Catholics on several social welfare issues. President Clinton consistently acted to extend abortion rights, culminating with a 1996 veto of a bill that would have banned a late-term abortion procedure that pro-life groups characterized as "partial-birth abortion." The Vatican called Clinton's decision "shameful" and New York's Catholic bishops accused the president of defending "infanticide."[94] At the United Nations International Conference on Population and Development in 1994, the Vatican had pointedly accused the Clinton administration of seeking to enshrine abortion as a universal right.[95] Yet in that same year, Clinton pursued closer connections between U.S. and Vatican economic assistance programs while the Republican Congress planned to curtail funding for foreign aid.[96] The Catholic Church supported Clinton's ambitions to provide government assistance to the poor and immigrants, and the president provided high-profile assistance to the majority-Catholic nations Ireland, Poland, and Mexico.[97] In the 1996 election, 53 percent of Catholics supported Clinton even though that same percentage had voted Republican in the 1994 midterm elections.[98] In January 1999 Clinton even obtained a meeting and photo opportunity with Pope John Paul II, although two papal knights—House Judiciary Committee chairperson Henry J. Hyde and chief investigative counsel for the committee David P. Schippers—were preparing the case for the president's eventual impeachment.[99]

While Clinton loosened the bonds Ronald Reagan had tied between the Republican Party and Catholic bishops, George W. Bush immediately set about recreating that political connection. Bush's brother, Florida governor Jeb Bush, had converted to Catholicism upon marrying a Mexican American Catholic. In the 2000 campaign, however, George W. Bush revived memories of his father's alienation of Catholics. Catholics (such as *New Republic* editor Andrew Sullivan) and non-Catholics (especially Bush's Republican primary opponent John McCain) berated the younger Bush's decision to speak at Bob Jones University, whose founder characterized Catholicism as "the religion of the Antichrist and a satanic system."[100] Yet most Catholics, especially the American Church's bishops, quickly forgave Bush, who apologized in the form of a letter to New York's Cardinal O'Connor, the longtime critic of those Catholic Democrats, such as Ferarro, who supported abortion.[101] Bush appealed to Catholic voters by defending the Vatican's observer status at the United Nations from critics of the Church's anti-abortion activism.[102] Catholic cardinals Edward Egan of New York, Anthony Bevilacqua of Philadelphia, and Bernard Law of Boston each joined Bush's campaign rallies and admonished Catholics in pastoral letters to vote for anti-abortion candidates.[103] Although Bush won the presidency with only 47 percent of the Catholic vote (he won a slight majority of white Catholic voters) in 2000, he continued to pursue high visibility with Catholic bishops. Less than a week after taking the oath of office, Bush dined at the District of Columbia's cardinal-designate Theodore McCarrick's residence with the papal nuncio and two other Catholic bishops. The Catholic bishops responded enthusiastically to Bush's creation of a White House Office of Faith-based and Community Initiatives, which they believed would help the church improve its hospitals and charitable social programs within its mission of exposing people to Christ's message.[104]

Bush's early decisions as president suggested that he greatly respected Catholic moral teaching. Even during the campaign, Bush sought instruction in Catholic social doctrine from the Reverend Richard Neuhaus, a Catholic convert and author and editor of a religious periodical, *First Things;* John DiIulio, University of Pennsylvania professor of politics; and Deal Hudson, editor of the conservative Catholic lay publication *Crisis.* He appointed Catholics as secretary of the Department of Health and Human Services (Tommy Thompson), secretary of the Department of Housing and Urban Development (Mel Martinez), and head of the Department of Homeland Security (Tom Ridge). Bush later promoted Catholics within his administration to attorney general (Alberto Gonzalez) and director of national intelligence (John Negro-ponte).[105] In a 2001 commencement address at Notre Dame University, Bush echoed Clinton's sermonizing style. While presenting his program for federal funding of faith-based charities, Bush cited "God's special concern for the poor" and Catholic layperson Dorothy Day, whose faith motivated her to dedicate her life to the poverty stricken.[106] Most significantly, Bush acted in accordance with the wishes of Pope John Paul II, who implored the president in a July 2001 meeting to prevent Congress from authorizing the creation of human embryos for experimental research. The pope's pleading appeared to contribute to the only veto of Bush's first term (of a bill passed by a Republican-dominated Congress with the support of many of Bush's evangeli-cal Protestant constituents).[107]

September 11's terrorist attacks greatly distracted Bush from this Catholic out-reach, however, by leading him into two wars upon which the Vatican frowned. While U.S. Catholic bishops defended Bush's right to seek justice in response to the harm done to innocent lives, they also warned the president to abide by national and in-ternational law and "sound moral principles." As the eighty-one-year-old pope read Bush's speech to Congress only two weeks after militant Muslims destroyed the World Trade Center, John Paul II decided to adjust his forthcoming speech in Kaz-akhstan, where he cautioned the United States against excessive military retribu-tion.[108] The pope spoke even more categorically against the U.S. invasion of Iraq in 2003. Despite an appeal through the pope's emissary just prior to the hostilities, the Bush administration defended its moral right to make war against Saddam Hussein's government.[109]

While Bush initially paid no immediate political price for ignoring the papal plea, the war's interminable nature served as a reminder of the variable character of the Catholic vote. Despite the opposition of a Catholic Democratic presidential nom-inee, Massachusetts Senator John F. Kerry, in the 2004 presidential election, Bush won a majority of Catholics (and 55 percent of white Catholics). A media consensus de-veloped that moral issues, such as homosexual marriage and abortion, persuaded Catholics and evangelical Protestants to vote for Bush, yet Georgetown University re-searchers concluded that fears of terrorism persuaded most Catholics voters to sup-port the president.[110] As the Iraq war dominated headlines and required more money and lives, Catholics repudiated the Republicans in the 2006 midterm elections. Dem-ocrats gained 51 percent of white Catholic and 72 percent of nonwhite Catholics votes.[111] In 2005 Bush had knelt in front of the decreased Pope John Paul II, making him the first U.S. president to attend a papal funeral.[112] A year and a half later, this precedent-setting sign of respect for Catholicism seemed a distant memory for Amer-ican Catholics.

While George W. Bush and Clinton mounted strong appeals to Catholics in the United States, the former's aggressive use of military force has alienated this group in a manner similar to his father. Clinton's willingness to negotiate with the Catholic hi-erarchy allowed him to overcome serious policy disagreements. While George W. Bush has defended the Catholic hierarchy's position on embryonic stem cell research, abortion, and federal aid to religious charities, the war on terrorism preceded these issues in his administration's priorities.

CONCLUSION

This story of White House outreach to Catholics demonstrates an apparent contradiction: the decline of a "Catholic vote" and the persistent pursuit of Catholic voters by presidents. While Democrats Roosevelt, Truman, Kennedy, and Johnson gained a substantial majority of Catholic votes, Catholics have not voted consistently on issues of public policy since the 1960s. The election of a Catholic president in 1960 contributed to this group's assimilation into mainstream American political life. As a result, Republican presidents Eisenhower, Nixon, Reagan, and George W. Bush have increasingly seized the opportunity to find common cause with Catholics. Why do presidents continue to reach out to Catholics? Perhaps because the three presidents who proved least willing to engage with Catholics—Ford, Carter, and George H. W. Bush—served only one term or less.

Yet will presidential appeals to Catholics continue even as the Church's hierarchy appears to wield less power than ever over its members? While presidents travel to Notre Dame University to address Catholics, this Catholic institution has increasingly adopted secular norms.[113] Although popes and American bishops insist upon the immorality of abortion, polling data suggest that U.S. Catholics largely disagree with the Church hierarchy's absolutism on this issue.[114] In the wake of the 2002 media exposure of widespread abuse of minors by clergy, the Catholic Church's persuasive power over its members' politics seems decreasingly significant.

In this period of weakened clerical authority, however, presidents possess an even greater ability to shape Catholic identity. By engaging the pope, a bishop, or a lay Catholic on moral and religious issues, the president appeals directly to the Catholic conscience. With so many challenges to Christian justice, the White House can employ the "bully pulpit" of U.S. media attention to set the Catholic agenda. In this way Democrats Franklin Roosevelt and Bill Clinton emphasized the Catholic Church's calls to governmental limitations on capitalism. During the cold war, Republicans Dwight Eisenhower and Ronald Reagan claimed a moral imperative to join with Catholicism's consistent outcry against communism's materialism and atheism.

While George W. Bush may have failed to create a consistent Catholic majority in the Republican Party, the president may have subtly planted the seeds for the sprouting of Catholicism in the United States. By promising to provide government aid to Catholic social organizations, opposing abortion, and vetoing experimental research on embryos, Bush aligned his administration with Pope John Paul II's plea for protection of life from conception to natural death. Although Bush's decisions to make war overseas contradicted the pope's appeals, the president appointed two Catholic justices to the Supreme Court. If the Court's current majority of five Catholics develops a legal philosophy consistent with Catholic moral teaching, historians may remember Bush as the president who reconstituted American Catholics as a voting bloc.

NOTES

1. James Garneau, "Presidents and Popes, Face to Face: From Wilson to Bush II" (John Tracy Ellis Lecture, The Catholic University of America, Washington, DC, October 26, 2005).

2. Mark Silk and John C. Green, "The GOP's Religion Problem," *Religion in the News* 9, no. 3 (2006): 2–4.

3. For example, see Glenn Feldman, "Unholy Alliance: Suppressing Catholic Teachings in Subservience to Republican Ascendance in America," *Political Theology* 7, no. 2 (2006): 137–79.

4. For a critique of the "swing" nature of the Catholic vote, see Mark M. Gray, Paul M. Perl, and Mary E. Bendyna, "Camelot Comes But Once? John F. Kerry and the Catholic Vote," *Presidential Studies Quarterly* 36, no. 2 (2006): 203–22.

5. This term refers to the office of the papacy, the bishop of Rome, who appoints bishops worldwide to manage the church's sacramental and social functions.

6. On soft power, see Joseph Nye, *Soft Power: The Means to Success in World Politics* (New York: PublicAffairs, 2004).

7. On the Swiss Guard, see Robert Royal, *The Pope's Army: 500 Years of the Papal Swiss Guard* (New York: Crossroad Publishing, 2006).

8. Thomas Fleming, *The Illusion of Victory: America in World War I* (New York: Basic Books, 2003), 131–34; Edward B. Parsons, *Wilsonian Diplomacy: Allied-American Rivalries in War and Peace* (St. Louis, MO: Forum Press, 1978), 69.

9. George Q. Flynn, *American Catholics and the Roosevelt Presidency, 1932–1936* (Lexington: University of Kentucky Press, 1968), 15–25.

10. Thomas Maier, *The Kennedys: America's Emerald Kings, A Five-Generation History of the Ultimate Irish-Catholic Family* (New York: Basic Books, 2003), 100, 117.

11. James Hennesey, *American Catholics: A History of the Roman Catholic Community in the United States* (New York: Oxford University Press, 1981), 260.

12. Gerald P. Fogarty, SJ, "Roosevelt and the American Catholic Hierarchy," in *FDR, the Vatican, and the Roman Catholic Church in America, 1933–1945,* ed. David B. Woolner and Richard G. Kurial (New York: Palgrave Macmillan, 2003), 18. See also Edward Kantowicz, "Cardinal Mundelein of Chicago and the Shaping of Twentieth-Century American Catholicism," *Journal of American History* 68 (June 1981): 52–68.

13. Philip Chen, "Religious Liberty in American Foreign Policy, 1933–41: Aspects of Public Argument between FDR and American Roman Catholics," in *FDR, the Vatican, and the Roman Catholic Church,* 129–31.

14. Monroe Billington and Cal Clark, "Catholic Clergymen, Franklin D. Roosevelt, and the New Deal," *Catholic Historical Review* 79, no. 1 (January 1993): 65.

15. James A. Farley, *Jim Farley's Story: The Roosevelt Years* (New York: McGraw-Hill, 1948), 174–78.

16. Richard Gribble, CSC, "The Other Radio Priest: James Gillis's Opposition to Franklin Delano Roosevelt's Foreign Policy," *Journal of Church and State* 44 (Summer 2002): 513–16.

17. Michael H. Carter, "Diplomacy's Detractors: American Protestant Reaction to FDR's 'Personal Representative' at the Vatican," in *FDR, the Vatican, and the Roman Catholic Church,* 184.

18. Charles R. Morris, *American Catholic: The Saints and Sinners Who Built America's Most Powerful Church* (New York: Vintage Books, 1997), ix.

19. For example, see Paul Blanshard, *American Freedom and Catholic Power* (Boston: Beacon Press, 1949); Paul Blanshard, *Communism, Democracy, and Catholic Power* (Boston: Beacon Press, 1951); Paul Blanshard, *The Irish and Catholic Power: An American Interpretation* (Boston: Beacon Press, 1953); Paul Blanshard, *American Freedom and Catholic Power,* 2nd ed. (Boston: Beacon Press, 1958). See also Paul Blanshard, *Democracy and Empire in*

the Caribbean: A Contemporary Review (New York: Beacon Press, 1947), and Paul Blanshard, *Right to Read: The Battle against Censorship* (Boston: Beacon Press, 1955).

20. Carter, "Diplomacy's Detractors," 190.

21. "Taylor Returning to the Vatican as Personal Envoy of President," *New York Times,* May 4, 1946; "Protestants Ask Taylor's Recall from Vatican in Visit to Truman," *New York Times,* June 6, 1946; "U.S. Envoy to Pope Called Temporary," *New York Times,* June 12, 1946; "Cardinal Fears 'Unhooded Klansmen' Foster Disunity," *Washington Post,* June 13, 1946.

22. Truman appeared to envision Taylor as a U.S. ambassador to global religious institutions. In a 1947 letter to his wife, the president mused about Taylor's future missions: "We are talking to the Archbishop of Canterbury, the bishop at the head of the Lutheran Church, and the Metropolitan of the Greek Church at Istanbul, and the pope. I may send him to see the top Buddhist and the Grand Lama of Tibet. If I can mobilize the people who believe in a moral world against the Bolshevik materialists, who believe as Henry Wallace does—'that the end justifies the means'—we can win this fight" (Elizabeth Edwards Spalding, "'We Must Put on the Armor of God': Harry Truman and the Cold War," in *Religion and the American Presidency,* ed. Mark J. Rozell and Gleaves Whitney (New York: Palgrave Macmillan, 2007), 101.

23. Seth Jacobs, *American's Miracle Man in Vietnam: Ngo Dinh Diem, Religion, Race and U.S. Intervention in Southeast Asia, 1950–1957* (Durham, NC: Duke University Press, 2004), 84.

24. Carter, "Diplomacy's Detractors," 192–94.

25. In 1953 Eisenhower's secretary of labor, Martin P. Durkin, was the only Catholic in the cabinet (James Reston, "President Discusses Driscoll as the Successor to Durkin," *New York Times,* September 13, 1953). In 1960 another Catholic secretary of labor, James P. Mitchell, received brief consideration as Richard Nixon's vice-presidential nominee (Thomas Carty, *A Catholic in the White House?: Religion, Politics, and John Kennedy's Presidential Campaign* [New York: Palgrave Macmillan, 2004], 87–88).

26. Jacobs, *America's Miracle Man,* 68.

27. In a February 1954 National Security Council meeting, Eisenhower argued for Catholic leadership in South Vietnam by drawing an historical analogy with Joan of Arc (whom the Holy See elevated to sainthood in 1920), who "had managed to defeat a large enemy and place a timid king upon his throne in France" (Seth Jacobs, "'Our System Demands the Supreme Being': America's Religious Revival and the 'Diem Experiment,' 1954–1957," *Diplomatic History* 25, no. 2 [Fall 2001]: 608). The State Department Division of Philippine and Southeast Asian Affairs included six Catholics among the sixteen candidates it favored as the leader of South Vietnam. Placing Diem at the top of the list, the report noted favorably that he "may have Vatican support" (ibid., 612).

28. See James T. Fisher, *Dr. America: The Lives of Thomas A. Dooley, 1927–1961* (Amherst: University of Massachusetts Press, 1997).

29. Donald T. Critchlow, *Phyllis Schlafly and Grassroots Conservatism: A Woman's Crusade, Politics and Society in Twentieth Century America* (Princeton, NJ: Princeton University Press, 2005), 80.

30. Carty, *Catholic in the White House?*; Thomas J. Carty, "Secular Icon or Catholic Hero?: Religion and the Presidency of John F. Kennedy," in *Religion and the American Presidency,* 101.

31. Harris Wofford, *Of Kennedys and Kings: Making Sense of the Sixties* (New York: Farrar, Straus, Giroux, 1980), 71. See also Scott Stossel, *Sarge: The Life and Times of Sargent Shriver* (Washington, DC: Smithsonian Books, 2004).

32. Maier, *The Kennedys*, 399; Lawrence J. McAndrews, "The Avoidable Conflict: Kennedy, the Bishops, and Federal Aid to Education," *Catholic Historical Review* 76 (April 1990): 289, 282, 294, 279–80.

33. McAndrews, "Avoidable Conflict," 289, 282, 294. See also Lawrence J. McAndrews, "Beyond Appearances: Kennedy, Congress, Religion, and Federal Aid to Education," *Presidential Studies Quarterly* 21 (3): 545–57.

34. Max Frankel, "The Pope and Politics: Kennedy Administration Overcoming Concern about Rome's Stand on Reds," *New York Times*, May 20, 1963, 2.

35. "Pope and President," *Washington Post*, May 2, 1963.

36. Arnaldo Cartesi, "Kennedy's Racial Policies Are Praised by the Pontiff," *New York Times*, July 3, 1963; the quotation is from Kenneth P. O'Donnell and David F. Powers, with Joe McCarthy, *"Johnny, We Hardly Knew Ye," Memories of John Fitzgerald Kennedy* (Boston, MA: Little, Brown, 1972), 432.

37. Ibid.

38. For example, Arnaldo Cortesi, "Pope Backs Plans to Ban A-Bombs and Halt Testing," *New York Times*, December 25, 1955.

39. Stossel, *Sarge*, 327–29.

40. Peter Grose, "Pope's Visit Poses Protocol Problems," *New York Times*, October 5, 1965.

41. James Hennesey, *American Catholics: A History of the Roman Catholic Community in the United States* (New York: Oxford University Press, 1981), 322.

42. Robert Dallek, *Flawed Giant: Lyndon Johnson and His Times, 1961–1973* (New York: Oxford University Press, 1998), 351.

43. Peter Hibblethwaite, *Paul VI: The First Modern Pope* (New York: Paulist Press, 1993), 505–6.

44. *America*, December 61, 1967, 735.

45. Father Cronin proved critical to Nixon's reputation as a successful foe of communism. Having worked with the Federal Bureau of Investigation in Baltimore, Cronin provided Nixon with critical information for congressional investigations of Alger Hiss's communist ties. Cronin continued to serve as Nixon's only speechwriter from 1940 until the 1960 campaign, when Kennedy's nomination for president encouraged the NCWC to remove him from the campaign for fear of public accusations of Catholicism's excessive participation in politics (Morris, *American Catholic*, 246–47).

46. Robert C. Doty, "Pontiff Urges President to Increase Efforts for Peace and Aid to Poorer Nations," *New York Times*, March 3, 1969.

47. Ibid.

48. Ibid.

49. Robert H. Phelps, "Nixon Won't Send Envoy to Vatican," *New York Times*, July 4, 1969; "Nixon Picks Lodge As Vatican Envoy," *New York Times*, June 6, 1970.

50. "Lodge Tells Nixon of Vatican Talks," *New York Times*, August 7, 1970; "Lodge, Nixon's Voice at Vatican, Gets Enviable Papal Audiences," *New York Times*, March 25, 1971.

51. Carty, *A Catholic in the White House?* 95–97.

52. William V. Shannon, "For God and Mr. Nixon," *New York Times*, August 17, 1972.

53. Theodore H. White, *Making of the President, 1972* (New York: Bantam Books, 1973), 306.

54. Shannon, "For God and Mr. Nixon." See also Timothy A. Byrnes and Mary C. Segers, "Introduction," in *The Catholic Church and the Politics of Abortion: A View from the States,*

ed. Timothy A. Byrnes and Mary C. Segers (Boulder, CO: Westview Press, 1992), 4–5; *Time,* September 24, 1984, 20.

55. Ibid.

56. David C. Leege, "The Catholic Vote in '96: Can It Be Found in Church?" *Commonweal,* September 27, 1996, 11–18; White, *Making of the President, 1972,* 258–65, 464.

57. "Vatican Denies Pope Sent Plea to Nixon," *New York Times,* December 28, 1972; Paul Hoffman, "Pope Calls Bombing Halt 'Ray of Light,'" *New York Times,* January 1, 1973.

58. Clayton Fritchey, "Billy Graham and Bombing: Not a Critical Word," *Washington Post,* January 6, 1973.

59. Lawrence J. McAndrews, "Late and Never: Ronald Reagan and Tuition Tax Credits," *Journal of Church and State* 42, no. 3 (2000): 467–84.

60. Douglas Brinkley, *The Unfinished Presidency* (New York: Viking, 1998), 456. This story came from a 1997 interview with the Clinton administration's United Nations ambassador Andrew Young, who claimed that several other officials cited *New York Times* reporter Richard Burt as the source for this quotation.

61. E. J. Dionne Jr., "Catholic Vote Hasn't Been Kennedy's for the Asking," *New York Times,* May 5, 1980; Gerald M. Pomper, "The Nominating Contests," in *The Election of 1980: Reports and Interpretations,* by Gerald M. Pomper, Ross K. Baker, Kathleen A. Frankovic, Charles E. Jacob, et al. (Chatham, NJ: Chatham House, 1980), 28–29.

62. Gerald M. Pomper, "The Presidential Election," *Election of 1980,* 71–73.

63. Paul Kengor, *God and Ronald Reagan: A Spiritual Life* (New York: Regan Books, 2004), 50.

64. Ibid., 201, 206.

65. Ibid., 210. Apostle Delegate Pio Cardinal Laghi is the source for this quotation.

66. Ibid., 200, 208–9.

67. Richard Halloran, "Proposed Catholic Bishops' Letter Opposes First Use of Nuclear Arms," *New York Times,* October 26, 1982.

68. D. J. R. Bruckner, "Chicago's Activist Cardinal," *New York Times,* May 1, 1983.

69. Charles Mohr, "Reagan Receives Bishops' Protest," *New York Times,* March 10, 1983.

70. Steven R. Weisman, "Reagan Calls on Catholics in U.S. to Reject Nuclear Freeze Proposal," *New York Times,* August 4, 1982.

71. Richard Halloran, "Minuet with Catholic Bishops over Nuclear War," *New York Times,* December 16, 1982.

72. For this reason, the U.S. Catholic bishops had generally opposed the idea of an ambassador to the Vatican. The NCCB director of social relations, Monsignor George Higgins, surmised that the vast majority of U.S. Catholic bishops opposed the opening of formal U.S. relations with the Vatican: "My guess is that in a secret ballot without any pressure from the Vatican, not 10 percent of the bishops would vote for it" (Kenneth A. Briggs, "Diplomatic Ties with the Vatican: For U.S., an Old and Divisive Question," *New York Times,* December 12, 1983.

73. Steven R. Weisman, "U.S. and Vatican Restore Full Ties after 117 Years," *New York Times,* June 11, 1984.

74. Steven R. Weisman, "Reagan and Pope Confer in Alaska on World Issues," *New York Times,* May 3, 1984.

75. Francis X. Clines, "Reagan Courts Ethnic Voters by Assailing Foes," *New York Times,* July 27, 1984; John Herbers, "Catholic Activism: Reasons and Risks," *New York Times,* September 23, 1984.

76. McAndrews, "Late and Never," 467–84; Steven R. Weisman, "Roman Catholic Clergy Is Site for Reagan Rally," *New York Times,* September 10, 1984.

77. John Herbers, "Catholic Activism: Reasons and Risks," *New York Times,* September 23, 1984.

78. All caps in original. Ed Magnuson, "Pressing the Abortion Issue," *Time,* September 24, 1984, 18–20.

79. Ferraro turned the issue of religious morality against Reagan by questioning the Christian character of Reagan's free market capitalism, which she deemed "terribly unfair" for failing to provide relief to the poor. Reagan replied by claiming that the immorality of abortion trumped such arguments: "How can [the Democrats] parade down the street, wearing compassion as if it were a cloak made of neon? They have no compassion for the most helpless of God's creatures [i.e., the unborn]." New York governor Mario Cuomo proposed personal questions to undermine Reagan's pursuit of the higher moral ground: "I'm not going to judge Ronald Reagan and ask why did you leave your first wife, was that a Christian thing to do, have you seen your grandchild?" (Francis X. Clines, "Reagan Courts Ethnic Voters by Assailing Foes," *New York Times,* July 27, 1984; John Herbers, "Religion Enters a Political Revival," *New York Times,* August 12, 1984; John Herbers, "Political and Religious Shifts Rekindle Church–State Issue," *New York Times,* September 2, 1984).

80. Wilson Carey McWilliams, "The Meaning of the Election," in *The Election of 1984: Reports and Interpretations,* ed. Gerald M. Pomper (Chatham, NJ: Chatham House, 1985), 172.

81. Bernard Weinraub, "Cautious Path for Bush's Europe Trip," *New York Times,* May 26, 1989.

82. Roberto Suro, "Vatican Is Blaming U.S. for Impasse on Noriega's Fate," *New York Times,* December 30, 1989.

83. George Weigel, *Witness to Hope: The Biography of Pope John Paul II* (New York: Harper Collins, 1999), 621–22.

84. Lawrence J. McAndrews, "Choosing 'Choice': George Bush and Federal Aid to Nonpublic Schools," *Catholic Historical Review* 87, no. 3 (2001): 454.

85. Ibid., 453–69.

86. Michael Wines, "Bush Tells Graduates That Family, Not Government, Can Cure Nation's Ills," *New York Times,* May 18, 1992.

87. Gwen Ifill, "Clinton Says Foes Sow Intolerance," *New York Times,* September 12, 1992.

88. Alessandra Stanley, "First Lady on Abortion: Not a Platform Issue," *New York Times,* August 14, 1992.

89. Lyman A. Kellstedt, John C. Green, James L. Guth, and Corwin E. Smidt, "Religious Voting Blocs in the 1992 Election: The Year of the Evangelical?" *Sociology of Religion* 55, no. 3 (1994): 311, 317.

90. Ifill, "Clinton Says Foes Sow Intolerance."

91. Ibid.

92. Ibid.

93. James L. Guth, Lyman A. Kellstedt, John C. Green, and Corwin E. Smidt, "America Fifty/Fifty," *First Things* 116 (October 2002): 19–26.

94. "Abortion Bill's Veto Assailed by Vatican," *New York Times*, April 21, 1996; Frank Bruni, "Clinton Veto on Abortion Is Criticized by O'Connor," *New York Times*, April 15, 1996.

95. Alan Cowell, "Vatican Says Gore Is Misrepresenting Population Talks," *New York Times*, September 1, 1994.

96. Alan Cowell, "Clinton Seeks Ties with Pope on Aid Groups," *New York Times*, December 22, 1994.

97. Todd S. Purdum, "Congenial Meeting after Plea for the Poor and Disadvantaged," *New York Times*, October 5, 1995.

98. Lee Walczak and Richard S. Dunham, "Can Clinton Keep Catholics in His Fold?" *Business Week*, April 15, 1996, 55; Thomas J. Reese, "An Election Footnote: Catholics Come Home to the Democratic Party," *America*, December 7, 1996.

99. James Bennet, "Papal Visit Spotlights Clinton's Bully Pulpit," *New York Times*, January 27, 1999.

100. Andrew Sullivan, "The New Double Standard," *New York Times*, March 12, 2000; Frank Bruni, "McCain Campaign Admits Calls to Catholics," *New York Times*, February 23, 2000.

101. Diana Jean Schemo, "Catholics Minimize Impact of Bush Visit to Bob Jones," *New York Times*, March 2, 2000.

102. Alison Mitchell, "Bush Sides with Vatican on Its Status at the U.N.," *New York Times*, May 27, 2000.

103. Jo Renee Formicola and Mary Segers, "The Bush Faith-Based Initiative: The Catholic Response," *Journal of Church and State* 44, no. 4 (Autumn 2002): 711.

104. Ibid., 703, 711, 715; Frank Bruni, "Bush Pushes Role of Private Sector in Aiding the Poor," *New York Times*, May 21, 2001.

105. Formicola and Segers, "The Bush Faith-Based Initiative," 711.

106. Bruni, "Bush Pushes Role of Private Sector in Aiding the Poor"; Formicola and Segers, "Bush Faith-Based Initiative," 706.

107. "Remarks by John Paul," *New York Times*, July 24, 2001; Kevin Sack, with Gustav Niebuhr, "After Stem-Cell Rift, Groups Unite for Anti-Abortion Push," *New York Times*, September 4, 2001.

108. Melinda Henneberger, "Pope, in Central Asia, Speaks Out against Any Overzealous Military Response by the U.S.," *New York Times*, September 24, 2001.

109. Although the Vatican spokesman qualified the pope's remarks by saying that the pope might support the use of violent force against terrorists ("Suppongo," or "I suppose," said papal spokesman, Dr. Joaquin Navarro-Valls, in Italian). See Melinda Henneberger, "Politics and Piety: The Vatican on Just Wars," *New York Times*, September 30, 2001; Elisabeth Bumiller, "Peace Envoy from Vatican in U.S. Talks with Bush," *New York Times*, March 4, 2003; "Religious Leaders Ask If Antiwar Call Is Heard," *New York Times*, March 10, 2003.

110. Gray, Perl, and Bendyna, "Camelot Comes but Once?" 203–22.

111. Silk and Green, "GOP's Religion Problem," 3.

112. Garneau, "Presidents and Popes, Face to Face."

113. Mark S. Massa, *Catholics and American Culture: Fulton Sheen, Dorothy Day, and the Notre Dame Football Team* (New York: Crossroad Publishing, 1999), 195–221.

114. John Tagliabue, "Are American Catholics Roman? Lost in Translation," *New York Times*, June 16, 2002.

PART IV
International Policy and the Vatican

11

THE UNITED STATES-VATICAN RELATIONSHIP

"Parallel Endeavors for Peace,"
Competing Visions of Justice

PAUL CHRISTOPHER MANUEL

*D*URING HIS MAY 2007 VISIT to Brazil, Pope Benedict XVI denounced the opposing economic systems of Marxism and capitalism. Benedict bemoaned "the painful destruction of the human spirit" done in the former communist countries, and he was equally harsh regarding contemporary capitalism and globalization, warning people against its "deceptive illusions of happiness."[1] North American observers were clearly pleased with his remarks on Marxism and its implied criticisms of the economic policies of Venezuelan president Hugo Chavez, but they were considerably less sanguine concerning his views on capitalism. To be sure, Benedict's warning statements on capitalism confront several key assumptions of American economic liberalism and are at the center of a deep philosophical cleavage between the Vatican and the United States in the contemporary world.

Strongly influenced by John Locke, mainstream American economic thinkers have long maintained that social justice is primarily a question of individual rights and freedom—the idea that a just society is one in which there are free and unfettered markets and a limited government. Locke tends to minimize the concept of community obligations and, in its stead, to elevate individual rights and freedom as the barometer of social justice. In this view, according to the classic formulation, the only legitimate function of government is the protection of each citizen's life, liberty, and property.[2]

The views expressed by Pope Benedict, and which originate in the one-hundred-year tradition of Catholic social teaching, run squarely against traditional American notions of capitalism, property rights, individualism, and personal choice. In the Catholic view, social justice is best defined as a relational concept—the ability of each person to fully participate as a member of a larger community. The key concept of poverty as "structural sin," for example, in which all members of a community have a duty to help the poor, is a central tenet of Catholic social teaching and may be understood to be a Catholic corrective to the American emphasis on individual freedoms and rights.[3] Expanding on this notion, Lisa Ferrari points out that "John Paul II writes of authentic human development rather than simply economic development and offers a 'theological reading of modern problems,'" in which he asks the faithful to reframe political and economic questions in terms of sin and "structures of sin."[4]

This chapter will examine the relationship between the Vatican and the United States in light of these divergent views. It will look at how they have cooperated and conflicted over the years by analyzing how the two sides have engaged in, following President Franklin Roosevelt's formulation, "parallel endeavors for peace," and then contrast that aspect of the relationship involving their competing visions of justice. Throughout, this chapter is interested in discovering a nuanced understanding of the nature of the relationship between these two global powers.

TWO DIFFERENT KINDS OF GLOBAL POWERS

The diverging worldviews of the Vatican and the United States have become significantly more important since the fall of Soviet communism. In the post–cold war world, the United States has focused much of its energies on exporting a liberal economic version of globalization, while the Vatican has fought for a preferential option for the poor, the needy, and the vulnerable in the global economy. As the United States proclaims to the underdeveloped world that free market capitalism is the means of escaping poverty, the Vatican seeks to temper American capitalistic enthusiasm with dire warnings against inordinate attachments to material things. Just as the United States is a political, social, and economic reality in the world, the Vatican is a leading moral voice in the contemporary global scene.

Although both the Vatican and the United States are currently powers with a global reach, James Kurth has insightfully argued that the Vatican and the United States are polar opposites in at least three fundamental ways. First, the Vatican is the smallest state in the world, whereas the United States occupies a vast landmass.[5] Next, the Holy See represents one Catholic faith in many nations across the globe, while the United States is one nation composed of many faiths. Third, the pope is the mediator for Catholics between the secular and spiritual worlds, while the United States is a society predicated in many ways on a strict separation between state and church.[6] They are not enemies, but they do offer the world very different prescriptions for achieving social, economic, political, and moral justice.

"PARALLEL ENDEAVORS FOR PEACE"

Two years before American entry into World War II, President Roosevelt penned a letter on December 23, 1939, to Pope Pius XII announcing his decision to appoint Myron C. Taylor as his personal representative to the pope.[7] Roosevelt spoke of the need for improved U.S.–Vatican relations, adding in his letter that "the people of this nation . . . know that only by friendly association among the seekers of light and the seekers of peace everywhere can the forces of evil be overcome. . . . I am, therefore, suggesting to Your Holiness that it would give me great satisfaction to send to you my personal representative in order that our parallel endeavors for peace and the alleviation of suffering may be assisted."[8]

The United States and the Vatican did successfully engage in "parallel endeavors for peace and the alleviation of suffering" and worked together during the rebuilding of Europe following the war. This effort helped to frame an important aspect of their relationship. Taylor remained in Rome until 1950 and later served as President Harry S. Truman's personal representative to the Vatican.[9] Truman then appointed Mark Clark to replace Taylor but was forced to withdraw the nomination following resistance from Congress; consequently, diplomatic relations between the Vatican and the United States were suspended for a period.[10]

As the cold war heated up in the 1950s, American presidents became increasingly aware of the important role the Vatican could play in the global anticommunist struggle. At a press conference on December 2, 1954, President Dwight D. Eisenhower expressed his admiration of the pope's "strong stand for peace, for liberty and freedom in the world, and his stand against communism."[11] With that statement, President Eisenhower identified three key themes that helped to frame the U.S.–Vatican relationship throughout the cold war, and especially in the 1980s. Elected in 1960, John Kennedy, as the first and thus far only Roman Catholic president of the United States, was acutely aware of the pope's moral influence around the globe and met with Pope Paul VI in Rome in July 1963 a few days after his "Ich bin ein Berliner" speech of June 26, 1963.[12] The tradition of appointing a personal representative to the Vatican continued under Presidents Richard M. Nixon, Jimmy Carter, and Ronald Reagan, and there were various meetings between American presidents and popes during the cold war.[13]

To be sure, the diplomatic relationship between the United States and the Vatican has been very complicated since the early years of the American nation. The United States opened consular relations with the Papal States in 1797, but formal diplomatic relations involving an exchange of ambassadors were not initiated until January 10, 1984. The strong influence of the anti-foreigner and anti-Catholic group known as the Know-Nothings in the mid-nineteenth century considerably slowed down the process of developing a relationship.[14] The Know-Nothings were in large part responsible for the 1867 legislation prohibiting the funding of an American embassy to the Holy See, which helped to delay formal U.S.–Vatican diplomatic relations for over a century. That legislation was finally repealed in 1983.

For its part, the Vatican, although a fact of international relations long before the American Revolution, is a particularly complex entity with a Byzantine institutional structure. The Vatican acknowledges only a fuzzy differentiation between its political and ecclesial institutions: the government of Vatican City and the Holy See. Yet they are, in fact, distinct offices. The Vatican's secretariat of state is assigned the formal responsibility to conduct foreign relations for Vatican City, and foreign diplomats are typically accredited to the Holy See. However, some sovereigns actually have diplomatic relations with the Catholic Church but not with the government of Vatican City.[15]

The 1980s were a particularly important time for relations between the Vatican and the United States. Pope John Paul II and President Reagan worked well together, and the two sides sought common solutions to East–West relations. President Reagan's personal representative to the Vatican was William A. Wilson, who diligently worked towards formal U.S.–Vatican relations, finally achieved in 1984.[16] Of course, as will be examined later in this chapter, the two sides voiced significant differences on social welfare policies during this time, but the foundational challenge of the period was the problem of Soviet communism. President Reagan and Pope John Paul II, along with Soviet Premier Mikhail Gorbachev, each played a critical role in the ending of Soviet communism; the end of Soviet-style communism in Eastern Europe represented a zenith in their "parallel endeavors for peace and the alleviation of suffering."

COMPETING VISIONS OF JUSTICE

In the aftermath of the cold war, the diverging worldviews of the United States and the Vatican have become significantly more pronounced. The United Nations Conference on Women of 1994 is an important case in point. Under President Bill Clinton, the United States led a movement at the conference to make abortion and family planning more accessible to women in the underdeveloped parts of the world, to help alleviate for these women some of the societal burdens of child rearing, and to empower them with educational and vocational training and employment opportunities. The Vatican strenuously worked to block this U.S.-led movement, arguing that it would essentially legalize the murder of unborn children throughout the world, and enlisted the support of many Catholic nations in Latin America in alliance with Muslim nations. The Vatican was successful, and its victory was secured when Pakistani prime minister Mohtarma Benazir Bhutto stated her opposition to abortion in the most forceful of terms: "Islam lays a great deal of stress on the sanctity of life. The Holy Book tells us: 'Kill not your children on a plea of want. We provide sustenance for them and for you.' Islam, therefore, except in exceptional circumstances rejects abortion as a method of population control. . . . Let me state, categorically, Mr. Chairman, that the traditional family is the union sanctified by marriage. Muslims, with their over-riding commitment to knowledge would have no difficulty with dissemination of information about reproductive health, so long as its modalities remain compatible with their religious and spiritual heritage."[17]

Bhutto, of course, spoke from her own religious tradition and convictions at the United Nations conference—but the success of the Vatican was to find significant points of moral harmony between the two great religious traditions and, in turn, to leverage their shared views into a significant anti-abortion, pro-traditional family, victory. Ferrari notes that the Clinton administration was stunned at how he was out-maneuvered by the Vatican's political savvy and diplomatic creativity.[18] With this, the Vatican let it be known that it would do whatever it could in the post–cold war world to block American policies it deemed immoral and dangerous.[19]

In light of John Paul II's strong condemnation of the American war in Iraq, the relationship has grown somewhat distant in the post-2003 period. Pope Benedict has also criticized American foreign policy, and his recent comments about the nature of globalization signal that key differences between the United States and the Vatican remain and may highlight the relationship in the years to come.

THE POST–1945 WORLD: CAPITALISM, AMERICAN STYLE

The defeat of fascism, the global emergence of the United States, the end of the European colonial empires, and the worldwide development of capitalism were widely understood as factors that would lead to a global growth of liberal democratic regimes. In the postwar world, American foreign policy emphasized the modernization of the poorer areas of the world by means of free-market capitalism.

In American universities of the 1950s and 1960s, scholars such as Seymour Martin Lipset, Deane Neubauer, and Philips Cutright placed heavy emphasis on industrialization and education as prerequisites to democracy. Their research pegged democratic institution creation to a set of economic and educational requirements; in their view, once a country passed through a so-called threshold level of economic development, it would likely become a democratic state as well.[20] Consequently, American foreign policy initiatives—including President Kennedy's Alliance for Progress and the Peace Corps—were grounded in the idea that the prospects for democracy in a country could be linked to its level of economic development, per capita income, literacy, and education. In particular, Kennedy was strongly influenced by Walter Rostow, a professor of economics at the Massachusetts Institute of Technology. Rostow argued in his important work, *The Stages of Economic Growth: A Non-Communist Manifesto* (1971), that the capitalist development model was the answer in helping the new nations of the so-called third world develop economically, thereby resisting worldwide communism.[21]

In this scenario, old-fashioned American know-how would be the magic elixir to lift the world out of poverty and tyranny. Economic development and wealth, an open class system, and capitalism were understood to be the universal prerequisite conditions for democracy. This assumptive posture informed President Kennedy's words at his 1961 inaugural speech, when he stated that "the world is very different now. For man holds in his mortal hands the power to abolish all forms of human poverty and all forms of human life."[22] That is, as long as there was economic development and modernization, democracy would follow. For most of the postwar period, then, the main operating assumption of American foreign policy has been that economic development and modernization are prerequisites to political democracy.[23]

Over the last fifty years, one result of American-style modernization has been the global expansion of capitalism, also known as globalization. Thomas Friedman's work, *The Lexus and the Olive Tree* (1999), insightfully argues that the world has been significantly transformed since the end of the cold war from one strongly marked by political and ideological division to an integrated, capitalist, and Web-based one. In many ways the product of American foreign policy initiatives of fifty years ago, the contemporary phenomenon of globalization, Friedman holds, is a new global system of international arrangements with its own set of assumptions, logic, and incentives: in short, the worldwide supremacy of capitalism has been achieved.

VATICAN CRITICISMS OF AMERICAN-STYLE CAPITALISM

The Vatican has long sought to point out the dangers of unfettered capitalism, and Pope Benedict certainly understands that Friedman's brilliant analysis aptly describes the contemporary global setting. He offered these thoughts on globalization while in Brazil: "Today's world experiences the phenomenon of globalization as a network of relationships extending over the whole planet. Although from certain points of view this benefits the great family of humanity, and a sign of its profound aspiration to-wards unity, nevertheless it also undoubtedly brings with it the risk of vast monopolies and of treating profit as the supreme value. As in all areas of human activity, glob-alization too must be led by ethics, placing everything at the service of the human person, created in the image and likeness of God."[24]

Indeed so, for if one's starting point in the discussion of economic theory and social justice is that all are made in the image of God, and that justice implies that human dignity and human rights precede rights such as those of private property and the right to unlimited accumulation of goods and money, then one's subsequent def-inition of justice would be rather different from the dominant liberal paradigm in American political and philosophical thought. Accordingly, the Vatican has always been very skeptical of capitalism, and it has developed a social teaching in response to the social challenges posed by industrialization known as Catholic Social Teach-ing. It represents a pragmatic solution to the serious economic, social, and political problems plaguing societies. Among other steps, this teaching focuses pastoral and re-lief efforts on the poor and seeks to make the Catholic Church itself a more welcom-ing, open, and just place for all, especially the poor.[25]

In sum, Catholic Social Teaching manifests a wariness with the Lockean empha-sis on individualism and its views regarding private property, and it seeks to recon-cile the traditional Christian and Catholic concerns for the dignity of human life with demands for political freedom and economic equality. For Leo XIII and subsequent popes, the Catholic Church has stood against excessive liberty for free market capi-talists (and remained wary of the liberal preference of individualism over commu-nity) and has guarded against the excessive equality of the socialists. In particular, the popes have feared three troubling characteristics of the growing socialist movement: its emphasis on materialism, its willingness to use violence to achieve its objectives, and its hostility toward religion.[26] Wariness of capitalism and socialism is critical to subsequent Catholic teachings about social justice.[27]

In his World Day of Peace message on January 1, 1972, Pope Paul VI offered the oft-quoted observation that "if you want peace, work for justice" as a critique of the condition of world poverty in the 1970s, and he has offered social justice as an anti-dote to revolutionary political movements. Later, he argued in his encyclical, *Populorum progressio,* that "genuine progress does not consist in wealth sought for personal comfort or for its own sake; rather it consists in an economic order designed for the welfare of the human person, where the daily bread that each man receives reflects the glow of brotherly love and the helping hand of God."[28] As such, the Vatican economic worldview represents something of a challenge for American economic policies.[29] The century-long tradition of Catholic Social Teaching challenges citizens to think in terms of community, with a preference for the poor and vulnerable in society.[30]

CONCLUSION

Following World War II, the United States became the world's most important global power for the first time in its history, whereas the Vatican has been a significant global player since the Portuguese discoverer Vasco da Gama reached the shores of India in 1498 and Pedro Álvares Cabral reached Brazil in 1500—bringing with them the Roman Catholic Church. As the world's largest economic power, the United States is a key global player; as the world's largest church, the Vatican offers an important moral voice. Pope Benedict's observations in Brazil are but a continuation of a hundred-year tradition of an ongoing Catholic critique of capitalism for its emphasis on consumerism, materialism, selfishness, secularization, and individualism. This teaching has increased awareness among Catholics and other people of good will of the important human issues at stake in economic relations. In the aftermath of the Second Vatican Council in the mid-1960s, the Roman Catholic Church assumed a new global identity as it sought to engage questions of economic justice and human rights in the modern world.

What of the future U.S.–Vatican relationship? A future pro-life Republican administration would certainly support some aspects of the Vatican's social policy, but not its economic ones, and a pro-choice Democrat would likely support some of the Vatican's economic views, but not its social ones—especially on abortion. Whichever party wins in the United States, its relationship with the Vatican will remain a dynamic one, with cooperation in their "parallel endeavors for peace" and conflict over their competing visions of justice.

In the end, their competing views may perhaps someday result in new global policies aimed at economic growth, the alleviation of human suffering, and the deepening of democratic legitimacy in civil society across the globe.[31] This is certainly part of what Pope Benedict had in mind when he made his comments in Brazil.

NOTES

1. www.iht.com/articles/ap/2007/05/14/america/LA-GEN-Pope-Brazil.php and www.usatoday.com/news/religion/2007-05-14-pope_N.htm. Benedict also stated that "the Marxist system, where it found its way into government, not only left a sad heritage of economic

and ecological destruction, but also a painful destruction of the human spirit." www.cnn.com/2007/WORLD/americas/05/13/pope.brazil.ap/index.html?eref=rss_ topstories. Benedict further warned that capitalism and globalization may give "rise to a worrying degradation of personal dignity through drugs, alcohol and deceptive illusions of happiness." The pope criticized abortion and same-sex marriage as well, and he called upon Catholic leaders to lead Brazil in a new direction respectful of life and of the poor and the vulnerable. See the Vatican website for his full comments, available from www.vatican.va/holy_father/benedict_xvi/speeches/2007/may/documents/hf_ben-xvi _spe_20070513_conference-aparecida_en.html.

2. See John Locke, *Two Treatises of Government,* ed. Peter Laslett, 2nd ed. (Cambridge, UK: Cambridge University Press, 2003). Also see Adam Smith, *The Wealth of Nations,* intro. by Alan B. Krueger (New York: Bantam Classics, 2003).

3. See *Sollicitudo rei socialis,* esp. n. 36–37. On a related point, this Catholic challenge is also directed against what is viewed as the "excessive individualism" of American politics and society. Stephen Carter aptly observes that the United States has both the highest rate of abortion and the highest rate of private ownership of firearms in the world. Carter further notes that American courts protect individual behavior such as the rights of the homeless to sleep in public libraries and other public places, even if offensive odors or unsanitary conditions threaten the use of public facilities for others. In Carter's words, "it is as though once an individual has made up his mind to do a thing, no matter how tasteless or repulsive, nobody else has legal recourse" (Carter, *Civility* [New York: Harper Collins, 1998], 219).

4. Lisa L. Ferrari, "The Vatican as a Transnational Actor," in *The Catholic Church and the Nation-State: Comparative Perspectives,* ed. Paul Christopher Manuel, Lawrence C. Reardon, and Clyde Wilcox (Washington, DC: Georgetown University Press, 2006), 36. Also see *Redemptoris missio,* n. 32, 37, 38, 58.

5. The 1929 Lateran Pact between Italy and the Holy See formally created the 108.7 acre Vatican City.

6. James Kurth, "The Vatican's Foreign Policy," *The National Interest,* Summer 1993, 43.

7. Pius XII served as pope between 1939 and 1958.

8. www.presidency.ucsb.edu/ws/index.php?pid=15853&st=Parallel+Endeavors+for+Peace &st1=.

9. President Harry S. Truman stated that "at my request the Honorable Myron C. Taylor is proceeding to Rome as my personal representative for further exchanges of views with His Holiness Pope Pius XII, on problems relative to the establishment of peace under a moral world order and to the alleviation of the human suffering still continuing in many parts of the world," available from www.presidency.ucsb.edu/ws/index.php?pid=12738&st= Vatican&st1.

10. See www.presidency.ucsb.edu/ws/print.php?pid=13971 and ://www.trumanlibrary.org/ truman-3.htm.

11. www.presidency.ucsb.edu/ws/index.php?pid=10147&st=Vatican&st1=.

12. www.brainyhistory.com/years/1963.html.

13. See Raymond L. Flynn, "Letter from the Vatican: Common Objectives for Peace," *SAIS Review*16, no. 2 (1996): 143–53. Between 1951 and 1968, the Vatican and the United States had no official diplomatic contacts. Flynn notes that President Nixon recommended a formal relationship when he appointed Henry Cabot Lodge as his personal representative to

the Vatican in 1969. President Carter appointed businessman David Walters as his personal representative to the Vatican in 1977, and the following year Carter named former New York City mayor Robert F. Wagner to that post. President Reagan appointed businessman William A. Wilson as his personal representative in 1971.

14. Ibid. In addition, Gene Burns, in *The Frontiers of Catholicism: The Politics of Ideology in a Liberal World* (Berkeley: University of California Press, 1992), observes "the immigrant, lower-class Catholics in this country experienced sporadic nativist attacks (e.g. anti-Catholic riots and burning of churches) into the early twentieth century, sometimes inspired by groups such as the Know-Nothings and the Ku Klux Klan. . . . One of the most common accusations was that they could not be true patriots because . . . their allegiance to a foreign pope necessarily took precedence over their allegiance to the United States" (74).

15. Ferrari, "Vatican as a Transnational Actor," 35.

16. The following is the list of United States ambassadors to the Holy See since formal diplomatic relations began in 1984: William Wilson served from 1984 to 1986; Frank Shakespeare from 1986 to 1989; Thomas Patrick Melady from 1989 to 1993; Raymond Flynn from 1993 to 1997; Corinne Claiborne Boggs from 1997 to 2001; James Nicholson from 2001 to 2005; and Francis Rooney from 2005 to the present. See http://en.wikipedia.org/wiki/United_States_Ambassador_to_the_Holy_See.

17. www.un.org/popin/icpd/conference/gov/940907211416.html

18. Ferrari, "Vatican as a Transnational Actor," 33. Also see Christine Gorman, "Clash of Wills in Cairo," *Time*, September 12, 1994, 56.

19. George W. Bush, a pro-life president, was influenced by Pope John Paul II during their meeting in the summer of 2001 to limit scientific experimentation on human stem cells, and the two men shared a similar concern with the life of the unborn. See archives.cnn.com/2001/WORLD/europe/07/23/bush.pope/ and www.zenit.org/english/archive/0101/ZE010124.htm#2025.

20. A classic expression of this literature may be found in the numerous works of political scientist Seymour Martin Lipset. Starting with his 1959 article, "Some Social Requisites of Democracy: Economic Development and Political Legitimacy," which appeared in the *American Political Science Review,* and in his noteworthy book, *Political Man: The Social Bases of Politics* (1960), Lipset gathered information related to economic development and computed averages for several countries. In each case, he found that the democratic countries were also the richer countries. Consequently, Lipset's research suggested that economic development improved a society's chances for democracy because it increased opportunities for widespread education, literacy, and wealth.

21. Walt Whitman Rostow, *The Stages of Economic Growth: A Non-Communist Manifesto* (Cambridge, UK: Cambridge University Press, 1971). Rostow served as an aide to Kennedy during the 1960 presidential campaign and then became JFK's deputy special assistant for national security affairs.

22. www.jfklibrary.org/Historical+Resources/Archives/Reference+Desk/Speeches/JFK/003POF03Inaugural01201961.htm.

23. This philosophical approach identifies traditional and modern societies as opposing ideal types. Traditional society is characterized by elitist and hierarchical structures, with ascriptive, particularistic patterns of authority and an extended kinship structure. Modern society is portrayed as having the opposite characteristics of these, being based on a rational, legalistic, and democratic authority system. Furthermore, the approach maintains

that a society based on traditional authority patterns and divided between rich and poor will probably result in some nondemocratic form of governance, whereas a democratic form of government will prevail in a modern, rational society with a large middle class.

24. www.vatican.va/holy_father/benedict_xvi/speeches/2007/may/documents/hf_ben-xvi _spe_20070513_conference-aparecida_en.html.

25. Contemporary Catholic thinking on social justice can be traced back to the papacy of Leo XIII (1878–1903), who wrote the important encyclical, *Rerum novarum: The Condition of Labor,* in 1891. Later, Pius XI picked up where Leo had left off and wrote the encyclical *Quadragesimo anno: After Forty Years,* in 1931. John XXIII built on these works with two additional encyclicals, *Mater et magistra,* in 1961, followed by *Pacem in terris* two years later. Combined, these encyclicals focused the attention of the Church squarely on the key social justice issues of the modern and industrializing world. Citing, among sources, scriptural passages and Thomas Aquinas, Leo XIII established a framework for a critical analysis of capitalist society from a Catholic perspective in *Rerum novarum.* Although generally optimistic about capitalism, Leo argued that Lockean liberals are wrong to think that economic life operates in a vacuum. To the contrary, he argues, economic life is intimately connected to human life and experience. It is simply not sufficient for those people engaged in economic life to focus on economics as if it did not concern human life. Rather, those engaged in economic life and activity are all required to take into account the basic needs of the individual and of the community. That is, profit and property rights are limited by the common good. See David J. O'Brien and Thomas A. Shannon, *Catholic Social Thought: The Documentary Heritage* (Maryknoll, NY: Orbis, 1992): 12–13, and David Hollenbach, SJ, *Claims in Conflict: Retrieving and Renewing the Catholic Human Rights Tradition* (New York: Paulist Press, 1979), 42.

26. Notably, Leo XIII's *Rerum novarum* proposes that a Catholic perspective on social justice under a capitalistic economy supports the idea that the state has a moral duty and an obligation to assist those in need. In the words of Leo XIII, "man is older than the state, and he holds the right of providing for the life of his body prior to the formation of any state" (O'Brien and Shannon, *Catholic Social Thought,* 16).

27. Pope John XXIII made a number of key contributions to Catholic social justice teaching. In 1961 he issued *Mater et magistra,* which deals with the question of social justice. In that encyclical he emphasizes the moral duty of the state to intervene in the marketplace to ensure that property is used for the common good. Two years later he authored the watershed encyclical *Pacem in terris,* which endorses the "welfare state" model of capitalism In particular, it supports the rights to life, food, clothing, shelter, medical care, culture, and education of all people. Certainly, when John XXIII called for the convening of Vatican II, his progressive thinking influenced many in the Church seriously to consider economic issues from a Catholic social justice perspective. See *Mater et Magistra* in *Catholic Social Thought.* Also see Donald Door, *Option for the Poor: A Hundred Years of Catholic Social Teaching* (Maryknoll, NY: Orbis, 1992), 147.

28. www.vatican.va/holy_father/paul_vi/encyclicals/documents/hf_p-vi_enc_26031967_ populorum_en.html.

29. The National Conference of Catholic Bishops in the United States entered the national debate on social justice in the United States with the publication of its pastoral letter, *Economic Justice for All* (Washington, DC: U.S. Catholic Conference, 1986). Published as a response to the economic policies being pursued by the Reagan administration, this letter sought to direct the attention of policymakers in Washington to the plight of the poor and

disenfranchised. Extending the Catholic concern with human rights and human dignity, the letter challenged the dominant liberal modes of thinking about justice and the economy in the United States.

30. See *Populorum progressio,* available from www.vatican.va/holy_father/paul_vi/encyclicals/ documents/hf_p-vi_enc_26031967_populorum_en.html. Pope Paul VI adds, "However, certain concepts have somehow arisen out of these new conditions and insinuated themselves into the fabric of human society. These concepts present profit as the chief spur to economic progress, free competition as the guiding norm of economics, and private ownership of the means of production as an absolute right, having no limits nor concomitant social obligations. This unbridled liberalism paves the way for a particular type of tyranny, rightly condemned by Our predecessor Pius XI, for it results in the 'international imperialism of money.' Such improper manipulations of economic forces can never be condemned enough; let it be said once again that economics is supposed to be in the service of man. But if it is true that a type of capitalism, as it is commonly called, has given rise to hardships, unjust practices, and fratricidal conflicts that persist to this day, it would be a mistake to attribute these evils to the rise of industrialization itself, for they really derive from the pernicious economic concepts that grew up along with it. We must in all fairness acknowledge the vital role played by labor systemization and industrial organization in the task of development" (ibid.).

31. www.vatican.va/holy_father/benedict_xvi/speeches/2007/may/documents/hf_ben-xvi _spe_20070509_welcome-brazil_en.html. Pope Benedict also said in Brazil that "the Church seeks only to stress the moral values present in each situation and to form the conscience of the citizens so that they may make informed and free decisions. She will not fail to insist on the need to take action to ensure that the family, the basic cell of society, is strengthened and likewise young people, whose formation is a decisive factor for the future of any nation. Last but not least, she will defend and promote the values present at every level of society, especially among indigenous peoples" (ibid.).

12

REFORMING THE VATICAN
The Tradition of Best Practices

Thomas J. Reese

*T*oo often, when anyone proposes the reform of church structures, the reformer is attacked for borrowing from the secular political field, as if this were intrinsically a bad thing. Such attacks are theologically unsound and historically ignorant.

This chapter makes three arguments: (1) the organization of the Vatican through history is not divinely inspired but is the result of the Vatican's adoption of practices from the secular political world; (2) the governance of the church is more centralized today than at any time in its history; and (3) to make the church more collegial, the Vatican must once again adopt the "best practices" of the secular political world.

This chapter is admittedly sketchy. To deal with the first point, the organizational development of the Vatican through history, would require a series of books, not one chapter. Likewise, describing the role of the pope in the church over almost two thousand years would take volumes. One could also go on and on when proposing reform. As a result, this chapter must be seen as the beginning of a conversation, not a definitive answer.

HISTORY OF THE ROMAN CURIA

When St. Peter, the first pope, arrived in Rome, he did not immediately appoint cardinals and set up the congregations and the other offices that exist in the Vatican today. He apparently had only a secretary to help him with his correspondence. In early centuries, the bishop of Rome had helpers much like those of any other bishop: priests for house churches, deacons for material assistance and catechumens, and notaries or secretaries for correspondence and record keeping.[1] By the fourth century, in imitation of the practice of the imperial court, notaries were a permanent fixture in the papacy. As staff to the pope, these men wrote letters and kept records of correspondence and other official documents. For example, they took minutes at the Lateran Council of 649 and prepared its acts. Because of the notaries' training and experience, popes sometimes sent them on diplomatic missions or to ecumenical councils in the East.

By the thirteenth century the Apostolic Chancellery was an important office, and the chancellor was the pope's principal adviser and assistant, just as chancellors were the principal advisers of European monarchs. The chancellery handled appointments of bishops and abbots as well as bulls and rescripts. Before becoming pope, John XXII (1316–44) had been chancellor to the French king. He used his expertise in organizing the chancellery to handle papal business. The chancellery was later eclipsed by the Apostolic Datary and then the office of the Privy Seal and ultimately the secretary of state. All of these offices had parallels in secular society.

Likewise, the College of Cardinals evolved from being the principal priests and deacons of Rome into a papal court that advised and elected popes. The cardinals often compared themselves to the old Roman Senate. As time went on and as papal business increased, the practice of consulting the College of Cardinals in meetings called consistories became common. At first the cardinals met monthly, but by the beginning of the thirteenth century they were meeting three times a week, on Monday, Wednesday, and Friday.[2] In many ways the pope and the cardinals functioned as a papal court similar to the royal courts of Europe during the Middle Ages, but the elective nature of the papacy gave to the College of Cardinals a unique role not enjoyed by the nobility in most nations. In exchange for electoral support, papal candidates made deals and promises that increased the power of the cardinals. Later, the power of the cardinals was severely curtailed by increasingly powerful popes, just as the power of nobles was curtailed by the rise of the absolute monarchs.

This brief history of the Roman curia shows, first, that the organization and structure of the Roman curia has changed over time, and second, that popes frequently borrowed or adapted practices from secular government and used them in the Church. One can conclude, therefore, that changing the organization and structure of the Vatican by using best practices from the contemporary political and corporate world would be in keeping with the long tradition of the Church.

A CENTRALIZED PAPACY

Church governance today is more centralized than it has ever been in the history of the Church. The papacy rules the Church with powers that would be the envy of any absolute monarch. The pope holds supreme legislative, executive, and judicial authority with few checks on his power. This can be seen especially in the appointment of bishops to dioceses around the world.[3]

In the first centuries of the Church, the local bishop was chosen by and from the people. In the ideal, the people of the community gathered in the cathedral where they prayed and selected a holy and talented man to lead them. In practice, irreconcilable factions supporting opposing candidates might clash, sometimes violently splitting the community. The faithful did not always speak with one voice.

As time went on, the selection process evolved to include the clergy, the people, and the provincial bishops in a system of checks and balances. Pope Leo I (440–61) described the ideal by saying that no one could be a bishop unless he was elected by the clergy, accepted by his people, and consecrated by the bishops of his province (the dioceses of a region are grouped together in a province under the leadership of a metropolitan archbishop).

The clergy knew the candidates better than the populace and were less likely to resolve their disputes by recourse to violence. At the same time, since he was to be the bishop of the community, he had to be acceptable to the people. The clergy's candidate would be presented to the people, who would normally indicate their approval by cheering. If they booed, the clergy might have to try again. To become a bishop, the candidate had to be consecrated by the bishops of his province under the leadership of the metropolitan archbishop. If he was unacceptable because of heresy or immorality or some other fault, the bishops could refuse to ordain him. Once consecrated, the bishop would usually notify the bishop of Rome, with whom he wished to maintain communion.

The problem with this democratic process was that it could be circumvented by powerful nobles and kings who had no respect for democracy. They could simply impose their desires on the Church through force or threats of violence. Thus, in 1016, Fulbert of Chartres writes, "How can one speak of election where a person is imposed by the prince, so that neither clergy nor people, let alone the bishops, can envisage any other candidates?"[4] The appointment of bishops by kings and nobles led to the corruption of the episcopacy when royal bastards and political favorites were chosen. Papal reformers from Gregory VII (elected 1073) onward saw their role as fighting off political influence in the selection of bishops.

In the East, episcopal synods (regional meetings of bishops) elected bishops. Even in the West, during the Middle Ages, the bishops of a province might elect a bishop with the man being ordained by the metropolitan archbishop, who was not allowed to ordain a bishop until after he had received the pallium from the pope.

It took the revolutions of the nineteenth century definitively to turn the tide when they wiped out most of the Catholic monarchs in Europe. But rather than returning the selection of bishops to the local church, it became the prerogative of the papacy to select bishops. This modern innovation is not in keeping with the long tradition of the Church. It led to the appointment of bishops who were loyal to Rome and would support its preeminence in the Church.

Likewise, the papacy's authority over doctrine and theological debate has grown. In the early centuries, regional or national councils of bishops helped define doctrine, coordinated church policy, and even provided a forum for judging bishops. The bishop of Rome might act as a court of appeals when bishops and councils disagreed. Bishops' conferences (national meetings of bishops that began in the nineteenth century) are the true successors of these councils, but the Vatican refuses to allow them to be called councils lest they start acting like the councils of old. Rome has limited the authority of bishops' conferences so that they can do little with out its approval.[5]

Ecumenical councils (meetings of bishops from all over the world) also had greater independence in the past, with some theologians even granting them the authority to impeach popes. Interestingly, this most uniquely ecclesial institution did not have a secular counterpart until the founding of the League of Nations in the twentieth century.

This quick review of the role of the papacy in the selection of bishops and in determining doctrine shows how power has been centralized in the papacy, especially in the last two centuries. Improved communications technology (beginning with the printing press, telegraph, and steam engine and continuing through television, fax, and e-mail) has helped the papacy exercise this power all over the world, despite the small size of its bureaucracy.

This centralization of power in the Vatican was a legitimate response to the political interference of kings and nobles in the life of the local church. Popes could stand up to kings better than the local church could. On the other hand, it should be remembered that sometimes nobles and kings were reformers of the church. It was the German king, Emperor Henry III, who in the eleventh century deposed three "popes" to begin a long line of reform popes, and it was another German king, Emperor Sigismund, who was able to end the Great Western Schism (1378–1417). Those were the days when the voice of the faithful was heard because it was backed with the sword. But even if centralization is seen as a legitimate response to the corrupting influence of the nobility, an argument can be made that such centralization is now not necessary and is in fact counterproductive.

POSSIBLE REFORMS

If history shows that the Church has always borrowed ideas and structures from civil society, then the question arises, what are some of the best practices in civil society that can help the Church today? Civil society has learned over the last two centuries that good government calls for (1) the elimination of the nobility; (2) the separation of powers; (3) the principle of subsidiarity (what can be done at a lower level of society should be done there); and (4) a system of checks and balances. Six reforms that reflect the best practices that have proven successful in civil society are presented below.

Make the Vatican a Bureaucracy, Not a Court

Most countries of the world have found that a royal court composed of a king and his nobles is not a good way to govern. While such courts might be good for tourism, few think that they are efficient or effective institutions in the twenty-first century. The Vatican today is still as much a court as a bureaucracy, with cardinals referred to as princes of the church and bishops acting like nobles in the court. This can be changed if no Vatican bureaucrat is made a bishop or a cardinal, whether he works in the Roman curia or as a nuncio. This would please the Orthodox, who consider a bishop without a diocese an abomination. One of the problems with nobles and bishops is that it is difficult to fire them, even when they are incompetent or when there is a change of government. Such a reform would also remind the Vatican bureaucracy that it is a servant of the pope and the college of bishops and is not itself part of the magisterium.

Strengthen the Legislative Bodies in the Church

At the same time that the role of the nobility in governance was declining in civil society, the role of independent legislatures was increasing. No political philosophy would depend on the executive for all wisdom and creativity. There is universal recognition that the synod of bishops, a meeting of bishops from around the world established by Pope Paul VI, has failed to rise to expectations. A useful reform would be to bar members of the Vatican bureaucracy from being a member of the synod of bishops. They could attend the synod as experts and staff, but not as voting members. All of the members of the synod should be elected by episcopal conferences; none should be appointed. The synod should also meet on a regular basis, say once every five years. It also needs committees to prepare agenda and documents between meetings. An ecumenical council should also meet at least once a generation.

Convert Congregations into Elected Synodal Committees

Vatican congregations and councils are committees of cardinals and bishops appointed by the pope and are responsible for various topics like clergy, liturgy, justice and peace, laity, evangelization, bishops, canon law, and so on. The Vatican cardinals on these committees are the most influential. The chair of the committee (called a prefect for a congregation and a president for a council) is also the head of the office with the same name. These offices advise the pope and implement church policy.

One important legislative function is oversight of the bureaucracy. Therefore, the members of Vatican congregations and councils should be elected by synods or by episcopal conferences so that they can act as policymaking and oversight bodies. Vatican bureaucrats should not be members of congregations, although they could attend meetings as experts and staff.

Create an Independent Judiciary

One of the most necessary elements in a governmental system under the rule of law is an independent judiciary. To allow the executive to indict, prosecute, judge, and sentence a defendant is today considered a violation of due process. The treatment of theologians and so-called dissidents by the Congregation for the Doctrine of the Faith is one of the scandals of the church. The potential for this maltreatment will continue as long as the CDF continues to act as policeman, prosecutor, judge, and jury. Retired bishops, for example, might make an appropriate jury pool.

Elect Bishops

As mentioned earlier, the appointment of bishops by the pope is a modern innovation. It follows a corporate model that sees the pope as the CEO and the bishops as branch managers of an international corporation. While the corporate model is highly centralized, political models recognize that local leaders need to be chosen by local citizens. Today it may be possible and advisable to return to the selection system endorsed by Pope Leo I, where the bishop is elected by the clergy, accepted by his people, and consecrated by the bishops of his province. If a bishop loses the confidence of his clergy and people, he should resign.

Strengthen Episcopal Conferences by Making Them Councils

Having everything decided by a centralized government is now recognized as a failed political strategy. Catholic social teaching speaks of the importance of subsidiarity in government policy and structures. According to the principle of subsidiarity, issues should be handled by the smallest or lowest authority possible. In ancient times, local and regional councils of bishops were important players in determining church teaching and discipline. They did so without referring every decision to Rome. Episcopal conferences, which now need Rome's approval for any important action, need to become episcopal councils and regain their ancient and independent policymaking role in the Church. They should not need to have every decision and document reviewed and ratified by the Vatican. They must be trusted to know what is best for their local church.[6]

CONCLUSION

Implementing these six reforms will not bring about the kingdom of God. No governance structure is perfect. Every reform has negative side effects. But these reforms would allow the Church to learn from the best practices of civil society so that it can implement a governance structure that follows the principles of collegiality and subsidiarity. It is noteworthy that most of these reforms are in fact returning to earlier practices and structures of the Church. Of course, spiritual reform and conversion are more important than structural reform. But this does not mean that structural reform is unimportant.

What are the chances of these reforms taking place in the Church? As a social scientist, I believe the chances for reform are close to zero. The Church is currently run by a self-perpetuating group of men who see such reform as not only threatening their power but also contrary to their theology of the Church. But as a Christian, I have to have hope.

Throughout Church history, we see periods of progress and decline. Although this is true of any organization or community, what distinguishes the Church is its openness to redemption that can renew Christians as individuals and as a community. Despite their weakness and sinfulness, Christians have faith in the word of God that shows them the way, Christians have hope based on Christ's victory over sin and death and his promise of the Spirit, and Christians have love that impels them to forgiveness and companionship at the Lord's Table. The future of the Church and any program of authentic reform must be based on such faith, hope, and love.

NOTES

1. For histories of the curia, see Ignazio Gordon, "Curia: Historical Evolution," in *Sacramentum Mundi: An Encyclopedia of Theology*, ed. Karl Rahner, Cornelius Ernst, and Kevin Smyth, vol. 2 (New York: Herder & Herder, 1970), 49–52; Giuseppe Alberigo, "Serving the

Communion of Churches," in *The Roman Curia and the Communion of Churches,* ed. Peter Huizing and Knut Walf (New York: Seabury Press, 1979); *Concilium* 127 (1979): 12–33; Reginald L. Poole, *Lectures on the History of the Papal Chancery Down to the Time of Innocent III* (Cambridge, UK: Cambridge University Press, 1915).

2. Petrus Canisius van Lierde and A. Giraud, *What Is a Cardinal?* (New York: Hawthorn, 1964), 95.

3. On the selection of bishops, see Thomas J. Reese, *Inside the Vatican: The Politics and Organization of the Catholic Church* (Cambridge, MA: Harvard University Press, 1996), chapter 9.

4. Jean Gaudemet, "Bishops: From Election to Nomination," *Concilium* 137 (July 1980): 11.

5. Brian E. Daley, "Structures of Charity: Bishops' Gatherings and the See of Rome in the Early Church," *Episcopal Conferences: Historical, Canonical & Theological Studies,* ed. Thomas J. Reese (Washington, DC: Georgetown University Press, 1989), 25–58.

6. See Thomas J. Reese, ed., *Episcopal Conferences.*

ACKNOWLEDGMENTS

Several of the chapters in this book are based on papers delivered at the sixth annual "Dilemmas of Democracy" conference (February 12, 2007) sponsored by the Institute for Leadership Studies at Loyola Marymount University in Los Angeles. We wish to thank Loyola Marymount University for its generous support for this conference, and Vivian Valencia, Charles Bergman, Kristina Rioux, and Theresa Tran for their assistance with the conference program.

John C. Green, Ted G. Jelen, and two anonymous reviewers gave especially careful readings of earlier versions of the manuscript and offered us many useful suggestions for improvements. We also appreciate the support of Georgetown University Press and the guidance of its director Richard Brown as we developed this project through its many stages.

CONTRIBUTORS

Richard Anderson is a research fellow at the Center for American Politics and Public Policy at the University of Washington and was the 2007 recipient of the Mary Gates research fellowship in American politics. His research is in the fields of public opinion and public policy, broadly examining how individuals and institutions react to change. For 2008–9 Anderson is a scholar in residence at the University of Aarhus, Denmark.

Matthew Barreto is assistant professor of political science at the University of Washington. His work examines the political participation and public opinion of Latinos and immigrants in the United States and his work has been published in the *American Political Science Review* and *Public Opinion Quarterly,* among other scholarly journals. In 2000 he was a research assistant for the Hispanic Churches in American Public Life (HCAPL) national survey of Latinos and Religiosity conducted by the Tomás Rivera Policy Institute.

Mary E. Bendyna is the executive director of the Center for Applied Research in the Apostolate and is a research associate professor at Georgetown University. She is a member of the Institute of the Sisters of Mercy of the Americas. Her political science research has focused on the relationships between religious values and political orientations. She has examined the political attitudes and behaviors of American Catholics and their role in contemporary American politics. Her research has appeared in books about clergy and American politics, the Christian Right, gender and politics, and PACs in congressional elections, and she has published articles in *Journal for the Scientific Study of Religion, Presidential Studies Quarterly, Journal of Church and State,* and *Sociology of Religion.*

Thomas J. Carty is associate professor of history and American Studies at Springfield College. He is the author of a number of studies on religion and politics, including a book about John F. Kennedy titled *A Catholic in the White House?* (Palgrave Macmillan, 2004; reissued in paperback in 2008).

William V. D'Antonio is emeritus professor at the University of Connecticut and a fellow at the Life Cycle Institute at The Catholic University of America. He is the coauthor of eight books and coeditor of four. His most recent book is *Voices of the Faithful* (Crossroads Publishing, 2007), a coauthored study of a Catholic lay social movement striving to help change the Church. He holds an honorary doctor of humane letters degree from St. Michael's College in Vermont and was a Fulbright senior fellow in Italy in 2004.

Brian Frederick is an assistant professor of political science at Bridgewater State College in Massachusetts. His research interests include the U.S. Congress, women and politics, and judicial elections. His work has appeared in *Public Opinion Quarterly, PS: Political Science and Politics, Judicature,* and *Politics and Policy.*

Michael A. Genovese holds the Loyola Chair of Leadership Studies and is a professor of political science and director of the Institute for Leadership Studies at Loyola Marymount University. In 2006 he was made a fellow at the Queens College, Oxford University. Genovese is the editor of Palgrave Macmillan's "The Evolving American Presidency" book series, and is also associate editor of the journal, *White House Studies.* He has lectured widely for the United States Embassy.

Mark M. Gray is a research associate at the Center for Applied Research in the Apostolate and is a research assistant professor at Georgetown University. His research has focused on household norms and political culture and how these relate to political participation and vote choice. His recent research includes several national-level polls of the Catholic population that examine Catholic culture, attitudes, and behavior. His research has appeared in books about changes in political parties, democratization, religious leadership, political corruption, and Catholic school choice, as well as articles in the *Journal for the Scientific Study of Religion, International Organization, Comparative Political Studies, Presidential Studies Quarterly, PS: Political Science & Politics,* and *Review of Religious Research.*

Kristin E. Heyer is associate professor of Christian ethics in the Department of Theological Studies at Loyola Marymount University. She is the author of *Prophetic & Public: The Social Witness of U.S. Catholicism* (Georgetown University Press, 2006) as well as articles that have appeared in *Theological Studies, The Journal of Peace and Justice Studies,* and *Political Theology.* She authored the sole chapter on Roman Catholicism in *Toward an Evangelical Public Policy: Political Strategies for the Health of Nations* (Baker Books, 2005).

Paul Christopher Manuel is the chief operating officer at the Institute for Global Engagement in Washington, DC, a think tank that advocates for religious freedom in the world. Manuel previously served as the executive director and cofounder of the New Hampshire Institute of Politics at Saint Anselm College, where he was professor of political science and internaational relations.

Adrian Pantoja is an associate professor of political studies and Chicano studies at Pitzer College, a member of the Claremont Colleges. Pantoja's research revolves around the Latino population, immigration, public opinion, and voting behavior. His research has appeared in a number of edited volumes and the journals *Political Research Quarterly, Political Behavior,* and *Social Science Quarterly,* among others. In addition, he has received the award for the Best Paper on Black Politics and twice won the award for the Best Paper on Latino Politics from the Western Political Science Association. Currently, he is editing a special issue on the 2006 immigrant rights protests for the journal *American Behavioral Scientist.*

Barbara A. Perry is the Carter Glass Professor of Government and founding executive director of the Center for Civic Renewal and the Virginia Law-Related Education Center at Sweet Briar College. In 1994–95 she served as the judicial fellow at the Supreme Court of the United States, where she received the Tom C. Clark Award for the outstanding fellow. For 2006–7 she served as a senior fellow at the University of Louisville's McConnell Center. In addition to publishing nearly thirty articles, she has written eight books, including *Jacqueline Kennedy: First Lady of the New Frontier* (2004) and her most recent book, *The Michigan Affirmative Action Cases,* published in 2007, both by the University Press of Kansas.

Thomas J. Reese was editor-in-chief of *America* from 1998 to 2005. Father Reese is a widely recognized expert on the U.S. Catholic Church and is frequently cited by journalists. He is author of a trilogy that examines church organization and politics on the local, national, and international levels: *Archbishop: Inside the Power Structure of the American Catholic Church* (Harper & Row, 1989), *A Flock of Shepherds: The National Conference of Catholic Bishops* (Sheed & Ward, 1992), and *Inside the Vatican: The Politics and Organization of the Catholic Church* (Harvard University Press, 1996). Reese currently serves as a senior fellow at the Woodstock Theological Center at Georgetown University in Washington, DC, specializing in religion and politics.

Mark J. Rozell is professor of public policy at George Mason University. He is the author of numerous studies on the intersection of religion and politics. Among his books are *Religion and the American Presidency* (Palgrave, 2007), and *The Values Campaign?: The Christian Right and the 2004 Elections* (Georgetown University Press, 2006). He is coeditor of the Georgetown University Press Religion and Politics series.

Margaret Ross Sammon is a PhD candidate in the Department of Politics at The Catholic University of America. She is writing her dissertation on the politics of the U.S. Catholic bishops.

Gregory A. Smith is research fellow at the Pew Forum on Religion and Public Life. He holds a PhD in government from the University of Virginia, where his doctoral research earned the 2006 Aaron Wildavsky Award given by the Religion and Politics section of the American Political Science Association for the best dissertation in religion and politics. He is the author of *Politics in the Parish: The Political Influence of Catholic Priests* (Georgetown University Press, 2008).

Matthew J. Streb is associate professor and director of undergraduate studies in the Department of Political Science at Northern Illinois University. He is the author of two books, *The New Electoral Politics of Race* (Tuscaloosa: University of Alabama Press, 2002) and *Rethinking American Electoral Democracy* (New York: Routledge, 2008), and the editor or coeditor of five other books. Streb has published more than twenty articles and book chapters, including pieces in *Political Research Quarterly, Public Opinion Quarterly, Social Science Quarterly,* and *Election Law Journal.*

Steven A. Tuch is professor of sociology and of public policy and public administration at George Washington University. His research interests focus on racial and ethnic inequality, public opinion, and social change in the postcommunist nations of central and eastern Europe, issues on which he has published extensively. He is coauthor (with Ronald Weitzer) of *Race and Policing in America: Conflict and Reform* (Cambridge University Press, 2006), coeditor with Yoku Shaw-Taylor of *The Other African Americans: Contemporary African and Caribbean Immigrants in the United States* (Rowman & Littlefield, 2007), and coeditor with Jack K. Martin of *Racial Attitudes in the 1990s: Continuity and Change* (Praeger, 1997).

John Kenneth White is professor of politics at The Catholic University of America in Washington, DC. He is the author of several books on American politics, including *The Values Divide: American Politics and Culture in Transition* (Chatham House, 2003).

INDEX